THE
YEAR-ROUND
HARVEST

THE YEAR-ROUND HARVEST

A Seasonal Guide to Growing, Eating, and Preserving the Fruits and Vegetables of Your Labor

Includes More Than **150** RECIPES for Your Garden Bounty!

CATHERINE ABBOTT AND **ALISON WOITUNSKI**

AVON, MASSACHUSETTS

Published by Adams Media, a division of F+W Media, Inc.
57 Littlefield Street, Avon, MA 02322. U.S.A.
www.adamsmedia.com

ISBN 10: 1-4405-2816-0
ISBN 13: 978-1-4405-2816-3
eISBN 10: 1-4405-3069-6
eISBN 13: 978-1-4405-3069-2

Printed in the United States of America.

10   9   8   7   6   5   4   3   2   1

Library of Congress Cataloging-in-Publication Data
is available from the publisher.

This publication is designed to provide accurate and authoritative information with regard to the subject matter covered. It is sold with the understanding that the publisher is not engaged in rendering legal, accounting, or other professional advice. If legal advice or other expert assistance is required, the services of a competent professional person should be sought.

—From a *Declaration of Principles* jointly adopted by a Committee of the American Bar Association and a Committee of Publishers and Associations

Many of the designations used by manufacturers and sellers to distinguish their product are claimed as trademarks. Where those designations appear in this book and Adams Media was aware of a trademark claim, the designations have been printed with initial capital letters.

This book is available at quantity discounts for bulk purchases.
For information, please call 1-800-289-0963.

Interior illustrations by Barry Littmann and Eric Andrews.
Wood image © 123RF.com

Contains material adapted and abridged from *The Everything® Grow Your Own Vegetables Book* by Catherine Abbott with a foreword by Meghan Shinn, Editor, *Horticulture* Magazine, copyright © 2010 by F+W Media, Inc., ISBN 10: 1-4405-0013-4, ISBN 13: 978-1-4405-0013-8; *The Everything® Root Cellaring Book* by Catherine Abbott with a foreword by Meghan Shinn, Editor, *Horticulture* Magazine, copyright © 2011 by F+W Media, Inc., ISBN 10: 1-4405-0468-7, ISBN 13: 978-1-4405-0468-6; *The Everything® Canning and Preserving Book* by Patricia Telesco with Jeanne P. Maack, Founder of Creative Canning Cuisine, copyright © 2009 by F+W Media, Inc., ISBN 10: 1-59869-987-3, ISBN 13: 978-1-59869-987-6; and *The Everything® Vegan Cookbook* by Jolinda Hackett with Lorena Novak Bull, RD, copyright © 2010 by F+W Media, Inc., ISBN 10: 1-4405-0216-1, ISBN 13: 978-1-4405-0216-3.

This book is dedicated to the people who continue to inspire the food in my life.

My dad, whose love of hunting, gathering, and raising food ensured that I would always care about what I ate and where it came from.

My coworkers and the youth at The Food Project, whose wisdom and passion inspired much of this book.

And Bart, who constantly reminds me that no matter what's on the plate, a perfect meal is one shared with the people you love.

CONTENTS

INTRODUCTION

For the at-home gardener, the growing season hums with productivity, life, and nourishment. Basic to human nature, the garden is a place where self-sufficiency and independence reign. Growing your own food allows you to exist outside the confines of the grocery store, giving you choices you might otherwise miss. Wanting to create a year-round lifestyle of at-home food production and consumption is a natural next step for those who relish the rhythm and health of the growing season. *The Year-Round Harvest* is designed to facilitate the steps necessary to extend the enjoyment of homegrown food well beyond the summer harvest. By learning how to grow earlier and for longer periods, learning the methods and options of growing indoors, and how to preserve and store your harvest, you are on your way to enjoying all the benefits of homegrown food year-round.

The Year-Round Harvest is a practical guide that approaches at-home gardening with a respect for, and understanding of, traditional and time-proven practices, while also embracing new technologies and developments in agriculture and food preservation. The beauty and simplicity of food production is within these pages—but you'll also find a plethora of new ideas and methods. This combination of traditional and modern approaches allows you to design a year-round system practical for your lifestyle. Whether you live in an urban, suburban, or rural area, whether you have no budget constraints or are growing your own food in an effort to be as thrifty as possible, *The Year-Round Harvest* provides the information necessary to create and implement an at-home food system that meets all your needs.

In this step-by-step approach, you have the freedom to decide which methods appeal to you and exactly how you can adapt them to your own garden. With easy-to-read illustrations, recipes, and instructions, you will learn how to properly assess your growing site, make soil amendments, and protect your crops from colder weather. Keeping the diversity of homes and growing spaces in mind, *The Year-Round Harvest* includes creative approaches to maximize your food production no matter what challenges you are faced with. You will learn when and how to use trellises, raised beds, terraces, and container gardens, as well as the ins and outs of drying, canning, pickling, freezing, and otherwise storing your food. How you decide to grow and store your food is up to you, and with *The Year-Round Harvest* as your guide, you will be able to make the best decisions for you and your family.

As the gardener and food enthusiast knows, the satisfaction of shared meals and bountiful harvests is a joy worth extending throughout the year. Our gardens and what we eat connect us to life's most meaningful ingredients—the land that sustains us, and the people around our table. With *The Year-Round Harvest* as your guide, you are soon to be enjoying the fruits of your labor throughout the year.

CHAPTER 1

YEAR AT A GLANCE

Understanding the strengths and challenges of your outdoor space is the first step to planning a successful garden. By maximizing strengths, thinking creatively, and viewing challenges as guidelines rather than limitations, your garden will be a unique reflection of your home and personality as well as an optimum growing environment.

Assessing the Basics

Sunlight, water, and soil are the key ingredients to a productive garden. Depending on the area you have to work with, the quality and quantity of these components can differ widely and can affect how you design your garden. Other factors, like wind, pests, drainage, and space can also affect how and what you can grow. The gardener turning an expansive suburban lawn into a vegetable garden is working with different variables than the urban resident converting a rooftop into a place to grow food. Both of these scenarios, and everything in between, can easily result in a beautiful and productive garden so long as all factors are assessed and understood early on.

Sunlight

Open sunlight for your garden is your top priority when deciding where to plant. While not all crops require the same amount of sunlight as others, the majority of your plants will need direct sunlight for at least 6 hours a day during the height of their growth.

Gardening in a Larger Space

If you have a yard or an outdoor space large enough to provide you with options for garden placement, then chances are you already have some idea as to where you would like to put your garden. There might be a spot in the yard that looks too vacant, or an area that you could access easily from the kitchen. Maybe you want the garden to be near an outdoor eating area or a space where your children like to play. When determining the consistency and directness of sunlight for your garden placement, you will want to observe the location you have in mind, but choose some other sites to observe as well.

By pinpointing and observing multiple sites, you can better gauge the quality of sunlight in each area. One spot might seem sunny enough on its own, but when compared to a different section of your outdoor space, you may notice that the sunlight in your spot is less present at certain points throughout the day, or that there is more consistent shade than you expected. It could turn out that the area that you were imagining for your garden is not the best option, but if you observe a few different locations at once, you'll be able to adapt your plans.

Hardiness Plant Zones

Hardiness plant zones are growing zones based on the average annual minimum temperature of an area. The U.S. Department of Agriculture (USDA) divides North America into eleven zones based on temperature. In order to understand the hardiness of certain plants, when

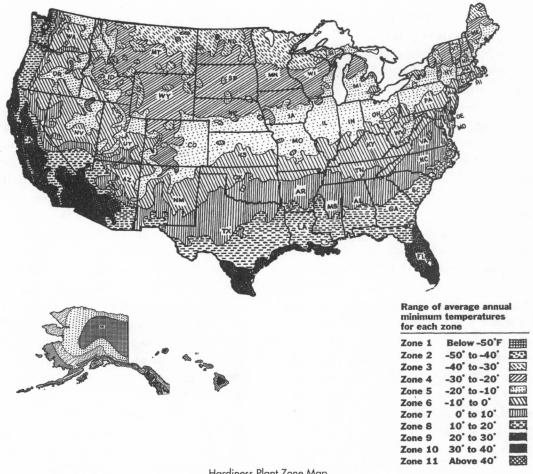

Hardiness Plant Zone Map

Range of average annual minimum temperatures for each zone

Zone	Temperature	
Zone 1	Below –50°F	
Zone 2	–50° to –40°	
Zone 3	–40° to –30°	
Zone 4	–30° to –20°	
Zone 5	–20° to –10°	
Zone 6	–10° to 0°	
Zone 7	0° to 10°	
Zone 8	10° to 20°	
Zone 9	20° to 30°	
Zone 10	30° to 40°	
Zone 11	Above 40°	

to plant, the best varieties for your garden, and how to care for plants throughout the colder months, you need to know which hardiness zone you are growing in.

Working with a Small Space

If there isn't much option for where your garden can go—for example if you have a very small yard, patio, deck, or an assigned community garden plot—then the goal of making your growing-site observations is to understand the type of sunlight your garden has access to. Being familiar with this beforehand will allow you to plant strategically. When observing your space, you want to determine if your garden area receives mostly direct sunlight, mostly shade, or a combination of both. Once you determine which category your garden space fits into, you can plant crops that will thrive in your particular environment.

Tree Cover and Shade-Producing Vegetation

Depending on the time of year you are making your observations, pay attention to trees and other vegetation that may not be in bloom but will have shade-producing foliage during the growing season. Nearby trees do not always rule out a potential garden location, but it is important to understand the scope of the shade they will produce. Knowing the type of tree or vegetation and assessing its relative health will help you to understand how much shade will be provided. If the area and the vegetation are new to you, talking to neighbors who are familiar with the specific tree or site is often the simplest way to get an idea of how much shade to expect. During my first season in a new apartment, I inquired about shade from a tree that was shared between my yard and my neighbor's. Not only did my neighbor (who had lived adjacent to my yard for decades) know exactly how much shade would be produced, but he was also able to fill me in on the drainage problems he had observed in my yard over the years. Because of this initial conversation, we ended up sharing the work of pruning the tree, as well as gardening tools, tips, and food throughout the year.

If you are unable to get the information you need from the folks living around you, a little research and common sense should be enough to give you a basic idea of how much shade to expect. If your outdoor space is tree-heavy, don't despair; often, pruning a few branches or cutting back some vegetation can open up plenty of sunlight for a productive garden.

The Best Time of Year for a Sunlight Survey

It will be easiest to make accurate assumptions about sunlight at times of the year when there is ample daylight and also during days when the sun is visible and present. For some this will mean that the fall and early spring will be the best time to observe potential garden sites (other than during the growing season itself) and also on a day when you can count on the sun being out. Having grown up in coastal New England and having lived in the Northwest, I can tell you that this might mean that you have to make observations over a span of several days if you're planning your garden at a time of year when sunlight is scarce or unpredictable.

In general, making observations at specific points throughout the day will allow you to accurately assess your access to sunlight. You can stagger these observations over a larger window of time by observing the garden site at different times on different days if you are unable to take note of the light at every hour (beginning in the morning until early evening) during a single day. Depending on where your garden is located in relation to where you live and work, it might take several days to develop a complete understanding of the sunlight in your garden site.

Making Conclusions: Consistency and Direct Light

If one area was fully immersed in sunlight during one third of the day, but without any direct sun for the remaining two thirds, this area does not have consistent sunlight despite receiving some direct light. A site that received partial to full sun throughout all parts of the day, but did not reach a point of receiving direct sunlight, has more consistency of sunlight but less direct sunlight. In an ideal situation, you do not need to choose between planting a garden in direct or consistent sunlight, as both direct and consistent sunlight would be present, although this is not always the reality.

Choosing a garden site that has a balance of consistent and direct light is important, but this variable is also flexible and the end balance will be different in each garden. There are benefits and challenges to the type of sunlight that your garden receives and it is important to consider how the variable of sunlight will interact with the other components of your garden. For example, a garden without any shade will require more water, whereas a garden that receives partial shade in the afternoon will use its water more efficiently. Likewise, a garden that gets too much shade might be more susceptible to fungus or mold growth in the soil. As you move through the steps of site assessment, you will continue to gather information about all the variables important to your garden. By the end of this section you will have an understanding of how all of these components interact with one another.

Water

Where your water access is and the size of your garden are important factors in determining garden site location. If you are planning to water your garden with a fixed irrigation setup, such as drip tape, a sprinkler system, or any other stationary system, your primary limiting factor is the length of your connecting equipment (typically a hose) and the area that this connection will have to cross in order to get to the garden. Your garden should not be any further than your connection can realistically reach. For some gardeners, this means paying attention to any terrain or obstacles that are not ideal to extend a hose across. A driveway, children's play area, or a heavily trafficked walkway or stairway are some areas you might want to avoid laying a hose or irrigation line across.

Rain Barrels

Creating a system to catch and conserve rainwater is the most inexpensive and environmentally conscious way to water your garden (other than relying on the rain itself). Depending on where you live and where your garden is located, this may or may not be practical. If possible, you will want to build a system that captures rainwater and transports it into a rain barrel where you can then decide when and how to release the water.

A basic rain-catch system uses tubing to capture rainwater from the gutters of your house, garage, or other buildings, and transports this water into a storage container that is elevated above the level of your garden. From this container, a hose or additional tubing can be connected to a water-release spigot that can be opened or closed. While the pressure of the water from a simple rain-barrel system is not great enough to use with a sprinkler system, the rain barrel in this system can easily be integrated with drip-tape irrigation or used to fill a watering can.

If you plan to build a rain-barrel system to irrigate your crops, you will want your garden to be located at a level lower than the rain barrel and within a reasonable distance. You can usually accomplish this elevation difference by positioning your barrel on a stand or blocks, putting it at a higher level than the garden. It is

important to keep in mind that a typical rain barrel will not have enough pressure to force water to move quickly through the irrigation line. The watering process in this system will be a slow one, but if built effectively, it will make irrigation efficient and require only very light lifting for the gardener. You can plan on having to open your water spigot and waiting several hours or even days (depending on the size of your garden) for the entire garden to be watered, but the only effort required from you will be turning the spigot on and off, and observing the plot to see when enough water has been distributed. The more hosing and irrigation line that the water has to travel through (how far away the garden is from the rain-barrel system and how much tubing is used within the system) will increase the amount of time watering takes.

Hand Watering

If you plan to water your garden by hand, either by filling a watering can or by extending a hose for each watering, it is particularly important that your garden be a reasonable distance from your water source. Even for the gardener with the best of intentions, a garden that is more than a quick walk away from a water source will most likely not be watered with as much attention and care as it would if water were easily accessible. This can translate into overwatering for some crops and underwatering for others if all plants are being given the same amount of water at

Rain Barrel System

the same time because of the amount of effort an individual watering can take.

One of the first gardens that I planted was located at the opposite end of the yard from the water source, which was a hose attached to a spigot on the house. Every time I watered the garden I had to uncoil the hose and recoil it. This particular garden was not located where I lived. The combination of these factors meant that the garden was often quickly and indiscriminately watered. All my crops received the same amount of water at the same time, and for some it was too much water, too little, or watering was ill-timed. By asking yourself the following questions, you will be able to think critically about how much distance from the water source to your garden is too far.

- On a daily basis, how much time are you willing and able to dedicate to watering your garden?
- If uncoiling and recoiling a hose will happen for each watering, how long is the hose and how much time and effort will be needed to extend it?
- How many times will you need to fill and refill your watering can to complete one garden watering?
- How much exercise are you willing and able to get during each watering?
- How heavy is a full watering can and how much is a reasonable amount to walk back and forth?

There are many factors that will affect how often your garden will need to be watered. How well the soil retains moisture and how sunny or wet of a growing season you have can drastically alter your watering schedule. Some growing seasons your garden may only need watering a few times during the entire season, and other summers you may find yourself watering every evening for several weeks. Depending on where you live, some of these factors might be predictable, and others may not be.

RAIN BARRELS WITH OR WITHOUT IRRIGATION

You do not need a full irrigation-line setup to warrant the use of rain barrels in your garden. If you decide that hand watering is a good fit for you and your garden, using a rain-barrel catch system to fill your watering cans is a much more resourceful way to water your plants—conserving both water and money.

Soil

The foundation of organic gardening is healthy soil. If you remember the mantra "A good gardener grows healthy soil and healthy soil grows healthy plants," and treat your soil accordingly, your crops will not only be productive but they will be highly nutritious as well. Since soil is the foundation of your garden, understanding the composition and characteristics of the soil you are working with is crucial for both short-term and long-term garden health. In order to properly assess your growing site, you will need to assess your soil.

Soil Testing and Deciding How to Grow

In urban and suburban areas, lead and heavy-metal contamination is a very real concern. If you are planning to garden directly in soil that is already present in your yard or outdoor space, you will want to test your soil before planting anything. Often the easiest way to do this is to contact the nearest state university to find out what your testing options are.

The Department of Plant, Soil, and Insect Sciences at the University of Massachusetts, for example, accepts and tests soil samples from home gardeners and commercial farmers at a minimal cost. In addition to testing for dangerous contaminants such as lead, this particular test also addresses soil health and productivity, providing the grower with specific information about what will grow best and any amendments to the soil that should or could be made. The turnaround time for the results is typically less than 2 weeks, and all you need in order to take samples is a small trowel, Ziploc bags, and a marker for labeling. To learn the exact steps and to print a soil sample order form, visit *www.umass.edu/soiltest*. The information you can receive from a soil test can often be the equivalent of knowledge that would otherwise take years to only partially understand.

Once you determine whether or not your existing soil is safe to plant in, you are equipped to decide whether to use raised beds as a cap for contaminated soil, or to plant directly in the ground in safe soil. Keep in mind that even if you already know that you want to go with a raised-bed approach, you still need to test your soil. Some soil can have heavy-metal levels high enough to warrant safeguards in addition to using raising beds. In some cases, you might decide that container gardening, which is explained later on in this chapter, is the best approach.

Raised Beds

Wood-framed raised beds are a common feature in urban and suburban gardening. Not only do they offer protection from soil contamination, but they also provide a tidy appearance, can be sized to fit in all different types of outdoor environments, and are easy to build. Raised-bed frames can be assembled at as much cost as you would like to put into the project. Depending on how particular you are about appearance, you can use any dimensional lumber that you already have, or

Raised Beds

you can purchase lumber that meets your specifications at your nearest lumberyard. As long as the wood has not been chemically or pressure-treated, it will suffice for building. The only other materials you will need for the frame are basic hardware (screws, nail, brackets) and a drill or hammer.

To fill raised beds, you will need to purchase soil or finished compost. This is often the most limiting factor because it can be expensive to purchase this much soil. But by doing a little research, you can avoid spending big bucks at your local garden center: Find out if there are any local composting facilities or other agriculture operations that will sell you unbagged soil or finished compost at a lower cost. If you have access to a pickup truck and can go get the soil or compost yourself, you can save even more money by eliminating any delivery charges. To give you an idea of how much soil you will need, a standard 12-inch-deep, 8-foot by 4-foot raised bed will need 32 cubic feet of soil.

Framed raised beds are perfect for yards that do not have one open space large enough for an entire garden. Using raised beds allows you to break up what would normally comprise one garden space, and spread the different components out over your entire outdoor area. For people who have limited outdoor space and/or yards with a diverse terrain and spotty sun coverage, framed raised beds offer versatility and a way to make the most of limited space.

Working with Existing Soil

Working with your existing soil is the best idea if it is safe and healthy soil to plant in and you have enough open space to do so. If you own the land that you are gardening, or are planning to garden on this land for at least several years, you will be able to undertake the care needed for long-term soil amendments, that will make working with your existing soil worthwhile.

When you get ready to prep your soil, which is discussed in the next chapter, it will be important to have an understanding of the basic characteristics of the soil you are working with. The easiest way to do this (in addition to reading the results from your soil test) is to dig around in your potential garden site. Is the soil rocky? Does it remind you more of clay or sand? Do you notice any worms or insect life?

Container Gardening

Using container gardens to grow food is not only practical but also a fast and easy way to enhance the aesthetics of any yard, deck, or other outdoor space quickly and inexpensively. Whether you live someplace where your only option is to grow food in containers, or you haven't the time or desire to convert your yard into a mini-farm, using containers to grow food is an easy way to quickly establish a garden just about anywhere.

When to Use

Container gardening can be a highly productive way to grow food when you

Old Wheelbarrow as a Container

Bathtub Garden

Plastic Tub Garden

don't have access to much outdoor space or healthy soil. Building inexpensive containers is easy and you can easily adapt containers for vertical growing. Containers are also easily moved, so they can be relocated in your outdoor space as necessary to achieve optimal conditions for your crops. If bad backs or other physical limitations are a concern, you will want to seriously consider using containers because of the flexibility in height and location that they provide.

Some vegetables have a shallow root system; others have much deeper roots and need more space to grow. When choosing any container for your vegetables, there are three important rules to remember: First, the container must be deep enough to hold enough soil to accommodate the plant's root growth. Second, it must be large enough for the plant to grow to maturity. And finally, water must be able to drain easily from the bottom of the container so the soil does not get waterlogged. The container can be any shape so long as it can fulfill these three essentials.

Common container gardens are comprised of basic pots and planters that you can buy at any garden center. For the gardener wanting to grow food more intensively, however, these containers can be limiting. A plastic storage tote with a lid is a good choice for container gardening. A typical 20-gallon tote is at least 12 inches deep, allowing for root space. By drilling drainage holes in the bottom of the tote, water can easily drain out so plant roots don't become waterlogged. If the tote container is elevated a few inches, the lid can be used as a drainage catch tray beneath it. You can also use a container that you already have on hand; reusing an old wheelbarrow or other household item can be a great way to avoid spending more money, of finding a new use for an old object, and even creating a decorative display.

What to Grow

Deciding what to grow is one of the most exciting parts of planning your garden. Now that you understand what type of plants grow best in your particular climate and the outdoor space you have to work with, it's time to think about what you like to eat. Think beyond the summer months of freshly picked salad items, all the way to what type of pumpkins you want to carve for Halloween, what you like to eat on Thanksgiving, and other favorite meals during the winter holidays and cold weather. Once you determine what you want to eat, what your storage options are, and which foods your household consumes the most of, you'll be ready to decide exactly what to grow in your garden. If you plan and plant correctly, you'll be enjoying your harvest well into the new year.

Getting Started—Thinking about Your Favorite Meal

It is often easier to think about what you want to plant not by which plants grow when—you can map that out later—but by category of food. A great way to get your kids, family, and friends excited about eating healthy is to involve them in this process. It is fun to sit down with your loved ones and make lists of what you like to eat together. When you do this, it's important to think about your whole diet throughout the year. A fun way to start this process is to break down your favorite meal into its plant-derived ingredients and see which ones you can grow at home. You'll be surprised at how many of the ingredients can easily come from your own garden. You might not be able to grow the peppercorn in your favorite sauce recipe, but you can certainly grow the tomatoes, onions, garlic, basil, and oregano. The more people you involve at this stage, the more people you'll have willing to lend a hand in the garden and join you in the fun of cooking and eating together throughout the year. You're also likely to get more ideas and a more creative crop plan if you make this a group effort.

Assessing Your Space and Consumption—Storage and Staples

After you've decided what foods you would like to eat from your garden, the next step is to think about what role these foods play in your year-round diet. Some foods, like lettuce, do not store well and are best enjoyed fresh from your garden— although you may be able to extend their growing season. Other foods, like tomatoes, can be eaten fresh as you pick them, and are also excellent to store frozen and canned as sauces, or dried in pieces. How you plan to cook with and store your harvest has a lot to do with what varieties you should choose to plant.

Storage

Depending on where you live, your ability and capability to store food will greatly influence what you choose to grow. Having some storage space available is a necessity for maintaining a balanced year-round diet that will keep you and your family happy and healthy during all of the seasons. While the ideal food-storage situation includes a basement or root cellar, a chest freezer, a dehydrator, a stovetop large enough to comfortably can food on, and a food pantry, you can still enjoy homegrown food year-round using just one or two of these storage methods, and almost all of them can be adapted to what you already have access to.

Since you'll be planning and planting in accordance with how you will be preserving and storing your harvest, you need to consider your food-storage situation before you can make any decisions about what varieties of plants to grow. If you have a lot of freezer space it makes sense to plan for food that is easily and best preserved by freezing. If you do not have a basement or a yard in which to build a root cellar, you may want to rethink planting large quantities of potatoes or anything else that is best stored underground. If your home already lacks much closet and cabinet space, canning all

your food might not be the best option. Think creatively—food storage is another area of year-round growing that is fun and easy to involve friends and family members in. If you choose to share storage space with a friend or neighbor, it's important to remember that this type of arrangement is beneficial to both parties only so long as you work out a food share agreement in the beginning.

Staples

Every household uses some foods more regularly than others throughout the year. In how many meals a day or a week do you use garlic or onion? Is there a favorite recipe that calls for a certain herb? What are you most likely to throw together when you're in a rush—is it a pasta-and-sauce dish or rice and beans? Do you eat a lot of spicy food? In my house, garlic is incorporated into at least one meal a day; onions, maybe two meals a day. The bread recipe that my friends and family regularly demand uses a lot of rosemary. I cook a tomato sauce at least once a week and if it isn't spicy, I don't want to eat it. This means that some of the staples in my household are garlic, onion, rosemary, tomatoes, and hot peppers. I also include potatoes and squash as staples because they store well in my basement and are so versatile in cooking. Think about the things you cook with and eat most often. Chances are, if you look around your kitchen right now, they're already on the shelves and in the cabinets that are most easily accessible.

Categorizing Your Choices and Choosing the Right Varieties

Once you have an idea of the storage and cooking qualities that are important to you for each type of food, you're ready to put your crops into the categories that will better help you organize your diet for the year. In order to have a well-balanced and diverse diet, you'll want to include things from most of the categories described below. It's up to you to adjust how much of each you want to grow. Based on your taste and unique needs, you might find yourself with more focus on some food types rather than others. It is okay to do this as long as you keep in mind that come winter, you're more likely to be happy with your diet if there's a good diversity of food.

Greens

Spicy salad mix, purple heirloom lettuce, arugula, spinach, frisée—the salad list is long and fresh greens are satisfying and easy to grow. Direct seeding is almost always successful and the plants germinate and mature quickly, allowing you to try many different types throughout the season. There are also many types of greens that can germinate in and withstand colder weather. This means that dependent upon your growing zone and your ability to shelter your crops, you can plan on fresh greens beyond the first frost. If you love your greens, it is important to include a variety that allows for fresh consumption as long as the season allows, and also for greens that you can enjoy in a preserved form. If you're new to the wide world of greens, consult any seed catalog to get ideas. Johnny's Selected Seeds catalog is a great resource that is sure to get you excited about your greens.

Tomatoes

A gardener's favorite. There is no other garden product that is so poorly represented by the grocery-store version. The world of tomatoes is a large one, and certain tomatoes are better used for different purposes. Slicing tomatoes are served fresh with slices of cheese, in a sandwich, or in a salad. San Marzana tomatoes, a variety of plum tomatoes, are famously best for Italian-style sweet sauces. Other tomatoes with more meat and less water, such as Romas, are best for canning, dehydrating, or making paste. Cherry varieties are fun, especially as a way to get kids in the garden, but are generally difficult to store and cook with; they are best used fresh. Make a list of what you would like to do with your tomatoes and then choose the varieties that will meet these needs. Depending on how much space you have for planting and storing, it's a good idea to start with one type of tomato for each different use.

Root Vegetables

If you have access to a cellar, the root veggies that you choose to plant, along with squash, will comprise the majority of your fresh food diet throughout the winter. Potatoes, onions, garlic, carrots, celeriac, rutabaga, turnips, radishes, kohlrabi, shallots, Jerusalem artichokes, sweet potatoes, swedes (rutabaga, or Swedish turnip), and cassava are enough to fill any root cellar. Depending on your style of gardening, a good idea is to choose your favorite root vegetables and then supplement these veggies with ones you would like to try. If you've never tasted a parsnip, I wouldn't recommend giving them half your garden space. Potatoes alone are an incredibly versatile vegetable; there are literally thousands of varieties, with extreme differences in tastes and colors. For families with kids, it's a great idea to plant potatoes in a variety of color—red, gold, purple, and even orange. Harvesting potatoes is like going on an Easter egg hunt and between the fun of digging them up and the beautifully bright colors, it will be easy to get your family eating potatoes in a form other than French fries.

Beans and Other Legumes

Beans will grow in almost any reasonably good garden soil. They grow best in a sandy, loamy soil with a neutral pH (acidity/alkalinity level). Beans do not like a lot of moisture before they germinate, but they do need regular watering once they have sprouted to produce tender beans. They are best harvested young when they are the most tender and need to be picked every few days so the plant knows it needs to keep producing more. If you leave the pods on the plant, the plant will take it as a sign to stop producing.

Brassica (Cabbage, Broccoli, Kale, and Brussels Sprouts)

Anything from the *Brassica* family is a good choice if you are hoping to eat fresh foods during the winter. Cabbage, kale, and Brussels sprouts do well in the ground up until the first frost. They also store well in your root cellar and can be enjoyed fresh for many months—important if you are serious about creating a year-round food system based on homegrown veggies. Incorporating a taste of green Brussels sprouts or crispy raw cabbage will make your family's winter meals more colorful and fresh.

Herbs

Herbs are hugely important if you care about flavor! The herbs that you grow yourself will have a stronger flavor than any herbs from a store. Herbs are also important because of their aromatic and medicinal qualities. Think about all the ways that you can use herbs—as tea, to make your home smell pleasant, to soothe coughs and colds, or to flavor your favorite dishes. Having a variety of herbs in your garden and diet will add fun, health, and flavor to the winter months and meals.

Squash and Pumpkins

Not only are squash and pumpkins great for storing, but they also mark the seasons in a way that other foods do not. In addition to the nutritional value and versatility that consuming and cooking squash provides, it's fun for younger family members to grow their very own

Halloween pumpkins. Don't forget about favorites like sweet potato and pumpkin pies! Squash dishes are important to holiday meals for a reason—they are actually in season during the fall and winter holidays. Squash and pumpkins do produce a significant amount of foliage per plant and also take up quite a bit of root-cellar space. This does not mean that gardeners working with a small space can't plant and store squash and pumpkins; you can, but you will have to be experimental and creative.

CURING PUMPKINS AND WINTER SQUASH

In order to get the most use and longevity out of the pumpkins and winter squash that you grow, it's important to cure these veggies after you harvest them. Cut the stems to the woody section, about four inches long, and allow the pumpkin or squash to stay in a dry, well-ventilated area for at least a week. After they have been cured, squash and pumpkins will last for months in root storage; otherwise they can actually start to rot within just a few weeks of being picked. If you harvest your jack-o-lantern pumpkin in early September, make sure to cure it so that it lasts until Halloween!

Peppers (Hot and Sweet)

If you like peppers, growing many different kinds is easy to do. Hot peppers add a spicy component to favorite meals, and for some, cooking with hot peppers and spice is a must. Even if you aren't a fan of spicy foods, growing and storing some hot peppers is important as a way to add versatility and depth to your cooking and eating. Sweet peppers come in many varieties that are excellent when added to family favorites like pizza or fajitas.

Heirlooms

Finding heirloom, or heritage, varieties that resonate with both your personal background and your climate is an exciting and interesting way to add a personal and creative touch to your garden. Heirloom varieties are those which continue to be propagated through open pollination, rather than through grafts and cuttings, and are adapted to a specific climate and culture. Not only are heirlooms often beautiful and more colorful than standard varieties, they also have history and meaning behind them. It is fun to grow purple carrots, tie-dyed tomatoes, or the same potato variety that was grown by your family generations ago. Depending on your level of gardening experience, it is important to remember that heirloom varieties are, generally speaking, less common because they often have smaller yields; can be more challenging to grow, transport, and store; and tend to grow best in climates similar to the one in which they originated. But don't let this scare you; most heirloom varieties are perfectly simple to incorporate into your garden. Consider that a practical approach to growing heirlooms might not be to plant an entire heritage garden your first season, but to try out a few different plants. For more information and for sources to buy heirloom seeds, Seed Savers Exchange is a nonprofit organization dedicated to saving and sharing heirloom seeds; it offers an excellent annual heirloom-seed catalog that is available online and in print.

How You Think about Food

One of the biggest differences between planning a backyard garden just for the fun of growing and planning a garden that you want to eat from year-round is changing your gardening mindset from planting and growing only the things you like to eat fresh in the summer—often salad ingredients like tomatoes and lettuce—to growing the staple crops that you're used to purchasing in bulk from the grocery store. It's exciting to learn that you can grow and store these foods yourself, and it also requires careful planning and forethought. In order to grow and store the best food for you and your family's diet, it's important to remember the basics— the foods that are the backbone and staples of your kitchen—as well as remembering to maintain an element of excitement and learning by trying new foods and new varieties of old favorites.

As you build your own food system at home, the work and tasks of raising, storing, and eating food will be tied to the season and time of year. Spring jumpstarts the labor of raising food, easing into the busyness and speed of summer. During the fall, the harvest wanes, and the focus changes to putting away the food for colder days. The winter becomes a time to relax, reflect, and plan for the coming spring. Your climate and the length of your growing season will determine the flow of your year, and the following model serves as a good example of what to expect in a four-season climate.

FOUR-SEASON GROWING PLAN

Winter: Garden planning; ordering seeds based on garden plans

Late Winter: Starting indoor seedlings

Early Spring: Begin direct seeding of early spring crops

Mid-Spring: Transplant seedlings to garden soil

Early Summer: Direct seed summer crops

Mid-Summer: Begin second plantings

Late Summer: Choose and establish season-extension system

Early Fall: Implement season extenders for fall crops

CHAPTER 2

PREPARING YOUR PLOT

Preparing and taking care of your soil is crucial to setting a healthy foundation for your garden. By properly amending and regularly adding nutrients to your soil, you will be able to produce healthy, delicious food from your garden. Before you plant anything, you need to heed the recommendations from your soil test results. Removing any obstacles from your gardening space, pruning shade producing branches, and adding compost to your soil will help to establish a healthy garden site.

Composting

Making and using compost is an important part of any gardening system. It does take some time and effort to get used to composting if it isn't already part of your lifestyle, but the rewards are worth it. Not only is composting a constructive way to use your kitchen waste and keep your garden site organized and free of debris, but by adding compost to your soil, you will increase productivity and soil health. There are many different methods of composting, and choosing the best one for you and your family will help to make composting an integral part of your family's routine and your garden's cycle.

Composting has experienced a surge in popularity, so the home gardener has many choices of bins. The type of bin you choose will depend on where it will be located, how much waste you will have, and how much time and energy you want to put toward making compost. Keep in mind, the following different methods described all involve using a large bin that will typically live outdoors. In the case of a worm bin, however, during some times of the year the worms will need to be warmer and will have to live in your garage, basement, or some other sheltered area.

Worm Composting

If you live in an apartment or condominium and do not have access to a backyard, composting with earthworms—a process known as vermiculture—can be an easy way to turn your kitchen waste into a nutrient-rich compost you can add to your garden. An earthworm has the ability to consume its own weight in soil and organic matter each day. It leaves behind castings that form a rich compost. A pound of earthworms will generally compost one pound of kitchen waste per day. It is also easy to build your own worm composting container.

The easiest way to build a worm bin to hold your earthworms is to use a standard 20-gallon/76-liter storage bin with a lid (the same kind described for use as a container garden).

1. Drill a line of small air holes around the top perimeter of the bin, and in the lid itself for air flow.
2. Drill a larger drainage hole in the bottom front of the bin, and attach tubing using a waterproof sealant to glue in place. This tubing will catch the liquid

from the worm castings, so you will also want to design a way to keep the tube elevated or closed until you want to access this "worm tea" to add to your garden.

There are several ways you can construct the interior of your worm bin, but I have found success using a tray system inside the plastic bin. Using this tray method, place two stacking perforated storage trays or drawers (the type you often see in bathrooms or on a desk) inside the bin, stacked on top of each other. Your worms will live in the bottom tray and will migrate to the top tray in search of food once they have consumed the contents of the bottom tray. By relocating to the top tray when all the food has been eaten in the bottom tray, the worms will separate themselves from their castings, as the castings will remain in the bottom tray, ready to be emptied out into your garden. After you add the castings to your garden, you can then place the emptied tray on top of the tray that now contains your worms and kitchen waste. You will continue with this rotation every time the bottom tray fills up and is processed into nutrient-rich castings. The bottom of the storage bin will slowly fill with worm tea, and you can use the drainage hole to access this powerful fertilizer when enough accumulates.

DRAINAGE FOR YOUR WORM BIN

To access worm tea from your bin, you can easily fashion a simple system made from drainage tubing long enough to attach to the lid with a string. When you want to drain the worm tea, merely untie the string and let the liquid flow out the tube. If you don't like the looks of this more basic model, you can attach a spigot that can be turned on and off to allow the liquid to drain out. Note that you will have to wait for a lot of worm tea to accumulate for this spigot method to be worth the effort.

What to Know about Worms

When you install your tray system inside the bin, you will want to create a simple worm habitat in the bottom bin. By adding a layer of newspaper, then soil or compost, and a layer of shredded newspaper, your worms will be ready to go!

The best worms for your worm bin are a type called red wigglers. You can purchase these at some garden centers and can also order them online; or if you have the time and energy, you can find them in your yard. You don't need very many to get started because they reproduce quickly to match their food supply. But you will need to carefully monitor your worm population and slowly increase their food supply so that the food supply is in balance with the number of worms in your bin—you don't want one to outmatch the other. Red wigglers can process most food waste, but you cannot feed them citrus, meat, bones, or dairy products. You can also add shredded newspaper and dryer lint to create a healthy, odor-free habitat.

Three-Bin System Composting

Constructing your own bin can save you money. You can use recycled materials, and make the bin the size that will best fit your needs. One common construction is a three-bin wood and wire system. It is designed to provide good air circulation, and each bin is usually 3 feet by 3 feet—the minimum size you need to make good compost. The first bin is used to collect debris, the second bin is where you start your pile, and the third bin is where you put the compost pile when it is nearly finished. This kind of structure will last a long time if you use rot-resistant wood like cedar or redwood.

Wire fencing or wire mesh can be used to make a compost bin as long as the holes are small enough to hold the materials you have. Bending the wire into a circular shape is often the easiest and the sturdiest way to set it up. You can also purchase wire bins that are made from galvanized metal mesh. They come in several shapes and sizes and are easy to set up.

Plastic Bin Composting

There are many different types of plastic compost bins on the market. Plastic bins are easier to move around, last longer than wooden bins, and protect your compost from the rain and sun. They come in round or square shapes; some have solid sides, and others have removable and stackable sides. Most have a capacity of 12 cubic feet, which is the size needed for your compost to heat up, but you can also find larger bins.

Tumbler Composting

Another option is to purchase a compost tumbler. Tumblers are convenient because every time you rotate the drum, you turn the material, which will make it decompose faster. However, compost material can become very heavy and it can be difficult to turn the barrel when it is full. Tumblers can also keep the material too wet, so you need to be aware of how much moisture you are adding to the bin.

What to Compost

There are a few key components to a healthy compost pile, primarily using materials that will decompose and are safe to enter the food system, and creating a balance of the different materials you use. Using compost is also an important part of organic gardening, and focusing on soil health will help you to create compost that is highly nutritious. First, and most important, the materials that comprise your compost pile need to be able to decompose. Common kitchen waste—like vegetable remains and coffee grounds as well as other household and garden items like wood, paper, and plant material—are commonly composted materials. It is important to remember that when you add your finished compost to your garden soil, the decomposed materials that comprise the compost will become a part of the system that produces your food, making it very important that the compost be made up of safe materials. The easiest way to do this is to focus on using organic materials that will add health to your garden and the food that you grow. The next step to a healthy compost pile is to create a mixture of different types of materials. Creating the right mixture will keep your compost pile healthy and free of strong odor. A properly balanced compost pile will have a mixture of green material, brown material, and manures or good soil. Too much green material will attract flies and give your compost a strong odor, and too much brown material will slow down the decomposition of the pile.

The green material adds nitrogen to your pile. Some common green-material items you can use are vegetable kitchen waste, animal or human hair, weeds that have not gone to seed, green garden debris, cut grass, and seaweed.

The brown material adds carbon to your pile. Some common brown materials are: thick vegetable stems such as from broccoli and corn stalks, coffee grounds, shredded dried leaves, small wood shavings, straw, hay, twigs, wood ashes, and sawdust.

Depending on where you live, many of these items might be easily found at home, but if you do not have enough material to get started check out your neighborhood for items you can use. It is important to remember that organic materials are best to add to your compost and that items from other sources should be identified before adding them to your pile. Do your neighbors have leaves you can rake up and use? Do they use their grass clippings? Be careful not to use grass clippings where pesticides have been used! If you live near

a beach, go foraging for seaweed. Coffee grounds are a great addition to a compost pile and often coffee shops will give coffee grounds away for free—but remember that unless they are organic, coffee grounds are often laced with pesticides. Accumulate these items and then build your pile all at once.

Materials to Compost

Green Materials	Brown Materials	Do Not Compost
Vegetable waste	Thick vegetable stems	Animal or human feces or urine
Weeds (before they have gone to seed)	Coffee grounds	*Large quantities of:*
Grass cuttings	Shredded dried leaves	Oils
Animal or human hair	Small wood shavings	Pine needles
Green garden debris	Straw	Meat products or bones
Seaweed	Hay	Oak leaves
	Twigs	Toxic materials
	Wood ashes	Anything treated with pesticides
	Sawdust	

Smaller materials will break down more quickly, so avoid putting large pieces of wood or cardboard into the pile. Shred large twigs, leaves, corn stalks, and broccoli stalks first or they will take a long time to decompose. Using a variety of materials with different textures will give your pile better air circulation, which will make better compost. A pile with only one or two materials in it will take longer to decompose.

There are certain materials that should never be put in your compost pile because they will not decompose or they may carry diseases that you do not want in the final product. Do *not* include any of the following items in your compost: dog, cat, or human feces; animal urine; or large amounts of oil, pine needles, meat products or bones, oak leaves, toxic materials, or materials treated with pesticides.

It is not usually necessary to add organic fertilizers to your compost because the green and brown matter will make rich compost on its own. But if you know your soil is deficient in a certain element or elements, then by all means add a little to your compost pile. Using organic fertilizers such as rock powder, blood meal, bone meal, cottonseed meal, kelp, greensand, and peat moss can be used to increase the nutrient level and to correct the pH if it is needed. Simply add a handful of any of these in between your green and brown layers. You can also add lime to neutralize the acidity in your compost. Dolomite lime is the best form to add because it has a combination of calcium and magnesium in it. Any garden center will carry a variety of soil amendments meant to adjust and correct the pH of your soil.

Growing Organically

At the base of organic gardening is the ideology that healthy soil grows healthy plants. This means more than simply avoiding synthetic fertilizers, herbicides, and pesticides. Organic gardeners strive to create a sustainable system of food production that uses resources wisely, in part by creating a closed cycle that minimizes the amount of off-site additions to your garden. Using organic garden practices means that your garden will result in higher yields, be healthier for a longer period of time, produce vegetables of higher nutritional quality, and will lower your carbon footprint.

There are specific methods used in organic growing, and every methodology described in this book is aligned with organic practices. Basic good organic gardening includes such things as making your own compost and adding it to your soil, using cover crops, and practicing crop rotation.

The restoration, preservation, and enrichment of the soil are the cornerstones of organic gardening. All plants need four basic requirements to grow: warmth, moisture, food, and light. Your garden soil provides the first three and the sun provides the fourth. The soil is a living system that needs care and attention to remain in a healthy enough state to provide plants with the nutrients they need to grow and produce fruits and vegetables.

Maintaining a healthy, fertile garden soil is extremely important to having a successful vegetable garden. Building good soil starts with knowing what soil type you have and how fertile it is. You then need to regularly use certain methods, such as adding amendments prior to planting in the spring, rotating your crops each year, and growing cover crops over the winter and during rotations to enhance and protect your existing soil. If your existing soil is poor, it can take several years to get your garden beds to a state of high fertility and good structure, but do not let that discourage you. Some very successful vegetable gardens started out with sandy or rocky soil.

In nonorganic or conventional methods, synthetic chemicals and pesticides are used to enhance the growth of the plant and to promote fruit or pod production. Nonorganic growing methods emphasize feeding the plant, not the soil. Using these artificial forms will make your vegetables grow, but they also deplete the soil fertility or soil structure. Most conventional growers produce dead soil; there are no replenished nutrients in the soil for the plants to draw from. Relying on something outside your soil to grow vegetable plants creates a vicious circle. You have to purchase more and more fertilizers, chemicals, and pesticides in order for the crops to grow each season.

Starting Your Own Seeds, Indoors and Outdoors

There are two ways to plant your vegetable seeds: directly outdoors into the soil or indoors in seed trays to be transplanted to the garden later. Different vegetable seeds have different requirements for germination and maturing; some need heat and some do better in cool weather. You must know the best way to start each of your vegetables. Most vegetable seeds will do well either way, but some vegetables, such as root crops, need to be seeded directly because they do not grow well if their roots are disturbed.

Vegetables best started by seeding directly into the soil include: beans, beets, carrots, corn, garlic, peas, potatoes, radish, rutabagas, salad greens.

Some vegetables are difficult to start outdoors because the seed needs a very specific temperature to germinate. These are best started indoors so you have more control over their growing conditions. Some examples are tomatoes, peppers, and eggplants.

WINDOW SEEDLINGS

Most homes have at least one window that gets enough sunlight to start a tray of seedlings, but depending on your climate, the amount and strength of sunlight might be a little too weak to give your seedlings the light and warmth that they need to start off strong. If your plants start to look long and spindly and not very robust, this means that the climate is not warm and sunny enough. By incorporating a few grow lights, or sometimes just a space heater, you can adjust your indoor climate to be warm and "sunny" enough to start successful seedlings at home.

Trellis and Staking

Some vegetable plants need support to grow and produce healthy fruits or pods. Tomatoes and cucumbers do best if they can grow upright so that the fruit is not lying on the ground and the plant can receive both light and air circulation. Some varieties of peas and beans can grow up to 6 feet high or more and need support, and many of the small fruit plants described in Chapter 5 require trellising. These climbing plants have vines that need to be able to attach to a structure of some sort in order to continue to grow taller. Some common vine and sprawling vegetables are climbing and runner beans, cucumbers, snow and snap peas, summer squash, and tomatoes.

It is important to know which plants will need staking or a trellis so that you can put these up just before you plant the seed or set out your transplants. If you wait, you can disturb the roots, which can cause stress, and the vines of different plants can grow into each other, making it difficult to place a stake or trellis without damaging the plants.

Growing vertically can save a lot of space, especially if you have a tiny garden site or grow in containers on your balcony. The plants are often healthier because they don't touch the wet or cold ground, and therefore attract fewer pests and diseases. Mildew and rot are common problems for many fruiting vegetables, so it's to your advantage to keep the fruit off the ground. When your plants grow upright, you can easily see the fruit to harvest. Gardening can be backbreaking work, and harvesting off an upright structure can alleviate some of this stress on your body.

Trellis and staking material can be purchased at most garden centers or from seed catalogs. You can also make structures of your own out of materials you have on hand. Plastic or nylon netting, wooden frames, wire cages, wooden stakes, or teepee structures are common types of trellises and stakes. With a little experimentation and ingenuity, most can be adapted to your garden's specific needs. When choosing which methods to use, the most resourceful thing you can do is to adapt materials you already have to meet your needs.

Companion Planting

Companion planting is a common method employed in organic gardening, and is also popular for space-conscious gardening necessary in suburban and urban areas. The basic idea of companion planting is to utilize the complementary components of different plants to create a system where crops are working together with less outside support to meet their needs. The classic example of companion planting is a system called the Three Sisters.

The Three Sisters system includes the three crops of squash, corn, and beans. This system has deep historical roots and is famously tied to stories of Native Americans teaching this system to European settlers. The plants that are employed comprise a traditional North American staple diet, since in addition to their complementary growing characteristics, their nutritional components complement each other well. There are different ways to employ the Three Sisters, but the general concept is that the corn stalk acts as a climbing support for the beans, the beans provide nitrogen to the soil, and the foliage of the squash acts as a cover to block out weeds. The best way to plant the Three Sisters is by using a mound system that alternates crops, and to pay attention to seed spacing, timing of plantings, and water drainage and absorption. You will also want to choose seed varieties that suit one another well.

Companion planting can also be used as part of an integrated pest management plan by finding a balance between the contributions of different plants and using crops as allies for one another. As you become more and more familiar with the different crops that you grow, you will understand what each one gives and takes, and can plant accordingly.

Maintenance and Upkeep: Watering, Weeding, Pest and Disease Control

One of the most rewarding parts of gardening is learning to apply the creative and critical thinking that is needed to problem-solve issues. Gardening is not an exact science and each season there will be new problems and new solutions to try out. Don't let this scare you. Learning how to adapt your system as you go, as well as how to plan differently for the next season, is exciting and fun. Half the fun in planning your garden during the winter is trying to figure out how to make everything run smoother than it did the year before.

Watering: Too Much or Too Little?

Your crops need water to grow, mature, and produce fruits, pods, or seeds for you to enjoy. The amount of water each plant requires depends hugely on your climate, your soil, and the type of fruit or vegetable. All of these variables make watering a complex subject. When you assessed your site, you already began the process of deciding what type of watering system would work best for you. In this section you will learn what underwatering and overwatering can look like. By applying this knowledge to the watering systems described in Chapter 1, you can adapt your watering systems as necessary.

Signs of Underwatering

A plant's roots must continually grow for the plant to stay healthy and produce its fruit, seeds, or buds. The roots draw the nutrients from the soil up into the plant to make it grow. Water allows the nutrients in the soil to be absorbed into the plant. If there is too little water, the roots cannot draw in the nutrients. As a result, the plant will not grow and mature as it should. You can water the surface or even the top several inches of your soil, but the plant roots need to go deeper into the soil to get more nutrients. This is why it is essential for regular deep watering when growing vegetables.

Wilted plants are one sign that you're not watering enough. If the plant can draw enough water to replace the amount that is evaporated from its leaves, it will remain upright and strong. If the plant is not getting the water it needs, it will quickly collapse. This causes severe stress to the plant and often death. It is important to water a plant that is wilted as soon as you can. It is important to take time every day to observe your plants so you can find and quickly fix potential problems. Your plants should appear strong, have a bright color, and look healthy. If you have young transplants, you need to give them a drink of water every day because their roots are very shallow and the top few inches of your soil can dry out very quickly. Too little water can lead to poor root development, which will make for an unhealthy plant.

Once your vegetable plants have begun to mature, watering them once a week is usually sufficient. For some plants, it is best to stop watering them altogether once they have matured. For example, onions and potatoes need less water as they get close to maturity.

If you notice any of the following signs in your plants, chances are they are not getting enough water:

- The plants appear small and very slow growing
- The plants are not producing very many fruits, seeds, or buds and the ones being produced are often misshapen
- The plants are diseased
- The plants are yellowish or pale in color, or the plants are wilting. (Some natural wilting may occur in the heat of the day, but if your plants do not

perk up by late afternoon, you do have a problem.)

Signs of Overwatering

Most gardeners go to great lengths to make sure they add enough nutrients to their garden beds. When the soil is moist, the water helps hold the nutrients to rock particles in the soil so the plant roots can absorb them. If there is too much water in the soil, a process called leaching occurs. The excess water drains lower into the soil and takes a lot of the nutrients with it. Vegetable plant roots grow to different depths, but most do not grow below 2½ feet. If the excess water has washed away the nutrients, there is less nourishment available for the roots to absorb. Without proper food, the plant will not grow and mature as you may expect it to.

Plants also need good air circulation to breathe. If the soil is saturated with water, there isn't any room left in the soil for air circulation. If the air supply is cut off for any length of time, the plant roots will rot, killing the plant. That's why it's crucial to know your own soil conditions. Keep a record of rainfall and regularly check the moisture in your soil either with a moisture meter or by digging into the soil with your hands or a small shovel to see how far down the moisture is. Water when needed. If you are a novice gardener, it can take time to get to know your soil and climate, so initially it is important to observe and jot down some notes to refer back to for the following season.

Combating Drainage Problems

You need fertile, well-drained soil to grow great vegetables; however, most gardeners are not blessed with perfect soil or the perfect garden site.

How do you make your soil healthier and get proper drainage if you live in a rainy climate or if you have soggy soil? What do you do if you have the opposite problem—a sandy soil that does not hold any amount of water? How do you increase the amount of moisture in this type of soil?

Adding organic material is the solution to both problems. It will help lighten heavy soil so the water can drain better, and it will add more organic material to the sandy soil to help hold the water in. Aged animal manure, compost, or well-drained topsoil will help. Add in as much as possible—several inches if you can get enough. It is important to add in organic matter every year because you inevitably lose soil through erosion and the process of harvesting your plants. Mulching—covering the soil around plants with organic material—is another way to protect your soil from being blown away or nutrients from being leached out. Using cover crops to hold in nutrients and prevent erosion is another important way to maintain your soil.

If you have an extreme problem with drainage, call a landscaper or other expert to assess the situation for you. Underground drainage pipes can help remove any excess water you may have in your garden site. A well-drained soil helps keep the plant roots from becoming water-logged, allowing them to absorb the nutrients and oxygen needed to grow and mature. A poorly drained soil leaves your vegetable plants more susceptible to root rot and soil-borne diseases, so get help with drainage if this is a problem in your garden site.

Controlling the Weeds

A weed is just a plant that grows where it is not wanted. This means that weeds will sometimes be vegetable plants that are growing where you did not intend them to be. You may find that a carrot plant, or some other misplaced veggie, snuck into a bed of greens. It's hard not to admire the determination of these plants, but in order to keep your garden organized and growing according to plans, you still need to remove these weeds.

It is important to keep your garden beds weeded when your vegetable plants are small so your plants get a good start. Weeds compete for the nutrients in the soil, often taking over and leaving your veggie plants without the valuable food they need to grow and mature. In this chapter you will learn different techniques to help keep your garden weed-free—or at least to help you keep them under control.

Know Your Weeds

Weed seeds are introduced to your garden by birds, the wind, and on the bottom of your shoes. If a soil will not support weeds, it will not support your vegetables, so weeds are a sign that your soil is fertile. Seeds are brought to the surface by digging or tilling the soil. Once they are exposed to the light, they start growing. Some weeds can grow very fast, stealing the light, nutrients, and space from your vegetable plants.

There are three types of weeds—annuals, biennials, and perennials. Annual weeds live for only one season, but they produce thousands of seeds to ensure their survival. They germinate in the spring, produce seeds in the summer, and die in the fall. The best way to control annual weeds is to pull them out or cut them off with a hoe before they go to seed. Annual weeds grow quickly, so you need to be on top of these so they do not spread their seed. Some examples of common annual weeds are knotweed, pigweed, purslane, lamb's quarters, and chickweed.

A biennial weed grows the first year but does not produce flowers or seeds until the second year of growth. The best way to control these weeds is to remove them from your garden in the first year of their growth so they have no chance of spreading their seeds. Common biennial weeds include burdock, mullein, and Queen Anne's lace.

Perennial weeds live for years. Some produce seeds and others spread via their roots or bulbs. Perennial weeds often have deep roots that creep underground, making them difficult to eradicate. To control them, you should dig them out, removing as much of the root as you can. You often have to pull these weeds on a regular basis in order to get all of the root system. Some common perennial weeds are dandelion, thistle, bindweed, chicory, plantain, wild sorrel, and dock.

Woody perennials include poison ivy, kudzu, some types of morning glory (which is a type of bindweed), and Japanese honeysuckle. These are often invasive and are spread mainly by birds that love the seeds of these plants. Some of these plants need only a piece of stem to come in contact with soil to begin growing, so they can multiply quickly.

Grasses are another invasive perennial weed. They can make some of the worst weeds because they produce a lot of seeds and the plants are difficult to uproot. Quackgrass and some varieties of bamboo are common grasses that are considered weeds, especially in the vegetable garden. These plants produce underground roots and stems, and new plants pop up several yards away from the parent plant, making them difficult to remove.

What Weeds Can Tell You

You can learn a great deal about your soil by observing the weeds that grow in your garden. They can point to soil imbalances such as poor drainage, lack of water, low fertility, lack of aeration, and nutrient deficiency. Certain weeds only grow in poor soil, which gives you an indication that you need to add more amendments and fertilize your garden area if you want to grow a successful vegetable garden. Correcting the imbalances in your soil often means you will be able to eradicate certain weeds. Taking your time to observe what weeds are growing in your garden area can be especially important if you are planning to start a new garden in a certain area, or if you are looking for some property to purchase with the intention of growing your own food or growing to sell.

Weed Your Garden

Spring brings new growth to your vegetable garden. The seeds begin to sprout and the transplants start to grow—and so do the weeds. Spring is the time to pay attention to your weeds. Weeds often grow faster than your vegetable plants, so weeds can overtake vegetable plants and steal the sunlight and nutrients your veggie plants need. It is easier to kill the weeds when they are small and the soil is moist rather than later when the soil is hard and dry. Always remove the weeds before they go to seed.

Getting on your hands and knees and pulling weeds (getting the roots if you can) is probably the best way to get rid of weeds in your vegetable garden. This can be time-consuming, but if you set aside time each week to do a patch, you will be pleasantly surprised that it can be easy to stay ahead of them. You can also use a hoe to speed up the process. Keep in mind, you cannot always replace the thoroughness of hand weeding by using tools, but you can find an efficient and thorough balance.

Mulch

After hoeing or weeding your garden bed, add mulch to the area. Weed seeds need light to germinate and grow, so the main function of mulch in weed control is to prevent light from reaching the seeds. Cover the area completely with up to four inches of mulch, leaving a few inches clear around the base of the plant stem. You'll often have mulch materials handy from your own garden. Two common materials are leaves and grass. Raking leaves and then running the lawn mower over them to shred them makes great mulch. Collecting your grass clippings in a mower bag is another mulch that costs no money and is easy to get. Just make sure you do not use pesticides on your lawn; you do not want to contaminate your vegetable patch. Mulching as a season extender is discussed in the next chapter. Keep in mind that you can create a mulching system that combats weeds and assists with season extension.

Mulch also has its disadvantages, however. Mulch can promote fungus and disease, especially if it keeps the soil too damp and cold. Slugs and mice love mulch, so use mulches sparingly if you live in an area where these are a problem. Using certain types of mulch can cause deficiencies in your soil. For example, pine needles are very acidic and may make it more difficult to grow vegetables in a soil that is already acidic. Sawdust uses up nitrogen to decompose, which it does at the expense of your plants. It is important to understand what materials are best for your garden site and the reasons why you are using mulch.

Other Ways to Control Weeds

One great way to prevent weeds is not to bring them into your garden. Keep any tools you work with clean. Remove any weeds that have gone to seed from your garden. When shopping for plants, make sure there are not any weeds in the containers. When you bring in hay or straw to your garden, make sure it is from a weed-free source. If it is not weed-free, you may soon find hay growing in your garden beds. Animal manures can have lots of weed seeds in them, so make sure you know what kind of bedding was used and what the animals were fed. All of these small things can make it easier to keep your garden free of weeds, or at least make sure you are not introducing new weeds to the area.

Growing a cover crop can smother weeds. By adding a cover crop you can enrich your soil as well as control weeds. Cultivate or dig the area and then sow the green manure thickly. Turn the green manure over before the weeds you are trying to control have a chance to set seed. To be most effective, you will need to grow and turn two or three cover crops in succession. By growing vegetables close together, you can reduce the number of weeds by shading any area from the sun. Grow your lettuces close together so they overlap each other or grow your squash under your corn to prevent weeds from getting any light.

Weeds Can Be Good

Weeds do have some benefits to your garden as well. Many perennial weeds are deep-rooted, which helps bring nutrients to the surface so your vegetable plants have access to them. The deep roots also aerate the soil, which can be helpful, especially if you have drainage problems in your garden site. Weeds will grow when most other plants will not and are beneficial for preventing soil erosion and for preventing leaching of nutrients due to heavy rainfall. Many weeds are a great food source for bees, butterflies, birds, and beneficial insects, which all help control unwanted pests and disease in your vegetable garden.

Weeds can be composted so long as they have been pulled before they go to seed. If you have only pulled a few weeds, you can leave them to dry in your pathway; however, if you have a whole bucketful of weeds, it is best to remove them from the garden, because they can attract pests. Place them into your compost instead; they are a good source of green matter.

Most gardeners consider comfrey and stinging nettle to be weeds, but these herbs can be added to your compost or used to make a nitrogen-rich fertilizer tea. Both of these plants draw up and store nitrogen in their leaves. When they are composted or made into teas, the nitrogen is released.

There are many edible weeds that you can harvest to use in cooking. Stinging nettle, dandelion greens, purslane, lamb's quarter, and burdock are all edible (and actually fetch high prices at some high-end farmers' markets). Comfrey and stinging nettle also are sold in teas and healing salves. It is important to do the research and know exactly what plant you are harvesting before you ingest it. However, once you know what weeds are edible or offer health benefits, you will have a whole new outlook and even more choices to add to your dinner table—and the weeds grew without any work on your part!

Pests and Diseases

Having healthy soil and a healthy garden environment is the best way to prevent pest infestation and diseases. In this chapter, you will get advice on how to make your soil healthy and how to implement good gardening practices. No garden is without pests and diseases, but the important thing is to control them before they become a problem. The secret is taking the time to observe your garden. You can keep your plants healthy by using natural controls and promoting beneficial insects.

Identify the Problem

Take the time every day or at least once a week to walk through your garden just to observe the plants. Ignore the weeds and do not stop to harvest; just take a few minutes to turn leaves over, check inside the cabbage leaves, and look closely for any insects or pests you may see. Doing this on a regular basis will allow you to

catch problems early on. Is a certain plant looking less healthy than it did last week? Are those new holes in the leaves? Is something eating the spinach? Are those cabbage flies around the *Brassica* plants? Do the tomatoes have spots or are they split? By observing the changes to your plants, you can determine whether there is a threat to the plant and act quickly. Keeping a journal of any problems you have had in your garden this season will help you to plan for next season. You can use the successes and failures as a jumping-off point for tackling problems in future seasons.

Soil Health

Having healthy, fertile garden soil is the best way to keep pests and diseases away. First, find out what kind of soil you have and correct any imbalances. Healthy soil will produce healthy vegetable plants. Healthy vegetable plants will not be stressed and will be less vulnerable to pests or diseases. Nutrient deficiencies, overwatering, and underwatering can make your vegetable plants more susceptible to pests and diseases.

If you till your soil when it is too wet or too dry, you can harm living organisms and earthworms in the soil. You can also change the soil structure, which can cause drainage problems, leaching of nutrients, and an overall unhealthy space for your plant roots to grow. Most gardeners are raring to go in the spring and want to get the garden going, but it is important not to till too early. Take this moisture test before you till in the spring: Squeeze a handful of soil. If it forms a firm hard ball, it is too wet; if it crumbles into dust, it is too dry. Soil that is just right will keep some shape but then easily crumble when you squeeze it.

Tilling or digging your soil in the fall will expose insects, larvae, and eggs to the elements, which can help destroy them. After you harvest an area you are going to leave bare, dig it up and let it sit for a week or so. Then either mulch the area or plant a green manure. Mulch will help keep the soil from getting too wet and will prevent leaching if you live in a rainy climate. On the flip side, mulch can also be a haven for pests such as slugs and can encourage mold and disease, so regularly check under the mulch for any larvae or eggs during the winter and spring.

Growing green manures is another way to keep your soil healthy. They are added in the fall and help keep the soil from being blown away by the wind. Green manures also prevent erosion and leaching of nutrients. Green manures are tilled under in the spring, which adds organic matter and nutrients to the soil, making the soil more fertile and healthier.

Organic Gardening Is Good Gardening, Practices to Employ

Organic gardening is nothing more than using practical and resourceful methods in your garden that limit the introduction of outside elements. By using common-sense approaches and focusing on maintaining a balance within the mini ecosystem of your garden, you will not only have to spend less money on introducing new things into your garden but you will also grow a garden that is healthier and enduring.

Keep It Clean

Maintaining a clean vegetable garden will go a long way toward keeping it free of pests and disease. Trash, garden debris, and diseased plants can be a haven for many pests and diseases. Remove weeds from the garden after they are pulled out. They can be put in the compost bin—or in the trash if they have gone to seed. If you have any diseased vegetable plants, make sure you put them into a garbage bag immediately after pulling them so you don't spread the problem into other areas of your garden.

When harvesting, make sure all the fruit is removed from the garden. If there are any moldy fruits, place them into the compost rather than leaving them on the ground. When a plant is matured and no longer producing, pull it out and place it into your compost. Debris that is left in your garden beds or in the pathways can easily become a home for many pests and diseases.

Always have clean, sharp tools. Take the time at the end of each day to clean your tools. Scrape off any mud or dirt from each tool and give it a good spray of water to clean it. This will remove any pests. This is especially important if you have been working with diseased plants or in an area infested by pests. Every few weeks, take a little more care and wash the blades thoroughly with soap and water and then sharpen and oil them. A clean, sharp tool will make your life easier when working in the garden and will ensure that you are not spreading pests and diseases around your garden.

Crop Rotation

Crop rotation is another essential practice to ensure a healthy garden. By growing your veggie plants in a different area each year, you will discourage pests and diseases in your soil. Each vegetable plant or family of plants requires different nutrients and attracts different pests and diseases. These pests usually live in the soil right where the plant was, so by moving your plants to a new area of the garden they will be less likely to survive. A good rule of thumb is not to plant the same vegetable or family of vegetables in the same area for four years.

Companion Planting

Companion planting is another practice that can help to keep pests and diseases away from certain plants. In this method, certain plants are grown together so that they help each other. One plant may attract beneficial insects that will eat common pests, keeping the other plants nearby healthier. Another plant may deter a pest, keeping the plant beside it healthier. For example, marigolds are sometimes planted around vegetable plants to keep insects away from the crops.

Plant Health

To have healthy vegetable plants, you need to start with healthy seeds and transplants. Buy your seeds from a reputable seller or—even better—save your own seeds, especially if you find a certain variety that does well in your garden. A reputable seller should be willing to answer all of your questions, provide you with information on where and how the seeds were grown, and give you growing tips. If your garden site is susceptible to certain pests or diseases, try to find seed varieties that are resistant to those problems. Seed catalogs have valuable information regarding different varieties of seeds. Choosing the right varieties of vegetable plants for your garden will help keep the soil and plants healthier.

SEED SAVING

The plants that produce the first fruits or pods are the plants you want to mark for seed saving. This is often difficult to do, as most gardeners cannot wait to harvest the first tasty produce of the season. But tie a ribbon in an obvious location on the plant you want to mark for saving seed so you'll be reminded not to harvest this plant. Simply remove the seeds from the plant when ready and store them out of reach of sunlight.

When you purchase plants or transplants, make sure they are healthy. Many gardeners have unknowingly brought pests and diseases into their gardens via transplants. Look closely at any transplants you are planning to bring home.

Check for any insects in the soil or on the undersides of the leaves, holes in the leaves, and evidence that insects have chewed the leaves. These are all signs that the plant may be infested. Make sure the plant looks healthy. The stem should be strong and thick, the leaves should be well-formed and bright green, and the plant should not be root bound.

LOCAL SEEDLINGS

Visiting local nurseries or garden centers that start their own plants from seed is often a safer way to purchase pest-free seedlings. Additionally, these seedlings have been grown in a climate and region that battles the very same pests and diseases that your own garden is also susceptible to. Buying seedlings locally will give your garden a healthy head start and also allows you to take advantage of the experience of local growers in your area.

Natural Animal and Pest Control

There are some easy ways to control any animal or pest problems you may still have, even if you are adhering to all the practices outlined in this chapter. It is important to observe your garden on a regular basis so you can catch any potential problems early on; problems are much easier to handle if only a few plants are infected.

Larger pests or animals can cause a lot of damage in vegetable gardens. Deer, elk, raccoons, squirrels, opossum, skunks, gophers, and bears like vegetables just as much as we do. Take the time to observe what kind of animal is entering your garden. They often come out and feed at dusk or dawn. If it's not a wild animal, maybe your neighbor's dog or cat is sneaking in and digging up your plants. Keep watch to see what is causing the problem.

Harmful Pests Versus Beneficial Insects and Animals

It takes time to get to know what is living in or entering your garden, and each year may bring a new problem. Learn by asking fellow gardeners, reading books, checking out the Internet, or asking questions at your local nursery or garden center. Check your local library, community education center, or food co-operative to learn about gardening classes offered in your area.

Vegetable gardening is a new experience each season because you cannot predict what will happen. Do not be afraid to experiment with new plant varieties and try out different natural controls. Stay away from pesticides when it comes to your vegetable garden; they will not make your soil healthier and will kill the beneficial insects as well as the pests. Pesticides in insects may also harm birds and other animals that feed on these insects. Attracting and keeping beneficial animals and insects in your garden brings you closer to having healthier plants and a more abundant vegetable harvest.

Birds, bats, toads, and snakes are all animals you want in your garden. They will keep slugs, snails, and many insects under control. You help attract wanted creatures by adding habitats and feeders, like bird houses, and water sources like bird baths and garden fountains, to your outdoor space.

Common Diseases

You may physically see a pest or insect, but it is more difficult to diagnose a plant disease because the symptoms can be similar to those caused by other factors like excessive heat or cold, nutrient deficiencies in the soil, or poor drainage. Having healthy soil, giving your plants proper water and fertilizer, and maintaining good garden practices minimizes your plants' vulnerability to many diseases. If you do have a recurring problem, it is important to learn what it is and to try to correct the cause.

There are four main types of pathogens that cause disease in vegetable plants— bacteria, fungi, nematodes (roundworms), and viruses. They all attack plants in different ways but produce some common symptoms in plants such as wilting, yellowing, and stunted growth. The pathogens can be spread in various ways. They can be blown around by the wind or carried in water. Animals, humans, garden tools, and other equipment can also transfer pathogens from plant to plant. Insects can carry a pathogen in their saliva and transfer it from plant to plant. When you are trying to diagnose a disease, it is important to learn the life cycle of the pathogen so you can avoid spreading it.

For a disease to occur, three elements must be present in your garden: a susceptible plant, a pathogen, and favorable conditions for the pathogen to survive. To control or manage plant diseases, you need to remove one or more of these elements. A disease cannot develop if one of these elements is missing. Pulling out and destroying the infected vegetable plant removes the pathogen. You can also make it difficult for pathogens to survive by creating an environment that is not compatible for them. For example, avoid overhead watering or take time to trellis a plant so it has better air circulation. Both of these measures make it more difficult for the pathogen to survive.

The best way to keep your vegetable garden free of pests and diseases is to have healthy soil, to give your plants the proper amount of water, practice crop rotation, and to keep your garden and tools clean. A healthy plant will be better able to fight off anything that comes its way. No vegetable garden will be totally free of all pests or diseases, and remember that you want beneficial insects and animals to stay around.

CHAPTER 3

SEASON EXTENDERS

It's not hard to sell the benefits of a longer growing season to the home gardener—more fresh food and a more consistently diversified diet for you and your family is reason enough to implement a season-extension plan as part of your home food system. Even in four-season and colder climates, you can significantly extend the growing period of your garden by adapting a few key tools and methods to your microclimate. By getting a head start early on in the season, and by keeping your garden going longer at the end of the season, your family will be able to eat fresh homegrown food for more months of the year, while still allowing for a gradual transition in and out of the fast pace and hard work that comes with the height of the growing season.

Thinking about season extension in creative and collaborative terms is important. On a very basic level, you can extend your growing season by protecting crops from conditions that are otherwise too difficult for them to withstand on their own. How to go about creating these systems of protection is different in every garden and every microclimate. There are many simple and traditional approaches to season extension and crop protection that do not require many resources to implement and maintain. Having a sense of experimentation and innovation is important, because there is no one way or right way when it comes to season extension (or gardening, for that matter).

In this chapter, different crop protection tools are explained to give you a full sense of each method. In your garden, you will find the most success if you are incorporating these tools into more comprehensive systems of crop protection and season extension. For example, using row covers in combination with low and high tunnels in colder weather strengthens the warmth-providing system that you are creating. Likewise, during late summer heat, using shade cloth to lower temperatures in your hoop house can assist in the germination of some late summer and early fall crops. Using mulching as the first step in a series of soil-warming procedures will add more depth and longevity to your season-extension system. In some cases, you will want to use one method on its own, but by having the knowledge of and access to each method, you can decide when and how to utilize the most appropriate system for the particular needs of your garden. Like everything with organic gardening, a diversified approach is more likely to yield the results you are looking for, and reassurance is provided by individual components serving as backup to one another.

Row Covers

Row covers are useful in a number of different ways. Referring to different forms of polypropylene material that is either draped directly over the plants themselves or resting just above the plants and supported by a hoop structure, the material in these coverings is also referred to simply as garden fabric or generally as low covers because of its proximity to the ground and crops during use. Depending on how and why you employ row covers, the benefits include frost and cold protection, temperature boosts to soil, water conservation, and pest control.

In regard to season extension, row covers are primarily beneficial because of their ability to create a consistency in soil and air temperature that is warmer than that outside of the area they are covering. The barrier that the fabric provides keeps warm air around the plants and in the soil, and also helps to conserve the soil's moisture and provide protection from pests and some weeds. Row covers can help to minimize drastic temperature changes between daytime and nighttime and also act as an important, although slightly weak shield against frost (offering only a few degrees of protection).

Using Row Covers

Thinking and planning for a longer season happens on both ends of the growing season—early in the spring and into the fall. Row covers can be used to help transition your crops into a productive season earlier in the spring and used to help extend growing when temperatures start to drop in the fall. Row covers, while extremely valuable, provide crops with temperatures only a few degrees warmer than that outside of the microclimate they create. These few degrees, however, are important protectors against late frosts, and serve some plants well with an early temperature boost in spring. In this way,

row covers are both valuable and also limited in their use. In order to get the full value out of your row covers, you want to use them efficiently, smartly, and often in conjunction with other season extenders.

Row Covers

In the spring, you can plant earlier by using row covers as protection for young crops. Some plants will respond better to this than others. Because row covers are only adding a few extra degrees of warmth to your crops, more vulnerable plants, such as tomatoes, will not be successful with garden fabric as their only protection. Hardier crops, like root veggies and some *Brassica*s, are more likely to be successful under the singular protection of row covers.

In order to succeed in protecting the health of your plants, you have to learn to balance light provision—an average row cover allows only about 70 percent of light in—with cold protection. This means that you will spend a certain amount of time laying covers down at night to retain heat and protect from frost, and that you will equally spend time uncovering crops to give them more sun and air ventilation. When wind is a factor, this can be trickier. You will need to hold your garden fabric down on its corners using weighted bags—like plastic bags filled with compost, sand, or other heavy material. Luckily, garden fabric is readily available in all sorts of sizes, including larger widths that will allow you to cover more space, without so many weighted bags needed to hold it in place. While simple enough, managing row covers in a way that effectively balances temperatures with light can be both time-consuming and labor-intensive.

Once your crops have matured and temperatures have become consistently warmer, you are finished using your row covers until the fall, when you can use them once again to provide the same balance of light provision and cold protection.

Row covers are extremely versatile because of their simplicity. They are used effectively in anything from small gardens to commercial farms precisely because of their adaptability. Combining row covers with the other season extenders described in this chapter will provide you with an array of options to best protect your crops and get them growing earlier in the spring and for longer in the fall.

Using Mulch

Mulch is useful in any garden as a tool to warm soil, provide protection, and control weeds. As a season extender, mulch works by protecting the root systems of plants as the weather becomes more harsh. By acting as a barrier from frost, snow, winds and cold temperatures, as well as raising the temperature of the soil, different mulches are better suited for different needs and conditions.

Plastic Mulch

On a basic level, black plastic mulching is used as a method of weed control, and using clear plastic mulch can warm soil by a few significant degrees. With new developments in agricultural products, there are variations of these two basic forms of plastic mulching available. Plastic mulching that combines the two characteristics of weed control and soil warmth is available. This mulching works by letting the heat-producing rays in, while also blocking out the light waves that would otherwise promote weed growth. In addition to this hybrid, plastic mulching comes in biodegradable forms, allowing for easier removal and/or incorporation in your garden. Plastic mulching is a straightforward way to warm soil for crops.

Leaves and Other Biodegradables

Using leaves you rake in the fall and/or hay or straw to mulch your garden is worthwhile for weed prevention and for the nutrients that are added to soil alone. Also noteworthy, though, is using mulch to warm and protect your soil and crops toward the end of the warmer temperatures season. Many people find success in mulching with straw and hay, and some will argue that one is better than the other.

In general, you can count on more weeds with straw mulching than you can with hay, although this can vary and should not necessarily sway you from using straw if it is more easily and inexpensively available to you than hay.

For my garden, I prefer a combination of both hay and dead leaves. Because I live in New England, I have unlimited access to fallen leaves during the fall. Since I have to wait until October for the leaves to begin accumulating on the ground, I typically start off by mulching my crops with hay that I am able to get from a friend who owns horses. I use any hay that is too "spoiled" (typically by exposure and dampness) for the horses to eat, and if I need to supplement this mulching base before there are leaves available, I use other biodegradables, such as old newspapers, to fill in the space. When the first leaves begin to fall, I rake them onto tarps and add them to the pre-laid mulch. I continue adding more layers of mulch as more leaves fall and end the process when there are no longer leaves left to add.

Straw Mulch

Tunnels, Hoop Houses, and Greenhouses

On the spectrum of season extenders, the greenhouse is the most permanent and intensive season extender to build, establish, and maintain. Hoop houses and high and low tunnels are the less permanent and simpler forms of greenhouses. Depending on your climate, space, time, and financial constraints, one of these options, or a combination, will do much to not only extend your season but to also increase your crop yields.

Low Tunnels

Low tunnels are similar to the hoop-structured row coverings described earlier in this chapter. The only significant difference is not in the structure (hoops are still used close to the ground and the crops) but rather in the material used to cover the hoops. While row covering uses different forms of materials, most common is a woven polypropylene that has the weight and movement of a lightweight blanket. Low tunnels, on the other hand, use the same plastic material as greenhouses, but draped over and attached to the hoop structure. Like mini hoop houses, low tunnels provide a barrier from the frost, wind, pests, and other factors that might be more common, or that crops are more susceptible to, at the beginning and end of the growing season. Low tunnels offer more wind and element protection than row covers, whereas row covering is singularly most effective for minimal heat increases and frost protection. Often, the combination of low tunnels and row covers can create a microclimate ideal in providing direct warmth and protection from other variables.

Because low tunnels are relatively close to the ground and close to the crops that they protect, they are efficient in creating and utilizing heat, and in conserving moisture. Depending on the size of your garden and how you decide to utilize low tunnels, these structures can be built tall enough to work in (although not necessarily tall enough to stand upright in), or so low to the ground that you have to move the plastic every time you want to cultivate.

The beauty of low tunnels is that they are simple to design and build. Depending on how you plan to use your low tunnels, you will need to create structures that balance this simplicity with an appropriate level of hardiness and permanence. If you are building tunnels that are large enough to work inside, then you will want to fasten the plastic to the hoops in a more permanent way than a tunnel that you will have to uncover every time you need to cultivate. Finding the right balance between semi-permanence and accessibility is key to low tunnel success.

Low Tunnel

High Tunnels and Hoop Houses Compared to Greenhouses

High tunnels and hoop houses are one and the same. These structures use the same frame structure as greenhouses do, but do not incorporate heat-producing elements like greenhouses do. For simplicity's sake, high tunnels are greenhouses without heat, and are the next step in season-extender progression after the more basic tunnels described in the previous section.

Both greenhouses and hoop houses can be used to start seeds that will be transplanted elsewhere and for direct seeding protection. The very visible difference with these two uses is that planting in a greenhouse is not usually done directly into the ground. These structures often have flooring that is permanent, and the trays holding seedlings are on tables. The other type of structure, the hoop house, involves planting in the ground that it shelters.

A greenhouse is often used as a temporary home to start seeds in trays and raise them until they are seedlings ready to be transplanted. A hoop house is typically used as the permanent home for direct-seeded crops or for seedlings that are being transplanted to the ground early on. In this way, hoop houses are used as protection for crops so that they can be grown earlier and for longer into the season. With this in mind, the most common way I have seen hoop houses used is for the creation of a space on the farm or garden that is specifically designated for crops that the grower plants successively throughout the year in order to always have something fresh growing.

At one of the farms where I work, the hoop house is always home to different forms of greens. We use this structure to house greens in a few different ways. Because this hoop house is a stationary structure (as opposed to hoop houses that are on rollers and can be moved around the farm), before the cold sets in, we transplant some crops from other parts of the unprotected fields into the hoop house to winter over. Primarily, we transplant mature kale and swiss chard plants into the hoop house in order to be able to harvest from them after the first frosts. We also direct seed salad mix and spinach in the early spring, and start some other greens (like chard) by planting transplants earlier than would be possible outside of the protection of the hoop house. All of this is fairly labor-intensive but the rewards are worth it when we are able to harvest greens almost year-round!

Greenhouses

Nowadays, greenhouses come in all sizes and styles, and are also heated in a variety of ways. Much of the decision-making around what size, style, and heating system depends not only upon your budget but also upon how and what you grow. For some people, it makes sense to grow one crop directly in the ground inside a greenhouse if it means you can harvest that crop earlier on and for a longer time. For others, the results are better if the greenhouse is used as a place to start all the different crops you want to grow, and to do so in trays that will later be transplanted outside of the greenhouse.

Like the mention I made of hoop houses that use rollers to move about the farm, mobile greenhouses are also a reality and are used by organic growers to promote soil fertility and health. The major difference, once again, between mobile greenhouses and mobile hoop houses is that greenhouses are heated. When following the organic growing principles of crop rotation and soil health, mobility of season-extending structures allows the soil and air protected by these houses to be a part of the natural cycle when not in use.

CREATIVE GREENHOUSE HEATING

Figuring out a cost-efficient way to heat a greenhouse is often the most limiting factor when it comes to establishing this particular structure. Depending on your abilities and the resources you have access to, there are creative ways that you can heat a greenhouse that do not use oil or gas heat. Using a wood stove if you have access to firewood or by strategically utilizing the heat from a compost pile are examples of innovative ways that you can add heat to your greenhouse inexpensively.

Hybrid Houses

For the at-home gardener whose primary goal is not monetary profit as much as it is to create a self-sufficient food system that will feed a family throughout the year, using a hoop house that can, when necessary, be heated and ventilated with a basic fan and heating system (even a space heater and a table top fan can work) is a hybrid that in many cases offers enough support and seasonal longevity for a family garden. The trick to success in using this type of semi-heated hoop/greenhouse is to make sure that your energy input does not outweigh the production output. What this means will be different to different people, but it probably won't be worth it to you to harvest a few tomatoes earlier in the season if the energy cost of each tomato was $10 in electricity and a significant increase in labor hours. If you are creative and experiment with different heating methods, however, you are likely to come up with a system that balances all of your expectations.

Hybrid Tunnel

Cold Frames

Like tunnel and house systems, the more traditional glass cold frame offers protection for crops in a way that can be manipulated according to what variables you are working with and against. Because

glass is a better insulator than plastic, the temperature increase that cold frames can provide is typically several degrees higher than that of a standard tunnel system.

Structurally, a cold frame is square-shaped, with a back side taller than the front, so that the top slopes downward. This top window is comprised of clear glass and can operate on a hinge system to open and close—opening to keep from overheating and closing to protect plants from cold. Some cold-frame systems open and close on their own by incorporating a wax-filled cylinder that works within a piston-and-spring system. The wax expands in the heat, forcing the window open, and shrinks when the temperature decreases, causing the window to close. Auto-ventilation systems like this cost about $60 per unit. Simpler systems are manually operated, often by propping a window open to rest on a notched rod. These same notches can then work to hold the window closed.

In some ways, cold frames fulfill the same needs as a hoop house, only on a smaller scale and with more intensity of heat. Because of the permanence that glass lends, cold-frame structures are often permanent structures. They can be stationary, remaining in place during the growing season, or permanent year-round. Or they can be moved around. Whether you choose to leave your cold frames outside all year or store them inside when they are not in use is a decision that ultimately reflects your climate and how sheltered an area your cold frame is installed in.

GLASS OVER PLASTIC

Major benefits of cold frames are that they last for a long time and glass creates a warmer climate than plastic. Glass also is much more durable than the plastics used in the other season-extension methods described in this chapter. Unfortunately, glass is also more expensive, although you can often find old windows that can be incorporated into a cold-frame design. Most people will probably agree that cold frames are more attractive than their plastic, hoop-framed counterparts. The permanence of their structure is also handy when looking for a designated area to harden off plants in. To harden off plants simply means to provide seedlings with a transition period from their indoor, more sheltered environment, to the more harsh outdoor environment. Allowing for this transition gives plants more of a chance of success and also makes them healthier and stronger in the long run.

Cold Frame

When and How to Use Cold Frames

Depending on the scale and style of your garden, cold frames may or may not be the best choice for you. Coming to a decision about this can take a season or two. Because of this, cold frames are best incorporated into a season-extension system that is already established. Because of the cost of glass and the permanence of the structures, installing cold frames in your first year of growing can eliminate much of your flexibility and sense of experimentation. You might end up deciding that you would like to install cold frames because the crop protection system that you developed involves using tunnels in much the same way as you would a cold frame, and therefore the switch to glass (with less waste and more permanence) is justified.

When installing a cold frame in your garden, there are a few important characteristics about the design and placement that will give you the most success. In order to get the most protection and warmest temperatures from your cold frame, you will want to install the frame where it will have southern exposure and northern protection. Ideally, this can mean having the back of the frame against a sheltered area (although not so much that it is in the shade). You will also want to build your frame so that the back wall is higher than the front wall. The result will be a frame that slopes downward and southward. The slope should always be one inch per foot, regardless of the size or shape of the frame.

Permanent or Temporary

If you are installing a cold frame that will be permanently located, you will want to prepare the area by digging out enough soil to rest the base of the frame in the ground. In doing so, you will better insulate the bed and support the frame itself. A good reason to build a permanent cold frame is to create an area to harden off plants in. You won't need to worry about decreasing soil fertility because these seedlings will live in their trays inside the cold frame until they are hardy enough to be transplanted into the ground without protection.

Another reason for a permanent frame might be that there is an ideal location naturally occurring in your outdoor space that you plan to utilize every year, like a small hill or slope that favors southern exposure and wind protection. If this is the case, and you will be using the ground soil to plant in, you will want to be sure to pay attention to your soil health.

A temporary cold frame can be placed on any level garden bed. The beauty of being able to move the cold frame around is that you apply its protection to any crops that may need it. In this way, more crops can benefit from the support of the cold frame. Temporary cold frames are easy to incorporate into crop rotation because they have fewer limitations than permanent structures. Keep in mind that, depending on the size of your cold frame,

moving the structure around will not necessarily be easy for one person to do.

Overwintering and Hardening Off

Many season-extension systems, like cold frames, can be used to meet overwintering and hardening off needs. The basic idea to all season extenders is to alter the microclimate of the plant slightly in order to provide minimal protection from the environment and to achieve a more perfect environment for the plant. When seasons change, plants need to adjust to the changes in their climate. By providing crops with protection during these changes you can increase the chances of their success as well as their overall productivity and healthy.

Overwintering

Overwintering refers to the process of protecting plants in a mature and dormant state throughout the winter. In some cases this means that you won't harvest from the plants during the winter, but that there will be an early harvest in spring as the mature plants transition back into a process of growth. For other crops this means that growth will stop in winter but that you can continue to harvest until there is nothing left to eat.

Not all plants are capable of surviving winter conditions. In general, varieties of plants that are described as winter hardy or frost hardy can withstand the winter if they are protected. Greens like spinach and some hardier lettuces, root veggies like carrots and turnips, and *Brassica*s like kale, collards, or Brussels sprouts are examples of crops that are commonly overwintered.

Many of the tools described in this chapter can be adapted to assist with overwintering. In particular, mulching and cold frames are two tools that can be employed, either separately or together, to overwinter crops. The easiest way to mulch crops for overwintering is to add biodegradables, such as described in the section about mulching in this chapter. Depending upon your specific region and the microclimate of your garden, mulching might be enough protection for some plants. For other plants, using a cold frame adds a necessary second layer of protection.

Hardening Off

With overwintering in the fall and transplanting in the spring, it is necessary to gradually increase the hardiness of your crops. When temperatures start to cool down in the fall, you want to ease the plants into the colder weather by adding mulch. If you plan to use additional protection through cold frames, you will want to add this component later on. It is helpful to think about hardening plants off in the fall much like you dress yourself with the change of seasons. If you started wearing your winter coat in the early fall, then come January, your winter coat would not feel warm enough. This same concept applies to plants. If you protect a bed of

crops with a cold frame in August, then the plants will never be able to adjust to colder temperatures. Your role as gardener is to ease them into the winter by offering transitional and gradual assistance.

In the spring, the same concept of easing crops into new temperatures applies. Seedlings that are started indoors will need to adjust to the cooler temperatures and harsher conditions of the outdoors gradually. Using strategies that are less protective than the greenhouse and yet more gentle than Mother Nature will harden off plants and make them stronger. Using a cold frame and/or row covers will help with this transition.

The concept of season extension is simple and so is the methodology around the tools used to make a longer season possible. Like anything in agriculture, we discover complexity as we adapt models to our specific needs. Luckily, much of the fun of growing your own food comes with problem-solving your way into the system that works best for your particular garden. Have fun using the tools and methods described in this chapter to create your season-extension system!

CHAPTER 4

PLANT TO PRESERVE— VEGETABLES

For the individual or family who wishes to consume a diet consisting primarily of food raised at home, vegetables are the most significant crop to be grown. This food group is packed with variety, nutrition, cultural significance, and important calories. Deciding what vegetables to grow should be taken seriously, but should also be fun.

In Chapter 1, you already started on some of the steps necessary to begin planning your vegetable garden when you began thinking about what you could grow in your garden space and what you and your family like to eat. This chapter outlines information about growing and preserving popular vegetable varieties. By incorporating the information from this chapter with what you and your family have already mapped out for your garden and diet, you will be able to develop a satisfying supply of homegrown food that will keep you well fed throughout the whole year.

What Vegetables Need

Sunlight and growing seasons are both important considerations, but you should also research the individual needs of the specific vegetable plants you have chosen to grow. Some vegetable plants grow best upright or vertical; others like to be protected from the hot sun, wind, or rain. All of these factors need to be considered when planning your vegetable garden layout.

The following is a list of vegetables that store well and are part of a balanced diet. You can use this list as a base for your food plan, but you should not feel limited by it. If a favorite veggie or a food that you are interested in trying to preserve is not listed below, you can find out if and how to preserve it with a little research. Don't forget—experimentation is one of the most fun parts of growing your own food!

Beans, Peas, and Perennial Vegetables

Freshly picked beans and peas are two of the tastiest treats from the garden. They are easy to grow in pots or raised beds, can be trellised to add structure to your garden, and have lovely flowers that enhance your vegetable garden's appearance. The other vegetables that will be discussed in this chapter—artichokes, asparagus, and sun chokes—are all perennial veggies; they die back in the fall and emerge again in the spring.

Beans

Beans are one of the easiest vegetables to grow. You sow the seeds directly into the garden, where they will germinate quickly in the right temperature and grow vigorously. Considering the small amount of space they take up in your garden, beans produce an awfully plentiful bounty. There are several different types of beans—bush beans (sometimes called snap beans), runner beans, pole beans, shelling beans for drying, lima beans, soybeans, and fava beans (sometimes called broad beans). Most varieties need warm soil to germinate, so they are usually planted in late spring. To tell whether it's time to plant your beans, walk barefoot on the soil at midday. If the soil feels cold, hold off for a while; if it doesn't feel cold, you're ready to plant. The exception to this is fava beans, which are a cool-weather bean and best planted in early spring.

Beans grow at various heights. Bush beans grow to a height of 16 inches; on the other end of the spectrum, pole and runner beans can grow up to 8 feet tall. The type of beans you want to grow will determine whether they need support.

Beans will grow in almost any reasonably good garden soil. They grow best in a sandy, loamy soil with a neutral pH. Beans do not like a lot of moisture before they germinate, but they need regular watering once they have sprouted in order to produce tender beans. They are best harvested young when they are the most tender, and beans need to be picked every few days so the plant knows that it needs to keep producing more beans. If you leave the pods on the plant, the plant will take it as a sign to stop producing.

Fresh beans won't last for much more than a week in your refrigerator, but they can be stored easily either by drying (preferred) or by canning or freezing. To freeze beans you will first need to blanch them (plunge them into boiling water for a short time) and only expect them to keep for several months in the freezer, versus the several years they can keep if they are dried. Beans that you buy from the grocery in bags are dried beans (versus canned beans that are also common in stores). Dried beans will store for several years if harvested and dried properly.

To cook dried beans, you will need to soak them overnight. After the beans have been soaked, you can slowly cook them over the span of several hours, adding a little oil (I prefer canola because its neutral flavor doesn't take away from the beans), salt, pepper, garlic, onion, and any other seasoning that you prefer. The beans should be cooked at a low heat and stirred occasionally to prevent burning or sticking. If you have a pressure cooker, you can achieve similar results to slow cooking but in about 40 minutes.

COOKING BEANS IN A PRESSURE COOKER

Cooking beans in a pressure cooker is one of the best ways to enjoy dried beans without the hassle of soaking and slow-cooking them. To achieve success with beans in your pressure cooker, follow the chart that came with your specific pressure cooker for water-to-bean ratio. It is best to bring the water to a boil before adding the beans. The trick to cooking unsoaked beans in a pressure cooker is to add a spoonful of oil to the water. This decreases the amount of foam that is produced, making it less likely to clog the pressure vent.

Peas

Peas are a cool-weather vegetable; they do best when planted in the early spring. If you live in a climate that has mild winters, do a second planting in mid-August for a fall harvest. Peas can withstand a little frost. They like a rich, well-drained soil that is not too high in nitrogen. They like organic matter, so mix in several inches of compost or aged animal manure when preparing the garden bed.

There are three different types of peas. Shelling peas are grown for the seeds. Snow peas have a flat edible pod and are often used in stir-fries. Snap peas have an edible pod and seeds that are eaten together. There are several varieties of each of these types of peas. Some peas will need to be staked; snow peas and snap peas can grow up to 5 feet high.

Peas need moisture to germinate, and they often germinate faster if the seed is first soaked overnight. Because peas are planted in the spring, it is important that the seed and plants do not get waterlogged or they will most likely rot. Peas are best stored frozen and can keep for several months in a freezer. They can also be dried and canned.

Perennial: Artichokes

The globe artichoke is easy to grow, is relatively disease free, and can make a stunning addition to any garden. It grows rapidly and can grow up to 6 feet tall and just as wide. It is a cool-season perennial vegetable that will grow vigorously and produce for 4 to 5 years. Just a few plants will produce enough artichokes for a small family.

The globe artichoke is known as an exotic plant, and it's not a common vegetable for most home gardeners. However, it is definitely worth growing, especially if you are looking to plant something new. This stately plant has gray-green leaves and produces flower buds that resemble elongated pinecones. The cones are green and layered with edible bracts, but the heart of the cone is the true delicacy. If the plant is left to mature, a large bud opens to reveal a purple thistle flower. This flower can be dried and is often used in floral arrangements.

Globe artichokes will produce some buds the first year but are best harvested in the second or third year after planting when they are producing between twelve and thirty buds on each plant. This is also about the time when they are becoming crowded and need to be divided. They require a cool period before they can flower but are sensitive to the cold and may only be grown as annuals if you live in a cold northern climate. Even if you live in a milder climate, it is best to cut the plants back to about 6 inches above the ground and protect the roots from freezing by using thick mulch.

Perennial: Sun Chokes

Sun chokes, often known as Jerusalem artichokes, are not related to the globe artichoke in any way. The "Jerusalem" tag came from a misunderstanding of the Italian word *girasole*, meaning "sunflower."

The term *artichoke* comes from an Arabic word meaning "thistle," which relates to the plant's appearance. It is a perennial vegetable that belongs to the sunflower family. The underground tuber is the part that is harvested and eaten.

Sun chokes will grow in any kind of soil and often grow quickly and prolifically. Plant tubers in the spring, giving them a large area to grow (they can grow up to 6 feet tall). They produce yellow flowers a little smaller in size than the common sunflower. When the leaves die back in the fall, the tubers can be harvested. They will overwinter in the ground and will taste sweeter after a frost. Sun chokes are a low-calorie alternative to potatoes.

Perennial: Asparagus

Asparagus is another perennial vegetable. Plant it in a permanent area; once planted, it will produce new shoots each spring and will do so for 15 to 20 years without too much work on your part. It is best to buy 1-year-old crowns, or rhizomes, as they take 3 years to grow from seed to harvest. In the first year of planting, resist cutting any of the spears so they can leaf out. The feathery foliage will nourish the roots, which in turn will give you more spears in the second year. In the second year, you can harvest the first few spears, but stop harvesting once the spears start to look spindly or have a diameter less than ¼ inch. In the third and following years, you will be able to harvest over a much longer season.

When preparing an asparagus bed, dig in generous amounts of compost or aged animal manure. This can be done by digging a trench a foot deep in your bed and then filling it with the 3 to 4 inches of organic material. Mix this with the existing soil. Lay the crowns in the trench and cover them with 2 inches of soil, but do not cover the tips of the shoots. As the plant grows, you can add more soil around the plant.

In the fall, cut back the fernlike foliage of the asparagus plant. This is also a great time to mulch the bed with aged animal manure to add nutrients to the soil as it decomposes over the winter. Leaves or straw can be added on top for more protection from the cold, but avoid mulching with sawdust, which is often too acidic for the plant.

Root Veggies

Root vegetables are grown for their edible roots. The veggies in this section are all easy to grow and have similar growing needs and soil conditions. Root veggies need a well-prepared garden bed with a light soil to grow their best. Here you'll find easy tips on how to grow some common root vegetables including beets, carrots, potatoes, radishes, and rutabagas. We will also discuss growing garlic, leeks, and onions, which are grown mainly for their roots but have some distinctive characteristics of their own.

Beets

Beets are a love-or-hate vegetable; either you love them or you have no desire to eat them at all. They are a great addition to any home garden because they are easy to grow, have a long harvest, take up a small amount of space in your garden, and can be stored. They have more than one edible part and can be eaten raw or cooked, so they are a very versatile vegetable. The young leaves are used with other baby greens in popular salad mixes. The mature leaves, beet greens, can be steamed for a nutritious side dish to add to any meal. The roots can be harvested as sweet and tender baby beets or they can be left to grow to maturity to be harvested as you need them all summer and fall.

The many varieties of beets give you more options than just a round red beet. You can buy seeds that will produce elongated roots, which have a milder taste. Beets can now be grown in a multitude of colors. There are white, yellow, orange, and striped varieties. Beets like a fairly rich soil that is free of rocks and debris. Add in aged animal manure and lime if needed when preparing your garden bed. Make sure your bed is well prepared with at least a foot of loose tilled soil for the roots to grow. Remove any lumps, rocks, or sticks from the soil so they don't impede the growth of the root. Beets are usually direct-seeded to your garden bed; however, they are slow to germinate, so mark the bed where they are planted. The seed can produce more than one plant; they will need to be thinned so there is only one plant for every 3 to 4 inches of garden soil as the seedlings start to grow.

To store beets you can pickle them, can them, or keep them in a root cellar. I often employ the first two methods by making and canning a beet relish and pickled beets, and storing both in glass cans. I do not store beets in my root cellar because they are not a favorite vegetable of mine and so I choose not to take up storage space for them in my root cellar. If you have a family that loves beets, however, they store well in large quantities if packed in peat moss in your root cellar or similar environment.

Carrots

Carrots are one of the most popular vegetables in the world. Pulling a baby carrot from the garden, wiping off a little dirt, and biting into it is an experience everyone should have. There is nothing better than a tender, freshly picked carrot! Carrots are great to grow if you have children around because carrots grow fairly quickly and can be picked at any size—and children love to pull them out of the ground.

The time-consuming part of growing carrots is the bed preparation. In order to grow their best, carrots need a deep, loose sandy soil that is free of debris. They are a great vegetable to grow in raised beds because the soil texture is often lighter than in a regular garden bed. If you have a heavy soil, it is important to dig in compost or aged animal manure to lighten the soil. However, if the soil is too fertile the carrots may get hairy and misshapen, and may not taste as good. It can take a few years to get your soil to the proper consistency to grow fabulous carrots. If there are any obstructions in the soil, the carrot will grow around them, producing oddly shaped roots. So before planting your carrot seeds it is important to take the time to break up any lumps of soil and pick out rocks that are larger than very small pebbles.

Carrots are a cool-season crop and are best planted in early spring to be harvested in the summer. If you live in an area where you get mild winters, plant another crop in late summer for a fall harvest. The carrot has its best flavor when grown in the full sun with cool nights. Carrots are direct-seeded and need to be kept moist in order to germinate, so you may have to water the garden bed two to three times a day until they germinate. Water carefully so as not to wash the seeds away. It is important to keep the soil moistened because the seeds may not be able to break through hard and crusty soil if the soil dries out.

To harvest large carrots so they do not break off, gently push the carrot downward into the ground and then pull it upward. This breaks the roots and makes the carrot easier to pull up.

When storing carrots, you need to remove the green, leafy tops. This is true whether you are storing them in your fridge (where they will keep in a sealed plastic bag for several weeks or more), freezing them (blanch them first), canning them (you will need to use a pressure cooker) or storing in your root cellar (carrots buried in sand and stored in a root cellar will keep for several months). If you want to store a large amount of carrots, or more than you have indoor space for, you can leave them in the ground covered with several inches of mulch and harvest as you need them, although they will become less sweet and will lose their tenderness the longer they are in the ground.

Potatoes

Potatoes are the most used vegetable in the world. They are nutritious, versatile, easy to grow, and ideal for storage. Potatoes are closely related to tomatoes; like tomato plants, potatoes produce sprawling and bushy vines above ground. However, potatoes produce tubers underground. They need a long growing season—approximately 4 months with continuous cool weather for best production. When preparing your potato bed, make sure the soil is well tilled with compost or aged animal manure added to it. Potatoes need a more acidic soil, so never lime in the area where they will be planted.

Potatoes are planted as early as you can get into your garden. They are grown from stem cuttings, which are also called seed pieces, or seed eyes. When planting, you can cut the seed potato into pieces; just make sure each section has at least three eyes. The potato plant can take up a lot of room and several plants will be needed for a small family to eat fresh potatoes. You'll want even more plants if you want to store potatoes for use during the winter months.

The potato seed does not need much water until it has sprouted above ground. After the vine starts to grow, keep mounding soil up against the new growth; this is called *hilling*. This allows the tuber to grow without being exposed to the sun; too much sun exposure will cause the potato to turn green. You can harvest young potatoes after the plant has flowered by digging around the base of the plant with your hands. The tubers are mature and ready to be harvested once the vine has turned brown and died back. Potatoes are excellent for storing and will keep for several months if stored properly. Make sure they are dry before storing them in a cool, dark area.

POTATOES, THE PERFECT FOOD

Potatoes are a nutrient-rich vegetable and comprise the majority of many native diets. By growing lots of different varieties of potatoes and storing them throughout the winter, you and your family will have most of the nutrition that you need to stay healthy. Did you know that the only essential nutrient potatoes lack is vitamin D? When cooked with milk, as in mashed potatoes, potatoes make a perfect superfood.

Rutabagas and Turnips

The rutabaga and turnip are closely related cousins. They are both cool-season crops, and like fertile, well-drained soil that is well tilled so the roots have a lot of space to grow. The young greens make a great addition to a salad mix or can be steamed as a healthy green vegetable. They are filled with calcium and other nutrients. The roots from both vegetables can be eaten raw but are most often cooked in soups or stews or mashed as a side dish.

The rutabaga has large yellow roots and is often called a *winter turnip* or *swede*. The young leaves can be eaten, but they get coarse once they mature. The rutabaga is a hardy, slow-growing root vegetable that is normally planted in early to mid summer and then harvested in the fall. Rutabagas are hardy enough to remain in the garden all winter and can be harvested as you need them. They need a fair amount of space because the roots can grow quite large, weighing 2 to 3 pounds each.

The turnip has a small, white, round root with a purple skin. It grows like a large radish. The greens can be eaten young or as mature leaves; turnips are sometime grown just for the leaves. Turnip seeds are planted in early spring and are best harvested before hot weather arrives. They can be grown during the fall as well but need more protection from frost than the rutabaga does. Turnips are not a fussy vegetable and will grow in most soil conditions. Both rutabagas and turnips store well in a root cellar or in similar conditions.

Leeks

Leeks require growing conditions similar to other alliums, like garlic and onions, which have been included in the herb chapter. These conditions are rich soil, a sunny area, and cool temperatures. Leeks are a biennial vegetable, which means they do not produce seeds until the second year of growth. If you are planning to save your leek seeds, this is something you will need to take into consideration.

Leeks can take 4 to 8 months to grow to prime size, which is usually about 1½ inches in diameter. They will produce tender young plants in the first year, but growing them into the second year will give you a longer harvest. Plant them on the edge of your garden or mixed in with your asparagus patch so they are not disturbed. Keep mounding the soil up around the plant as it grows to keep the bottom part of the leek a nice white color.

When harvesting your leeks, gently lift them from the ground using a garden fork. The best way to store leeks is to leave them in the ground over the winter. You won't be able to access them once the ground freezes, but the following spring, you will have a super early vegetable to harvest and enjoy. Make sure they are mounded with soil and mulched with a good covering of chopped leaves or straw. To prepare leeks for cooking, wash them thoroughly to get the soil out from between the leaves.

Heat-Loving Veggies

These heat-loving veggies are mainly known as semi-tropical vegetables and need a lot of heat and warm soil to grow well. Soil temperatures must be warm for the seeds to germinate and the plants cannot handle any cold weather, especially during the seedling stage. In northern climates, these vegetables usually need to be started indoors in early spring and then transplanted out once the weather is warm enough.

Corn

Freshly picked corn dropped into a pot of boiling water is sweeter than anything you can buy in the supermarket because the sugar within the kernels has not yet turned to starch. Corn is a vegetable that can be planted in a newly cultivated garden area. It is hardy and tough, giving it the ability to grow and survive where many other vegetables would not. Corn does take up a fair amount of garden space, but it is definitely worth finding a place for in your backyard garden.

There are many different varieties of corn. For any of them to be successful, they need lots of space, warm weather, fertile soil, and water. Each corn stalk will produce one or two cobs, so you need a large garden area to plant your corn in order to get a good quantity of cobs. Corn likes a rich, warm soil (above 50°F) and needs at least 8 hours of sunlight a day to germinate. It is best planted on the northern side of your garden so it does not block the sun from reaching your other vegetables.

Corn needs to be pollinated, meaning the male flowers from the tassels need to reach the female flowers, which is the silk on the ears. This is usually done by the wind. It is best to plant corn in blocks; that way, the corn pollen from the tassels can easily spread to other plants. When choosing your varieties, make sure they cannot cross-pollinate. It is best to choose only one variety of corn if you have a small garden. If you have a larger garden and choose to grow different varieties, make sure there is some distance between each variety, or choose to plant varieties that will mature at different times.

Corn tastes best when eaten fresh, but is still worthwhile to preserve. You can easily freeze the kernels for several months. You can also dry corn on the cob and use the individual cobs for popcorn. These dried cobs will last for several months to a year but are limited in their use for anything other than popcorn.

Cucumbers

Cucumbers need to be pollinated, so it is important to know whether the variety you choose is a hybrid or a standard. Standard varieties have both male and female flowers on the same vine; insects or the wind will do the pollinating for you. The male flower comes out first and looks like a miniature cucumber. The female flower is identified by a swollen ovary just behind the male flower. Hybrid varieties have separate female and male plants and will need to be pollinated by hand. If you have saved cucumber seeds from the past or a friend has given them to you and you are not sure of the variety, check the plant as it grows to see what kind of flowers it is producing.

If there is only a male or a female flower, no fruit will form. Go to your garden center and purchase another plant that will pollinate the first one for you.

Cucumbers can only be preserved in a brine and then either frozen or canned. You can use these pickled and frozen cucumbers in salads year-round, as their pickled flavor is milder than the more traditional, canned pickles.

Eggplants

Eggplants need hot weather and rich soil in order to grow their best. This vegetable is much more common in Europe than it is in North America; however, if you enjoy a great moussaka, try growing eggplants in your backyard or in a container on the patio. Eggplants are in the same family as tomatoes and peppers, so if you plant them in the same area it is easier to do your vegetable rotation.

The most common eggplant variety produces a large, purple, oval-shaped fruit. You can also find varieties that have yellow, green, and white fruit and others that form rounded or cylindrical fruit. These can all add color to your garden and are definitely fun to show off to your guests.

If you live in a cool climate, it is best to start your eggplants from seed indoors in early spring and then transplant them out when warmer weather arrives. Eggplants need full sun and lots of heat, so they are an ideal candidate for a greenhouse or a more sheltered but sunny spot in your garden. Each plant will produce between eight to ten fruits.

Peppers

Peppers come in various shapes, from chunky to long and skinny and round to conical. You'll find them in shades of green, red, orange, and yellow. Their flavors range from mild and sweet to sizzling hot. Sweet peppers are also known as bell peppers because of the shape of the fruit. They are often harvested when green; that way, the plant produces more fruit. When left on the plant to mature, bell peppers will turn either yellow, orange, or red depending on the variety. Hot pepper plants grow taller and have narrower leaves than the bell varieties, and their fruit can range in size from about 1 to 7 inches long.

Peppers are a little touchy to grow. They need lots of full sun, warm daytime temperatures, cool nighttime temperatures, fertile soil, and lots of water. Sweet peppers need a little less heat than hot pepper varieties. When preparing your garden bed, add compost or aged animal manure. Peppers can then be seeded directly if you have a long growing season; however, they often do better started indoors in early spring and transplanted out once the temperature reaches 65°F.

Peppers are a very popular vegetable, either cooked by themselves or with other foods. They are also eaten raw in salads or as appetizers. When preparing to use your pepper, cut it in half, remove the stem, and rinse away the seeds. Fresh or dried hot peppers need to be handled carefully because the oils in the pepper skin can burn your skin or eyes. It is suggested that you use rubber gloves and hold the hot pepper under water when preparing it. Remove the seeds from a hot pepper if you want to cut down the heat; the seeds add to the hot taste.

Both sweet and hot peppers can be frozen, dried, or canned. If you're a fan of spicy foods, keeping a dried string of your favorite hot peppers in your kitchen is both functional and pleasing to look at.

Squash

Squash is an easy vegetable to grow, and each plant can produce a large number of fruits. There are two types of squash—summer and winter. The main differences between these are the amount of time they take to mature and how well they will store once harvested. Summer squash is a warm-weather vegetable that is eaten before the fruit has fully matured. The skin and seeds are eaten as part of the whole fruit. Winter squash takes longer to mature and is usually harvested in the late summer or fall. It usually has a larger fruit than summer varieties and the skin is tough and inedible. The seeds are often removed before cooking as well. Some varieties, such as pumpkin squash, produce lovely edible seeds that are delicious when roasted.

Squash like a rich soil with plenty of organic matter. They often grow best in the compost pile. They are a vine vegetable that can spread 6 to 8 feet across, so make sure you give them lots of room when planning your garden layout. Squash can be direct-seeded or put out as transplants, which usually depends on the length of your growing season. Each plant—especially the summer zucchini squash—can produce lots of fruit seemingly overnight, so one or two plants are usually enough for any family. Winter squash can also produce several fruits from one plant, but if cured properly they will store for several months so you can enjoy them over time.

Squash plants require lots of water. Since the leaves become very large, it is best to water the plant by hand or with drip irrigation around the base of the plant so the water reaches the roots. Squash leaves are more susceptible to mildew if they get wet.

If cured properly, winter squash will store for several months. You cure squash by leaving the cut fruit in the sun for several days. You will need to turn the squash or pumpkin every few hours to ensure equal exposure. Protection at nighttime is also necessary and can be achieved either by covering or by bringing inside.

Tomatoes

There is nothing tastier than a ripe tomato that you have just picked off the vine. Tomatoes are one of the most popular vegetables eaten in North America, and most gardeners love to grow them. Most people think of a tomato being round and red, but there are several varieties that produce yellow and orange fruit and others that produce fruit that is pear- or plum-shaped. The size of the tomato can range from 1 to 6 inches in diameter,

depending on the variety you choose. One plant will produce an abundance of fruit for you to enjoy.

Tomatoes will grow well in any backyard as long as it is sunny and hot. They do well in containers and in greenhouses, especially if you live in a cooler climate.

Tomatoes are best started indoors, where you can regulate the temperature so they will germinate. Tomato seeds need 10 to 12 weeks of growth before they are ready to be transplanted into the garden or a container. It is important that you harden off your tomato plants, introducing the plants to the cool outdoors gradually over several days' time when you are ready to transplant your tomato plants.

Unlike most plants, tomato plants like to be planted deep. Bury at least half of the stem underground to give the plant a strong root base. Tomatoes are best grown upright on supports. This allows the stem of the plant to grow tall without breaking from the weight of the fruit. It also keeps the fruit from touching the ground and allows air circulation around the plant.

Gardeners often give tomato plants either too much or too little water. When you first transplant a tomato plant, water it every few days until it is well established. Once the plant reaches 2 to 3 feet tall, the roots are probably just as deep; a little water each day will not reach where the roots need it the most. Tomatoes need a deep watering once a week or every ten days. Fruit that starts to split is one sign that the plant is not getting enough water.

If you are planning to grow your tomato plants in containers, it is best to choose dwarf or hanging varieties unless you have a very large container. A standard tomato needs a container at least 18 inches deep.

GREEN TOMATOES

If you have lots of green tomatoes, by wrapping them in newspaper and keeping them in a cardboard box in a warm room, they will gradually ripen, giving you fresh tomatoes through the fall. Using this method, tomatoes that I harvested green in August have taken until November to ripen—tasting just as fresh as if they had been picked from the vine.

Brassicas

Also known as the cabbage family, this group of vegetables includes such favorites as broccoli, Brussels sprouts, cabbage, cauliflower, and kale. This chapter offers advice and growing tips for all of these wonderful veggies. They are cold-hardy vegetables that produce a lot of food for the space they use. They grow well in most soil types. Adding shredded leaves to the area where you will be planting the following year will help to produce fabulous *Brassica*s for you.

Broccoli

Broccoli is a cool-season crop and is probably the easiest of all the *Brassica* family to grow. Most varieties will produce one large head averaging about 6 to 8 inches in diameter. Once this head is cut off, the plant will continue to produce side branches with smaller heads. Keep cutting these before they flower and you will be able to harvest broccoli from one plant for several weeks.

The broccoli plant may *bolt* if the weather gets hot. This means the plant will go to flower more quickly than it normally would in cooler weather. It is best to plant broccoli early in the spring (April) and then again in late summer if you have a mild fall and winter.

Broccoli often does best transplanted. This allows you to start your plants indoors so they get more growth before the heat of the summer arrives. The best way to store broccoli is by freezing. Before going into the freezer, broccoli should be soaked in salt water to remove dirt and pests. After soaking for about 30 minutes, the broccoli can be chopped into smaller pieces.

Brussels Sprouts

Brussels sprouts look like little palm trees with lumps growing from the plant stem, or trunk. The bumps, which are usually 1 to 2 inches in diameter, are the Brussels sprouts. They are often called baby cabbages because they look like miniature cabbages. Each plant should produce between 50 and 100 sprouts.

Brussels sprouts are a cool-season vegetable and the taste is improved by a light frost. Like most other *Brassica*s, these vegetables like fertile, well-drained soil to grow in. The plant is slow growing and can stay in your garden into the late fall, so long as it is harvested before the first frost. To store indoors, you want to leave the roots attached to the plants and hang them upside down in your root cellar as soon as they are harvested.

Cabbage

Cabbage is another easy-to-grow vegetable in the *Brassica* family. It grows well in most soils and is a cool-season crop. It is best to plant this vegetable in early spring for a summer harvest or in late summer for a fall harvest. The mature cabbage forms a head from a rosette of thickened leaves. The cabbage head can be round, pointy, or flattened depending on the variety. The leaves can be richly colored and textured. There are green varieties that produce light green leaves and red varieties with purplish red leaves. The Savoy cabbage has crinkly leaves. There are short-season and long-season varieties.

THE MANY USES OF CABBAGE

Cabbage can be eaten cooked or raw. Sauerkraut (cooked cabbage) and coleslaw (raw cabbage) are two of the most common cabbage dishes. Cabbage contains a good amount of vitamin C and some vitamin A. Its nutritional and storage qualities make cabbage a common staple in many countries. Try cabbage in your soups, tacos, and burgers, either raw or cooked. A medium head of cabbage will give approximately 2 pounds of cabbage or about 12 cups of shredded cabbage.

Cabbage, like all *Brassica* vegetables, is susceptible to a variety of soil-borne diseases, so crop rotation is essential in order to keep your garden healthy. Once you have planted *Brassica*s in an area, do not plant them in that spot again until at least four years after the first crop. Like Brussels sprouts, cabbage can stay in your garden into the late fall and can be stored indoors in a root cellar or similar environment.

Collards

Collards are another cold-hardy vegetable in the *Brassica* group. Their leaves look like cabbage leaves but do not form a head like a cabbage and collards are grown to be cooked rather than eaten raw. Collards are usually planted in the summer for harvesting in the fall and winter. The leaves of a mature plant are sweeter after a frost. The collard plant can also take the heat, so it is one of the few cooking greens that will do well all summer long.

Collards need a rich soil and a lot of water in order for the leaves to stay tender. When working the soil, add 3 inches of compost or aged manure to the garden bed. Collards also do best with regular fertilization. Use a nitrogen-rich fertilizer every few weeks, which will give them the nutrients they need to grow fast, develop a nice green color, and taste tender.

Kale

Kale has high levels of vitamin C and calcium and the highest levels of beta carotene of all the green vegetables. It is a hardy vegetable. Kale will survive over the winter and the leaves are more tender and sweet once they have been touched by frost. Kale will easily go to seed and spread throughout your garden, so pull the plants out before the seeds spread if you want to contain it.

There are several different varieties of kale, which are easily distinguishable because of their color and leaf. The most common are probably the green, curly-leaf varieties. Some other varieties are Red Russian, which have gray-green leaves with a purplish stem; Lacinato, or dinosaur, which has a dark blue-green leaf; Redbor, which has dark red leaves; and Improved Siberian, which has flat green leaves.

The following recipes were chosen because of how well they feature vegetables that can easily be grown at home.

Parmesan Sprouts with Prosciutto

Serves 4 as a side dish

This is a deliciously rich way to enjoy these small Brassicas! If you have the patience, wait to harvest your sprouts after the first hard frost to ensure the best flavor.

2 tablespoons butter

2 cloves garlic, minced

2 ounces thinly sliced prosciutto, slivered

1 pound Brussels sprouts, cleaned and halved

1½ tablespoons all-purpose flour

1 cup cream

2 tablespoons port wine

Kosher salt and ground pepper to taste

⅓ cup freshly grated Parmesan cheese

1. Melt butter in a large frying pan over medium-high heat.
2. Add garlic and prosciutto. Simmer for 2 minutes, stirring regularly.
3. Add sprouts. Simmer for 5 more minutes.
4. Sprinkle flour evenly over the sprouts. Stir.
5. Slowly add cream, followed by the port wine. Simmer about 13 minutes until the sprouts are nearly fork tender.
6. Remove from heat, add half of the cheese, and stir well.
7. Store in freezer-safe containers. Label and date.

Freezer Tip

Once this dish is done, you can freeze it whole in an oven-ready dish or portion it out into individual servings. It will need to be cooked for 20 minutes at 350°F. Serve with additional freshly grated Parmesan cheese.

Vegetable Stock

Makes 8 quarts

Making vegetable stock is one of the handiest and most cost-efficient skills you can learn. You can adapt this recipe to use any extra vegetables, including the ends and parts of vegetables removed when preparing a meal.

14 quarts cold water
2 pounds peeled carrots, cut into 1-inch pieces
2 pounds peeled parsnips, cut into 1-inch pieces
1 bunch leeks, rinsed well and chopped fine
12 stalks celery, cut into 1-inch pieces
3 large onions, peeled and quartered
4 large sweet red peppers, seeded and cut into 1-inch pieces
4 large tomatoes, seeded and diced
4 medium turnips, peeled and diced
6 cloves garlic, peeled and minced
6 bay leaves
2 teaspoons dried thyme
1 cup fresh parsley, chopped
1 tablespoon black peppercorns
2 teaspoons fine sea salt

1. Combine all ingredients in a large stockpot. Bring to a boil.
2. Cover and reduce heat to low. Simmer for 2 hours.
3. Uncover and simmer for 2 additional hours to concentrate flavors.
4. Strain stock through several layers of cheesecloth in a colander. Discard veggies and seasonings.
5. If canning, ladle stock into sterilized jars, leaving 1-inch headspace. Wipe rims. Cap and seal. Process in a pressure cooker at 10 pounds pressure for 30 minutes for pints or 35 minutes for quarts.

Stock Tip
When you know you're going to be making vegetable stock, prepare ahead of time. Keep your clean vegetable ends and pieces in a food storage bag in the freezer and add them to the stock water for increased flavor.

Tomato, Mushroom, and Barley Soup

Serves 4

This recipe is a classic and you can substitute any other grains for the barley, just be sure to cook them first. A hearty treat during the long winter.

1 cup chopped onion
⅔ cup chopped carrot
16 ounces coarsely chopped tomatoes
Juice from the tomatoes
1 cup sliced celery
1 teaspoon dried savory leaves
1 cup quick-cooking barley
2 cups sliced white or cremini mushrooms
Salt and pepper to taste
1 tablespoon olive oil
1 quart water

1. Over medium heat, heat olive oil in a saucepan until hot. Add onion, carrots, and celery, and cook just until onion is tender. Stir in herbs and cook for 1 more minute.
2. Add the water, tomatoes with their juices, barley, and mushrooms. Heat until boiling. Cover and cook for 10–15 minutes or until barley is tender.

Roasted Sweet Peppers

Roasting veggies is easy, and peppers are one of the most delicious roasted vegetables. Once you master this simple method, you can apply it to many recipes, including the Roasted Red Pepper Pesto recipe in this book.

To roast any sweet pepper, simply cut in half and remove the seeds. Place skin side up on baking sheet and broil until the skins turn black. You can also add olive oil to the peppers prior to broiling, which will help the skins to come off, but you should wrap the peppers in aluminum foil to prevent burning.

Roasted Red Pepper Pesto

The combination of roasted red peppers and pesto creates a perfect summertime flavor and can be made in larger batches to freeze. Toss with pasta to add color and flavor to your favorite meals.

1 cup roasted red peppers
1 cup packed fresh basil
3 cloves garlic
¼ cup grated Parmesan
1 teaspoon balsamic vinegar
3 tablespoons olive oil
1 teaspoon sugar (optional)
Salt and pepper to taste

1. Process all ingredients in food processor (don't add salt and pepper yet) until smooth.
2. Season with salt and pepper.
3. Mix with pasta or use as a spread.

Cream of Broccoli Soup

Serves 6

A comforting meal, enjoy this soup in the wintertime, using frozen broccoli and dried herbs.

2 pounds broccoli, cleaned and cut into 1-inch pieces

1 cup chopped onions

3 garlic cloves, minced

½ teaspoon dried thyme leaves

1½ cups vegetable stock

½ cup light cream

6 tablespoons sour cream (optional)

3 tablespoons milk (optional)

Salt and pepper to taste

1 tablespoon olive or canola oil

1. Heat oil in a large saucepan until hot.
2. Add onions and garlic and cook for a few minutes until tender.
3. Add broccoli and thyme and cook for 2 minutes.
4. Add stock and heat until boiling. Then reduce heat, cover and simmer for 10 minutes or until broccoli is tender.
5. Process the soup in a blender or food processor until smooth.
6. Return to saucepan, add cream, and heat over medium heat until hot enough to serve. If desired, you can combine the sour cream and milk and add to individual bowls of soup just before serving.

Summer Squash Pasta

Serves 4–6

A fast and easy summertime dish and a great way to use up some of the zucchini and summer squash!

> 1 hot red pepper, sliced in half without seeds
> 2 garlic cloves
> 4 cups sliced summer squash or zucchini
> 1 cup fresh flat-leaf parsley, minced
> ½ pound pasta
> 6 tablespoons olive oil
> Sea salt to taste

1. Heat oil in a skillet until hot.
2. Add garlic and pepper, and cook until the garlic turns a golden color. Take the skillet off the heat and remove the garlic and pepper, keeping the now-flavored oil in the pan.
3. Reheat the oil, add the squash slices, and fry for several minutes.
4. Take off the heat and add parsley and sea salt.
5. Meanwhile, boil water for the pasta. Once boiling, cook the pasta until it is *al dente*. Drain and rinse under cold water, then mix with the squash parsley sauce.

Sesame Carrot Salad

Serves 4–6

This recipe is a great way to use your freshly harvested carrots during the summer, or carrots pulled from your root cellar during the colder months. This dish can be served warm, and it is also very good chilled and goes well as a side dish with soups or rice dishes.

3 cups shredded or very thinly sliced carrots

2 teaspoons tamari soy sauce

2 teaspoons sesame oil

1 teaspoon sea salt

1 cup orange juice

1 tablespoon rice syrup

3 tablespoons roasted, unhulled, black sesame seeds

1. Combine all ingredients except for carrots and sesame seeds in a saucepan and bring to a boil. Cover and simmer for 5 minutes.
2. Meanwhile, gently roast the sesame seeds just long enough to release flavor.
3. When the sauce and seeds are done, combine all the ingredients and serve either warm or chilled.

Eggplant Baba Ganoush

Makes 1 cup

You can use the delicious eggplant baba ganoush as a spread on crackers or bread, or like any other sandwich spread.

2 medium eggplants

3 tablespoons olive oil, divided

2 tablespoons lemon juice

1 cup tahini

3 cloves garlic

1 teaspoon cumin

1 teaspoon chili powder (optional)

1 teaspoon salt

1 tablespoon chopped fresh parsley

1. Preheat oven to 400°F. Slice eggplants in half and prick several times with a fork.
2. Place on a baking sheet and drizzle with 1 tablespoon olive oil. Bake for 30 minutes or until soft. Allow to cool slightly.
3. Remove inner flesh and place in a bowl.
4. Using a large fork or potato masher, mash eggplant together with remaining ingredients until almost smooth.
5. Adjust seasonings to taste.

Fresh Basil Bruschetta

Serves 4

You can use this bruschetta as a dip for crusty bread, or you can top halved fresh bread with it, drizzle olive oil on top, and toast in the oven. Either way, it's a delicious, fresh summertime appetizer.

2 large tomatoes, diced small
3 cloves garlic, minced
¼ cup chopped fresh basil
2 tablespoons olive oil
Salt and pepper to taste

Combine all ingredients in a bowl and allow to sit for at least 15 minutes so it can marinate. You can also add a little balsamic vinegar if preferred.

Fried Zucchini Sticks

Serves 4

You don't have to deep-fry these zucchini sticks, just sauté them in a bit of oil if you prefer. This is a great snack for kids!

¾ cup flour
1 garlic clove, minced
1 teaspoon fresh basil, minced
½ teaspoon fresh oregano, minced
¼ teaspoon salt
4 zucchinis, cut into strips
Oil for frying
Homemade ketchup for dipping

1. In a large bowl or pan, combine flour, garlic, basil, oregano, and salt.
2. Lightly toss the zucchini strips with the flour mixture, coating well.
3. Heat oil in a large skillet or frying pan. When oil is hot, gently add zucchini strips to pan.
4. Fry until lightly golden brown on all sides. Serve with vegan ranch dressing or ketchup.

Broccoli and Pasta Herb Soup

Serves 4

This is a great wintertime recipe that can be made with frozen broccoli and dried herbs. It can also be used in the summertime with fresh broccoli and fresh thyme.

> 5½ cups vegetable stock
> 4 garlic cloves, minced
> 2½ teaspoons dried thyme leaves
> 3 cups broccoli florets
> 2½ cups fusilli pasta, uncooked
> Salt and pepper to taste

1. Heat the veggie stock, garlic, and thyme in a saucepan and bring to a boil.
2. Stir in pasta and broccoli, and reduce heat.
3. Simmer uncovered for 10 minutes or until pasta is *al dente* and the broccoli tender.
4. Add the lemon juice, salt and pepper, and serve.

Zucchini Salad

Serves 4

This recipe is a perfect summer dish with its simplicity and fresh taste. It is also a great zucchini recipe to add to your repertoire during prolific zucchini harvests.

> 4 small zucchinis
> ¾ cup lemon pepper dressing*
> 2 teaspoons dried oregano, or 2 tablespoons fresh oregano
> 8 large lettuce leaves, Boston lettuce works well

Wash zucchini and remove the ends. Slice thinly lengthwise, mix with dressing and oregano, and allow to marinate for several hours at room temperature. Serve on lettuce leaves.

> ***Lemon Pepper Dressing***
> 1 mashed garlic clove
> 2 tablespoons fresh lemon juice
> 1 tablespoon wine vinegar
> ½ cup olive oil
> A dash of sugar
> A dash of sea salt
> ½ teaspoon cracked pepper

Stir all ingredients together vigorously.

Pico de Gallo

Makes 1½ cups

Possibly my favorite thing to make in the summertime. Using fresh, homegrown tomatoes, cilantro, onions, and garlic sets this salsa far above anything you can buy at the store.

> 2 good-sized tomatoes
> 1 medium yellow onion
> 1 bunch cilantro
> 1–2 limes
> Salt and pepper to taste
> ½–1 tablespoon honey (optional)
> 1 teaspoon tamari soy sauce (optional)

1. Depending on the size of your tomatoes and what tomato-to-onion ratio you prefer, I generally chop up 2 good-sized slicing tomatoes for 1 onion. Chop both tomatoes and onions uniformly into small, but not fine, pieces.
2. Finely chop a bunch of cilantro, adding more or less depending on your taste. Combine all ingredients in a bowl.
3. Roll the lime on the table or countertop to help release juices. Quarter lime and squeeze as much juice as possible into the mixture.
4. Add salt and pepper to taste.
5. Add more lime juice if necessary. Depending on the variety and quality of your ingredients, adding honey and soy sauce can help to bring out the flavor. Try adding a little to taste.

Spicy German Dijon Potato Salad

Serves 4

Tangy deli-style German potato salad requires potatoes that are thinly sliced and not overcooked. This vegan version is just as good—if not better—than any other recipe you'll find.

4 large potatoes, precooked and cooled
2 tablespoons olive oil
½ yellow onion, sliced thin
⅓ cup water
⅓ cup white or apple cider vinegar
1 tablespoon Dijon mustard
1 tablespoon flour
1 teaspoon sugar
2 scallions, chopped
Salt and pepper, to taste

1. Slice potatoes into thin coins and set aside.
2. In a large skillet, heat onions in olive oil over medium heat and cook until just barely soft, about 2–3 minutes.
3. Reduce heat and add water, vinegar, mustard, flour, and sugar, stirring to combine. Bring to a simmer and cook until thickened, just 1–2 minutes.
4. Reduce heat and stir in potatoes, scallions, and bacon bits. Season with salt and pepper to taste.

Cucumber Cilantro Salad

Serves 3

Cooling cucumbers and cold creamy yogurt are coupled with a dash of cayenne pepper for a salad that keeps you guessing.

4 cucumbers, diced
2 tomatoes, chopped
½ red onion, diced small
1 cup soy yogurt, plain or lemon flavored
1 tablespoon lemon juice
2 tablespoons chopped fresh cilantro
Salt and pepper to taste
¼ teaspoon cayenne (optional)

1. Toss together all ingredients, stirring well to combine.
2. Chill for at least 2 hours before serving to allow flavors to marinate. Toss again just before serving.

Lemon Cumin Potato Salad

Serves 4

A mayonnaise-free potato salad with exotic flavors, this one is delicious either hot or cold.

- 1 small yellow onion, diced
- 2 tablespoons olive oil
- 1 teaspoon cumin
- 4 large cooked potatoes, chopped
- 3 tablespoons lemon juice
- 2 teaspoons Dijon mustard
- 1 scallion, chopped
- 1 teaspoon cayenne pepper
- 2 tablespoons chopped fresh cilantro (optional)

1. Heat onions in olive oil just until soft. Add cumin and potatoes, and cook for just 1 minute, stirring well to combine. Remove from heat.
2. Whisk together the lemon juice and Dijon mustard, and pour over potatoes, tossing gently to coat. Add scallions, cayenne pepper, and cilantro, and combine well.
3. Chill before serving.

Spicy Sweet Cucumber Salad

Serves 2

Japanese cucumber salad is cool and refreshing, but with a bit of spice. Enjoy it as a healthy afternoon snack or as a fresh accompaniment to takeout.

> 2 cucumbers, thinly sliced
>
> 1 teaspoon salt
>
> 1 cup rice wine vinegar
>
> 1 teaspoon sugar
>
> 1 teaspoon sesame oil
>
> 1 teaspoon red pepper flakes
>
> 1 onion, thinly sliced

1. In a large shallow container or baking sheet, spread cucumbers in a single layer and sprinkle with salt. Allow to sit at least 10 minutes.
2. Drain any excess water from the cucumbers.
3. Whisk together the rice wine vinegar, sugar, oil, and red pepper flakes.
4. Pour dressing over the cucumbers, add onions, and toss gently.
5. Allow to sit at least 10 minutes before serving to allow flavors to mingle.

Pesto and New Potato Salad

Serves 4

A simple side dish if served hot, or potato salad if served cold, these creamy pesto potatoes are a lively and creative way to use tender new potatoes.

1 cup pesto such as Herb Pesto or Spinach Pesto (see Index for recipes)
1 cup mayonnaise
2 pounds new potatoes, chopped and cooked
3 scallions, chopped
⅓ cup sliced black olives
Salt and pepper, to taste

1. Whisk together pesto and mayonnaise, and toss with potatoes and remaining ingredients.
2. Season generously with salt and pepper to taste.

Barley Vegetable Soup

Serves 6

Barley and vegetable soup is an excellent "kitchen sink" recipe, meaning that you can toss in just about any fresh or frozen vegetables or spices you happen to have on hand.

1 onion, chopped

2 carrots, sliced

2 ribs celery, chopped

2 tablespoons olive oil

8 cups vegetable broth

1 cup barley, uncooked

1½ cups frozen mixed vegetables

1 14-ounce can crushed or diced tomatoes

½ teaspoon parsley

½ teaspoon thyme

2 bay leaves

Salt and pepper to taste

1. In a large soup pan or stockpot, sauté the onion, carrot, and celery in olive oil for 3–5 minutes, until onions are almost soft.
2. Reduce heat to medium-low, and add remaining ingredients except salt and pepper.
3. Bring to a simmer, cover, and allow to cook for at least 45 minutes, stirring occasionally.
4. Remove cover and allow to cook for 10 more minutes.
5. Remove bay leaves, season with salt and pepper to taste.

Potato and Leek Soup

Serves 6

With simple earthy flavors, this classic soup is a comforting starter.

1 yellow onion, diced
2 cloves garlic, minced
2 tablespoons olive oil
6 cups vegetable broth
3 leeks, sliced
2 large potatoes, chopped
2 bay leaves
1 cup whole milk
2 tablespoons butter
¾ teaspoon salt
⅛ teaspoon black pepper
½ teaspoon sage
½ teaspoon thyme

1. Sauté onions and garlic in olive oil for a few minutes until onions are soft.
2. Add vegetable broth, leeks, potatoes, and bay leaves, and bring to a slow simmer.
3. Allow to cook, partially covered, for 30 minutes until potatoes are soft.
4. Remove bay leaves. Working in batches as needed, purée soup in a blender until almost smooth, or to desired consistency.
5. Return soup to pot and stir in remaining ingredients. Adjust seasonings and reheat as needed.

Easy Roasted Tomato Soup

Serves 4

Use the freshest, ripest, juiciest red tomatoes you can find for this super-easy recipe, as there are few other added flavors. If you find that you need a bit more spice, add a spoonful of nutritional yeast, a dash of cayenne pepper, or an extra shake of salt and pepper.

6 large tomatoes

1 small onion

4 cloves garlic

2 tablespoons olive oil

1¼ cups soy milk

2 tablespoons chopped fresh basil

1½ teaspoons balsamic vinegar

¾ teaspoon salt

¼ teaspoon black pepper

1. Preheat oven to 425°F.
2. Slice tomatoes in half and chop onion into quarters. Place tomatoes, onion, and garlic on baking sheet and drizzle with olive oil.
3. Roast in the oven for 45 minutes to 1 hour.
4. Carefully transfer tomatoes, onion, and garlic to a blender, including any juices on the baking sheet. Add remaining ingredients and purée until almost smooth.
5. Reheat over low heat for just 1–2 minutes if needed, and adjust seasonings to taste.

Curried Pumpkin Soup

Serves 4

You don't have to wait for fall to make this pumpkin soup, as canned pumpkin purée will work just fine. It's also excellent with coconut milk instead of soy milk.

1 yellow onion, diced

3 cloves garlic, minced

2 tablespoons butter

2 cups pumpkin purée*

3 cups vegetable broth

2 bay leaves

1 tablespoon curry powder

1 teaspoon cumin

½ teaspoon ground ginger

1 cup soy milk

¼ teaspoon salt

1. In a large soup or stockpot, heat onion and garlic in margarine until onion is soft, about 4–5 minutes.
2. Add pumpkin and vegetable broth and stir well to combine. Add bay leaves, curry, cumin, and ginger, and bring to a slow simmer.
3. Cover and allow to cook for 15 minutes.
4. Reduce heat to low and add soy milk, stirring to combine. Heat for just another minute or two until heated through.
5. Season with salt to taste and remove bay leaves before serving.

*Purée Your Own

Now that you're growing your own pumpkins, there's nothing like fresh-roasted pumpkin! Make your own purée to substitute for canned. Carefully chop your pumpkin in half, remove the seeds (save and toast those later), and roast for 45 minutes to an hour in a 375°F oven. Cool, then peel off the skin, and mash or purée until smooth. Whatever you don't use will keep in the freezer for next time.

Cream Cheese and Butternut Squash Soup

Serves 4

This is a rich, decadent soup, a wonderful comforting treat in the middle of winter. Top with a mountain of homemade croutons or serve with crusty French bread.

> 2 cloves garlic, minced
> ½ yellow onion, diced
> 2 tablespoons olive oil
> 3½ cups vegetable broth
> 1 medium butternut squash, peeled, seeded, and chopped into cubes
> 1 teaspoon curry powder
> ¼ teaspoon nutmeg
> ¼ teaspoon salt
> 4 ounces cream cheese

1. In a large skillet or stockpot, sauté garlic and onions in olive oil until soft, about 3–4 minutes.
2. Reduce heat to medium-low and add vegetable broth, squash, curry powder, and nutmeg. Simmer for 25 minutes until squash is soft.
3. Working in batches, purée until almost smooth, or to desired consistency. Or, if squash is soft enough, mash smooth with a large fork.
4. Return soup to very low heat and stir in cream cheese until melted, combined, and heated through. Adjust seasonings to taste.

Fiery Basil, Eggplant, and Tofu Stir-Fry

Serves 3

Holy basil, also called tulsi, *is revered in Vishnu temples across India and is frequently used in Ayurvedic healing. It lends a fantastically spicy flavor, but whatever basil you have in your garden will also do.*

3 cloves garlic, minced
3 small fresh chili peppers, minced
1 block firm or extra-firm tofu, pressed and diced
2 tablespoons olive oil
1 eggplant, chopped
1 red bell pepper, chopped
⅓ cup sliced mushrooms
3 tablespoons water
2 tablespoons soy sauce
1 teaspoon lemon juice
⅓ cup fresh Thai basil or holy basil

1. Sauté the garlic, chili peppers, and tofu in olive oil for 4–6 minutes until tofu is lightly golden.
2. Add eggplant, bell pepper, mushrooms, water, and soy sauce, and heat, stirring frequently, for 5–6 minutes, or until eggplant is almost soft.
3. Add lemon juice and basil, and cook for another 1–2 minutes, until basil is just wilted.

Sesame Soy Asparagus and Mushrooms

Serves 4

Fresh asparagus in season has such a vibrant taste, and if you have an asparagus crop, you should give this recipe a try. Fresh asparagus needs very little enhancement. If you can't find fresh asparagus, don't bother trying this with dull store-bought asparagus; it's not the same at all!

1 pound fresh asparagus, trimmed and chopped
¾ cup chopped mushrooms
2 teaspoons sesame oil
1 teaspoon soy sauce
½ teaspoon sugar
2 tablespoons sesame seeds (optional)

1. Preheat oven to 350°F.
2. Place asparagus and mushrooms on a baking pan and roast for 10 minutes.
3. Remove pan from oven; drizzle with sesame oil, soy sauce, and sugar, and toss gently to coat.
4. Roast in oven for 5–6 more minutes.
5. Remove from oven, and toss with sesame seeds.

Cajun Collard Greens

Serves 4

Like Brussels sprouts and kimchi (Korean sauerkraut), collard greens are one of those foods that folks tend to either love or hate. They're highly nutritious, so hopefully this recipe will turn you into a fan if you're not already.

1 onion, diced

3 cloves garlic, minced

1 pound collard greens, chopped

2 tablespoons olive oil

¾ cup water or vegetable broth

1 14-ounce can diced tomatoes, drained

1½ teaspoons Cajun seasoning

½ teaspoons hot sauce (or to taste)

¼ teaspoon salt

1. Give your collards a good rinse, then tear the leaves off the middle stem.
2. Fold or roll all the leaves together, then run a knife through them to create thin strips, similar to a chiffonade cut used for herbs. The stems can be added to a vegetable broth or to your compost pile.
3. In a large skillet, sauté onions, garlic, and collard greens in olive oil for 3–5 minutes, until onions are soft.
4. Add water or vegetable broth, tomatoes, and Cajun seasoning. Bring to a simmer, cover, and cook for 20 minutes, or until greens are soft, stirring occasionally.
5. Remove lid, stir in hot sauce and salt, and cook, uncovered, for another 1–2 minutes, to allow excess moisture to evaporate.

Lemon Mint New Potatoes

Serves 4

Potatoes are an easy standby side dish that goes with just about any entrée, and this version with fresh mint adds a twist to the usual herb-roasted version.

10–12 small new potatoes, chopped
4 cloves garlic, minced
1 tablespoon olive oil
¼ cup chopped mint
Salt and pepper to taste
2 teaspoons lemon juice

1. Preheat oven to 350°F. Line or lightly grease a baking sheet.
2. In a large bowl, toss together the potatoes with the garlic, olive oil, and mint, coating potatoes well.
3. Arrange potatoes on a single layer on baking sheet. Roast for 45 minutes.
4. Season with salt and pepper, and drizzle with lemon juice just before serving.

Summer Squash Sauté

Serves 2

Green zucchini and yellow squash absorb flavors like magic, though little enhancement is needed with their fresh natural flavor. Toss these veggies with some cooked orzo or linguini to make a main dish.

1 onion, chopped
2 cloves garlic, minced
2 tablespoons olive oil
2 zucchinis, sliced into coins
2 yellow squash, sliced thin
1 large tomato, diced
1 teaspoon dried oregano
1 teaspoon dried basil
Salt and pepper to taste
2 teaspoons hot chili sauce (optional)

1. Sauté onions and garlic in olive oil for a minute or two, then add zucchini, yellow squash, and tomato. Heat, stirring frequently, for 4–5 minutes until squash is soft.
2. Season with oregano and basil, and heat for 1 more minute.
3. Stir in hot sauce.

Garlic Green Beans

Serves 4

Perfectly balancing the crispness of green beans with the bite of garlic, this recipe will liven up any serving of green beans.

1 pound fresh green beans, trimmed and chopped
2 tablespoons olive oil
4 cloves garlic, minced
½ teaspoon crushed red pepper flakes
Salt and pepper to taste

1. Boil green beans in water for just 3–4 minutes; do not overcook. Or steam for 4–5 minutes. Drain and rinse under cold water.
2. Heat olive oil in a skillet with garlic, green beans, and red pepper flakes. Cook, stirring frequently, for 3–4 minutes until garlic is soft.
3. Taste, and season lightly with salt and pepper.

Sweetened Roast Squash

Naturally sweet squash is delicious in this simple, quick side. Serve as is, scooping out of the skin, or remove the soft flesh and give it a quick mash.

1 butternut, acorn, or spaghetti squash
1 teaspoon sea salt
4 tablespoons orange juice
4 tablespoons maple syrup
Nutmeg or ginger to taste

1. Preheat oven to 400°F.
2. Chop squash in quarters, and scrape out seeds. Place in a large casserole dish. Sprinkle each chunk of squash with a bit of sea salt, 1 teaspoon of orange juice, and 1 tablespoon maple syrup, then a shake of nutmeg or ginger.
3. Cover with foil and bake for 40–45 minutes until squash is soft, basting once or twice with any extra sauce.

Steamed Rosemary-Pepper Squash

Serves 4

Sweet butternut squash is delicious with just a touch of seasoning. This lightly seasoned squash recipe is easy to make, simple, and delicious.

| 1 butternut squash
| 1 teaspoon sea salt
| 2 teaspoons dried rosemary, finely chopped
| 2 teaspoons freshly ground black pepper

1. Chop squash in half lengthwise, and scrape out seeds. Place in a large casserole dish. Drizzle olive oil on the flesh side. In a small bowl, combine the salt, rosemary, and black pepper; mix. Sprinkle each half of the squash with the seasoning.
2. Place the seasoned squash halves cut side up in a stovetop pan large enough to hold them lengthwise and deep enough to add water without it boiling over. Pour in a couple of inches of water, cover, and heat over medium-low heat.
3. Steam for 40–45 minutes until squash is soft.

Baked Potato Fries

Serves 3

Brown sugar adds a sweet touch to these yummy potato fries. If you like your fries with a kick, add some crushed red pepper flakes or a dash of cayenne pepper to the mix.

4–5 large potatoes, sliced into fries
2 tablespoons olive oil
¼ teaspoon garlic powder
½ teaspoon paprika
½ teaspoon brown sugar
½ teaspoon chili powder
¼ teaspoon sea salt

1. Preheat oven to 400°F.
2. Spread potatoes on a large baking sheet and drizzle with olive oil, tossing gently to coat.
3. In a small bowl, combine remaining ingredients. Sprinkle over potatoes, coating evenly and tossing as needed.
4. Bake in oven for 10 minutes, turning once. Taste, and sprinkle with a bit more sea salt if needed.

Maple-Glazed Roasted Veggies

Serves 4

These easy roasted veggies make an excellent holiday side dish. The vegetables can be roasted in advance and reheated with the glaze to save time if needed. Parsnips can also be substituted with one large potato.

3 carrots, chopped
2 small parsnips, chopped
2 sweet potatoes, chopped
2 tablespoons olive oil
Salt and pepper to taste
⅓ cup maple syrup
2 tablespoons Dijon mustard
1 tablespoon balsamic vinegar
½ teaspoon hot sauce
Extra salt and pepper (optional)

1. Preheat oven to 400°F.
2. On a large baking sheet, spread out chopped carrots, parsnips, and sweet potatoes. Drizzle with olive oil and season generously with salt and pepper. Roast for 40 minutes, tossing once.
3. In a small bowl, whisk together maple syrup, Dijon mustard, balsamic vinegar, and hot sauce.
4. Transfer the roasted vegetables to a large bowl and toss well with the maple mixture. Add more salt and pepper to taste.

Roasted Garlic, Zucchini, and Onions

Serves 4

Roasting veggies brings out their natural flavors, so little additional seasoning is needed.

6 whole cloves garlic

4 zucchinis, chopped

1 onion, chopped into rings

1 tablespoon balsamic vinegar

1 tablespoon olive oil

Salt and pepper, to taste

1 teaspoon fresh thyme

2 teaspoons nutritional yeast (optional)

1. Preheat oven to 400°F.
2. Arrange the garlic, zucchinis, and onions on a baking sheet. Drizzle with vinegar and oil, and season with salt and pepper, tossing to coat well.
3. Roast in oven for 20–25 minutes, then toss with fresh thyme, nutritional yeast, and additional salt and pepper to taste.

Dried Tomato Risotto with Spinach and Pine Nuts

Serves 4

The tomatoes carry the flavor in this easy risotto—no butter, cheese, or wine is needed. But if you're a gourmand who keeps truffle, hazelnut, pine nut, or another gourmet oil on hand, now's the time to use it, instead of the butter.

1 yellow onion, diced

4 cloves garlic, minced

2 tablespoons olive oil

1½ cups Arborio rice, uncooked

5–6 cups vegetable broth

⅔ cup rehydrated dried tomatoes, minced

½ cup fresh spinach

1 tablespoon chopped fresh basil (optional)

2 tablespoons butter (optional)

Salt and pepper to taste

¼ cup pine nuts

1. Heat the oil and butter in a large saucepan or deep fry pan over a medium heat. Add onion, cooking for 1–2 minutes before adding the garlic. Cook the garlic for another 1–2 minutes but do not let it turn brown.
2. Stir in the uncooked rice and allow to cook for 3–4 minutes, being careful to not let it burn.
3. Stir in the tomatoes and spinach and allow to cook for 3 minutes, stirring frequently.
4. Pour in the vegetable broth, one cup at a time. Allow the rice to absorb each cup of broth by stirring and cooking for 3 minutes between each cup.
5. Once all the liquid has been absorbed you can turn off the heat and stir in the pine nuts.
6. Add salt and pepper and top with basil.

Spanish Artichoke and Zucchini Paella

Serves 4

Traditional Spanish paella is always cooked with saffron, but this version with zucchini, artichokes, and bell peppers uses turmeric instead for the same golden hue.

3 cloves garlic, minced
1 yellow onion, diced
1 cup white rice, uncooked
1 15-ounce can diced or crushed tomatoes
1 green bell pepper, chopped
1 red or yellow bell pepper, chopped
½ cup artichoke hearts, chopped
2 zucchinis, sliced
2 cups vegetable broth
1 tablespoon paprika
½ teaspoon turmeric
¾ teaspoon parsley
½ teaspoon salt

1. In the largest skillet you can find, heat garlic and onions in olive oil for 3–4 minutes, until onions are almost soft. Add rice, stirring well to coat, and heat for another minute, stirring to prevent burning.
2. Add tomatoes, bell peppers, artichokes, and zucchinis, stirring to combine. Add vegetable broth and remaining ingredients, cover, and simmer for 15–20 minutes, or until rice is done.

Latin Rice with Corn and Peppers

Serves 4

This rice recipe loads up the veggies, making it hearty enough for a main dish. And you can easily use your frozen or canned veggies if fresh ones aren't available.

2 cloves garlic, minced
1 cup rice, uncooked
2 tablespoons olive oil
3 cups vegetable broth
1 cup tomato paste (or 4 large tomatoes, puréed)
1 green bell pepper, chopped
1 red bell pepper, chopped
Kernels from 1 ear of corn
1 carrot, diced
1 teaspoon chili powder
½ teaspoon cumin
⅓ teaspoon oregano
⅓ teaspoon cayenne pepper (or to taste)
⅓ teaspoon salt

1. Add garlic, rice, and olive oil to a large skillet and heat on medium-high heat, stirring frequently. Toast the rice until just golden brown, about 2–3 minutes.
2. Reduce heat, and add vegetable broth and remaining ingredients.
3. Bring to a simmer, cover, and cook until liquid is absorbed and rice is cooked, about 20–25 minutes, stirring occasionally.
4. Adjust seasonings to taste.

Mushroom and Rosemary Wild Rice

Serves 4

This earthy and fragrant dish is a wonderful comfort food and can be served as either a side dish or as a main course. It can also be used as a stuffing for a turkey or chicken; just add bread!

1 tablespoon chopped fresh rosemary
1 yellow onion, diced
2 tablespoons olive oil
1 cup sliced mushrooms
1½ cups wild rice, uncooked
4½ cups vegetable broth
2 tablespoons butter
½ teaspoon lemon juice
¼ teaspoon ground sage

1. In a large pan, heat rosemary and onion in olive oil until onions are just soft, about 3 minutes. Add mushrooms, and heat for another minute.
2. Add wild rice and vegetable broth, and bring to a simmer. Cover and cook 40–45 minutes until rice is done and liquid is absorbed.
3. Remove from heat and stir in remaining ingredients.

Greek Lemon Rice with Spinach

Serves 4

This Greek spanakorizo is seasoned with fresh lemon, herbs, and black pepper.

1 onion, chopped
4 cloves garlic, minced
2 tablespoons olive oil
¾ cup rice, uncooked
2½ cups water or vegetable broth
1 8-ounce can tomato paste
2 bunches fresh spinach, trimmed
2 tablespoons chopped fresh parsley
1 tablespoon chopped fresh mint or dill (optional)
2 tablespoons lemon juice
½ teaspoon salt
½ teaspoon fresh ground black pepper

1. Sauté onions and garlic in olive oil for just 1–2 minutes, then add rice, stirring to lightly toast.
2. Add water or vegetable broth, cover, and heat for 10–12 minutes.
3. Add tomato paste, spinach, and parsley. Cover, and cook for another 5 minutes, or until spinach is wilted and rice is cooked.
4. Stir in fresh mint or dill, lemon juice, salt, and pepper.

Spinach Pesto

A flavorful twist on traditional pesto, spinach pesto is a great way to make a thicker and more flavorful sauce or spread. Use this pesto as a pasta sauce, or serve it on your favorite bread or crackers.

1 cup loosely packed fresh spinach
3 tablespoons fresh basil, finely chopped
2 garlic cloves
1 tablespoon Parmesan cheese, grated
2 tablespoons olive oil
1–2 teaspoons lemon juice
Salt and pepper to taste

1. Mix all ingredients except lemon juice, salt, and pepper in a food processor until smooth.
2. Add lemon juice.
3. Allow the mixture to stand for 3 hours. Add salt and pepper to taste just before serving.

Squash and Sage Risotto

Serves 4

Risotto is easy to make, but it does take a bit of effort with all the stirring! This earthy recipe works well with just about any kind of squash. You can also use any squash you have frozen or canned.

3 cloves garlic, minced

½ yellow onion, diced

2 tablespoons olive oil

1½ cups Arborio rice, uncooked

5 cups vegetable broth

2 whole cloves

1½ cups roasted puréed pumpkin, acorn, or butternut squash

1½ teaspoons sage

⅓ teaspoon salt

¼ teaspoon pepper

1. In a large skillet, sauté the garlic and onions in olive oil for 3 minutes over medium-high heat. Add uncooked rice and cook for 2 more minutes, stirring frequently to lightly toast the rice.
2. Add ¾ cup vegetable broth and cloves, and stir well. When most of the liquid has been absorbed, add another ½ cup broth, stirring frequently. Continue adding vegetable broth ½ cup at a time until rice is just tender and sauce is creamy, about 20–25 minutes.
3. Reduce heat to medium-low and stir in puréed squash and ¼ cup vegetable broth. Continue to stir well and cook for 4–5 more minutes.
4. Stir in sage and season with salt and pepper.
5. Allow to cool, stirring occasionally, for at least 5 minutes. Risotto will thicken slightly as it cools. Remove cloves before serving.

Eggplant Puttanesca

Serves 4

Salty and garlicky puttanesca is a thick sauce traditionally served over pasta, but try it over a more wholesome grain, such as quinoa or even brown nice.

3 cloves garlic, minced
1 red bell pepper, chopped
1 eggplant, chopped
2 tablespoons olive oil
2 tablespoons capers, rinsed
⅓ cup sliced kalamata or black olives
½ teaspoon red pepper flakes
1 14-ounce can diced tomatoes
1 tablespoon balsamic vinegar
½ teaspoon parsley

1. In a large skillet or saucepan, sauté the garlic, bell pepper, and eggplant in olive oil for 4–5 minutes until eggplant is almost soft. Add capers, olives, and red pepper flakes, and stir to combine.
2. Reduce heat to low and add remaining ingredients. Cover and allow to simmer for 10–12 minutes until juice from tomatoes has reduced.
3. Serve over cooked pasta or rice.

Lemon Quinoa Veggie Salad

Serves 4

Depending on when you make this dish, you can use fresh or frozen veggies. Fresh broccoli and tomatoes work well.

1½ cups quinoa
4 cups vegetable broth
1 cup frozen mixed veggies, thawed
¼ cup lemon juice
¼ cup olive oil
1 garlic clove, minced
½ teaspoon sea salt
¼ teaspoon black pepper
2 tablespoons chopped fresh cilantro or parsley (optional)

1. In a large pot, simmer quinoa in vegetable broth for 15–20 minutes, stirring occasionally, until liquid is absorbed and quinoa is cooked. Add mixed veggies and stir to combine.
2. Remove from heat and combine with remaining ingredients. Serve hot or cold.

Baked Spinach Tart

Serves 4–6

Unlike the dull, dark leaves of spinach purchased in the frozen foods aisle at the grocery store, this mouthwatering tart featuring fresh greens from your garden is bursting with bright flavor and color.

2 large eggs
1 cup plain nonfat or whole milk yogurt
1 cup feta cheese
1 cup shredded mozzarella cheese
1 bunch fresh spinach, well rinsed, wilted, and chopped
½ cup chopped onion
Salt and freshly ground black pepper to taste
1 (9-inch) unbaked deep–dish pie shell
½ pint grape tomatoes

1. Preheat the oven to 350°F.
2. Beat the eggs until foamy. Stir in the yogurt, feta cheese, mozzarella cheese, spinach, and onions, mixing well until combined. Season with salt and pepper.
3. Spoon the mixture into the pie shell and push the tomatoes into the top of the mixture.
4. Bake for about 40 minutes or until the mixture is firm to the touch. Let it cool slightly before slicing and serving.

Mediterranean Potato Salad

Serves 4

This potato salad works for all different varieties of potatoes. It's especially good if you've grown multiple varieties in your garden.

2 pounds assorted potatoes, cooked and cooled
1 bunch scallions, thinly sliced
1 cup grape tomatoes
2 hardboiled eggs, quartered
1 cup chopped Italian flat-leaf parsley
¾ cup pitted Niçoise olives
3 tablespoons bacon bits
2 tablespoons mayonnaise
2 tablespoons buttermilk
1 tablespoon olive oil
1 teaspoon smoked paprika
Salt and freshly ground black pepper to taste

1. Cut the potatoes up until they are of a uniform size. Put them into a salad bowl and add the scallions, grape tomatoes, eggs, parsley, olives, and bacon bits.
2. Whisk together the mayonnaise, buttermilk, olive oil, smoked paprika, salt, and pepper until well mixed. Dress the salad, tossing gently to coat all the ingredients. Serve.

Artichoke and Spinach Pesto Pasta

Serves 4

Spinach and artichoke with pesto is an impossibly delicious combination.

1 cup basil
1 cup spinach leaves
3 cloves garlic
½ cup pine nuts or walnuts
1 tablespoon lemon juice
½ teaspoon sea salt
¼ teaspoon pepper
2 tablespoons olive oil
1 cup chopped artichoke hearts
2 tablespoons butter
1 tablespoon flour
¾ cup milk
2 cups cooked pasta

1. Process together the basil, spinach leaves, garlic, nuts, lemon juice, nutritional yeast, sea salt, and pepper until almost smooth. Add olive oil, then artichoke hearts, and process until artichokes are finely diced.
2. In a small saucepan, melt the butter and stir in the flour to form a paste. Add milk, and heat until thickened.
3. Remove from heat and stir in basil and spinach pesto mixture.
4. Toss with prepared pasta and avocado.

Lemon, Basil, and Artichoke Pasta

Serves 6

The earthy rosemary, basil, and lemon flavors would complement gnocchi well; otherwise use a grooved pasta, such as corkscrews, to catch the sauce.

12 ounces pasta, cooked
1 6-ounce jar artichoke hearts, drained and chopped
2 large tomatoes, chopped
½ cup fresh basil, chopped fine
½ cup sliced black olives
2 tablespoons olive oil
1 tablespoon lemon juice
½ teaspoon rosemary
Salt and pepper to taste

Over low heat, combine the cooked pasta with the remaining ingredients, combining well and heating until just well mixed and heated through, about 3–4 minutes.

CHAPTER 5

PLANT TO PRESERVE— SMALL FRUIT

Small fruits are a great way to introduce at-home fruit production to your garden and year-round food supply. Requiring little maintenance once established, small fruits are perennials and will satisfy your and your family's fruit needs for years to come. Extremely adaptable to container gardening and with a wide range of hardiness zones, small fruit plants are easy to grow organically and can be incorporated into almost any home garden system. Planting fruit is also an investment, and for the gardener and food enthusiast, fruit grown at home will easily pay off in the decades that many of these plants produce for.

Many types of fruit will only grow in very warm and tropical regions, yet there are some that grow well in colder regions. The wide distribution of tropically grown fruits often gives people the impression that their fruit consumption has to come from plants that are not local to their region. Unless you live in one of the hottest planting zones, it's time to switch your thinking about where you get your fruit calories (and the vitamin C and potassium supplied by fruit consumption) if your goal is to produce the majority, or all, of your family's diet at home. In this chapter you won't learn how to grow bananas, oranges, or mangos, but you will learn how to grow strawberries, blueberries, raspberries, and blackberries.

Strawberries

Strawberries are a classic summer fruit and one of the easiest fruit plants to grow. Growing in small, bushy clusters, strawberries are perennials and depending on climate variation and the particular type of strawberry, you can expect to get anywhere from 2–5 years, and sometimes longer, out of your plants. The strawberries that you grow yourself are by far superior to any strawberries that you can find at the grocery store and are a wonderful addition to your garden plans and year-round diet.

Planting Strawberries

Strawberries prefer full sun and nutrient-rich, slightly acidic soil. They are also serious nutrient consumers. The soil that your berries grow in needs to be replenished regularly in order to get the most productivity and years out of your plants. Some growers go so far as to uproot their strawberry plants in the fall and keep them in containers during the winter in order to add compost and organic matter to the soil before returning the berry plants to the ground in the spring. In colder zones this method is also useful as a way to ensure that your plants survive during winters with extreme temperatures, although in many zones, mulching is enough protection.

When planting these heavy-feeding berry plants, it is important to add organic matter to the soil a couple of weeks prior to putting the plants in the ground to ensure that your strawberries start off in a nutrient-rich soil. Adding organic fertilizers after the plants are in the ground is also helpful.

In addition to feeding your strawberry plants, it is also important to protect them from cold over the winter, extreme heat in summer, weed growth, and pests. Mulching is the best tool to cover most of these areas, and a heavy application of a basic mulch (like straw or hay) will keep your roots cool during the heat of summer, will offer protection from severe winters, and will also limit weed growth.

Regular monitoring of your strawberry plants is important to keep away root-eating pests. The best way to control pests is by prevention. By removing rotting berries and unhealthy leaves, you can stay ahead of insect problems. Birds offer a more serious threat, but you can drape birdproof netting over your strawberry plants when they begin to ripen.

Strawberry Runners

Strawberries are started from small plants (these plants propagate by sending out runners). If allowed to extend themselves, these runners will help to continue your strawberry productivity and longevity by producing new young plants each year. For the healthiest and most productive strawberry crop, you should plant with enough space to allow these runners to grow. June-bearing varieties produce more runners than ever-ready and day-neutral varieties and will therefore need more space. Best planted in rows, June-bearers should be spaced about 2

feet apart, with 3 to 4 feet between rows, whereas ever-ready and day-neutrals only need to be spaced about ½ a foot apart, with only 2 feet between rows.

Tending Your Patch

In order to maintain healthy and productive strawberry plants for years, it is necessary to renovate your strawberry patch after each harvest. This simply means that you should thin your rows of berries by removing any older plants and leaves. You can do some of this by hand and your work will be made easier if you also mow over your strawberries in order to thoroughly remove excess leaves. Be sure to set your mower at a high enough setting so as not to damage any plants. When you are done renovating, the remaining strawberry plants will need some extra attention. It's a good idea to add a considerable amount of fertilizer as well as to put down new mulching.

Strawberry Varieties

There are three types of strawberries: the June-bearer, the ever-ready, and the day-neutral. These berries all differ in their flavor, in the quantity of their crops, and whether or not they produce only at one particular time during the year, rather than throughout the year. Both ever-ready and day-neutrals can be harvested in their first year, whereas June-bearers cannot be harvested until their second year.

June-bearing strawberries produce one bumper crop of strawberries in late spring that is perfect for making a large batch of preserves. This variety is known best for its small berries, deep in color and intensely luscious in flavor. These little berries are a burst of flavor in your mouth and will do well to remind you of warmer weather when you enjoy them in their preserved form in the wintertime. In addition to their concentrated flavor, June-bearers are the best strawberries to make preserves with because all the berries on June-bearing plants will be ready at the same time. For the gardener wanting to keep a supply of berries through the winter, planting a crop of June-bearers will ensure a pantry of fruit preserves. These berries can also be frozen, but don't expect them to retain their shape and appearance as well as the large, firm strawberries you can buy at the grocery store; but their delicious flavor will remain intact.

Ever-ready berries produce three crops of berries throughout a season, and typically begin producing after June-bearers in early summer and will continue until the fall in most areas. This variety produces fewer berries than the other two but is still a popular fruit with gardeners because of its continual production throughout the year and because of its ability to adapt to most climates. The flavor of this berry is less intense, yet its consistency and continual growth will keep you in fresh strawberries throughout the summer.

Day-neutral strawberries are similar to the ever-ready in that they produce throughout the summer. As the name

suggests, this variety is not affected by day length, and will continue producing into the fall, ending the season with a plentiful crop. In general, day-neutrals produce more berries, with better flavor, than the ever-ready variety. They do not, however, withstand high heat as well as the ever-ready. For these reasons, both varieties are popular, and often one is better suited to your region than another.

Many gardeners plant all three of these varieties in order to have a continual supply of strawberries from spring until fall. Planting a combination of June-bearer, ever-ready, and day-neutral types will ensure a good supply of strawberries beyond the warm weather if you plan to preserve the majority of your June-bearing crop.

Traditional strawberry preserves are a popular favorite and will keep well beyond the following June (if you can keep your family from eating them all!). Freezer jam is also a popular, raw version of the traditionally canned, cooked jams. Cleaned and frozen whole strawberries are also useful to have on hand for smoothies, milkshakes, and pastry and cake toppings as well as for use in any baking or cooking that calls for whole berries.

Blueberries

Blueberries are a favorite berry to grow, particularly so in colder regions because of their ability to withstand severe winters. Blueberries are native to North America, and varieties that are adapted to many different regions are available. Because blueberries prefer full sun and are also extremely hardy, these plants are ideal for almost any climate. Including these lovely flowering bushes in your home garden is an easy way to enjoy homegrown fruit no matter where you live.

There are four different types of blueberries, most easily recognized by their differing heights: lowbush, highbush, half-high, and rabbiteye.

Lowbush

Commonly referred to as wild blueberries, lowbush is the shortest type, reaching a height of up to 18 inches. These are the famous Maine blueberries, and are also popular in other cold climates. Lowbush blueberries are winter hardy as far north as hardiness zone 3. The recognizably small berries on these plants are intensely sweet and make wonderful preserves.

Highbush

Highbush varieties produce the larger round berries that are commonly sold in grocery stores. These plants can reach 6 feet in height and prefer warmer temperatures. These large round berries are winter hardy in zones 4 and up.

Half-High

Half-high varieties are a hybrid variety and are a compromise between the temperature requirements and taste of the lowbush and highbush varieties. The berries are a medium size, and these plants are just as hardy as the lowbush variety,

although the berries are not as intensely flavorful. True to their name, half-high blueberries are taller than lowbush, but not as tall as highbush varieties.

Rabbiteye

Rabbiteye blueberries are the tallest type of blueberry plant. When well pruned, these bushes grow to around 10 feet tall; unpruned, up to 20 feet. Rabbiteye blueberries are best suited for zones 7 and higher because their thick skin protects berries from extreme heat. They are commonly grown in the Southwest and produce a berry not much larger than the lowbush varieties.

Soil Requirements for Blueberries

Success with blueberry plants has a lot to do with the care they receive in the first year they are planted, as well as with the soil they are planted in. One of the most important factors in growing blueberries is soil acidity: Blueberries will do best in soil with a pH between 4 and 5. Soil that has a pH higher than 5 will need to be amended before any plants can go in the ground. If you are working with soil with a pH significantly higher than 5 (7 and up, or alkaline), you should consider planting your blueberry plants in containers or raised beds.

In addition to the pH level, blueberries like a loose, moisture-retentive, sandy loam that also drains well. In order to maintain and fertilize the soil that your blueberries grow in, you can add any fertilizer that is specific to acid-loving plants.

Planting Blueberries

Most blueberries are self-pollinating, but productivity will be better if you enlist the help of bees by planting different varieties of berries.

For the home gardener looking to plant berries for more than just a tasty snack during the summer months, you will want to plant about two plants per person, or slightly less if you are planting many other types of berries. Because you will be planting more than just a couple of plants, it makes more sense to plant your blueberries in rows so that you can dig a trench that will hold multiple plants, versus digging individual holes. You will also have more long-term success with soil health if you prep by the bed, and not by the hole.

Lowbush varieties need the least amount of space, and depending upon the variety, should be planted 1 to 3 feet apart with about 4 feet between rows. Because lowbush varieties have low-lying male parts, it's important to encourage runners to develop on the lowest level. When planting, cover the lowest part of the plants with a little bit of soil to encourage growth of these parts.

Highbush, half-high, and rabbiteye varieties should all be planted with about 5 feet between plants, and up to 10 feet between rows. These bushes should be planted 3 inches deeper than the root ball size.

Pruning Blueberries

Pruning is particularly important during your blueberry plant's first year. Pruning can seem daunting if you're new to it, but it's actually quite easy. It helps if you think of this task in terms of your general goal, which is to stimulate growth. By removing parts of the plant that require energy to sustain but which do not produce, you are enabling the plant to redirect that energy into fruit production. Likewise, pruning excess or weakly producing parts helps the plant not to overproduce, which can weaken and shorten both the lifespan and long-term productivity of a blueberry plant.

When you prune, you should do so in the spring, and you want to remove all nonvigorous and dead wood growth. Any stems that are more than an inch thick should be removed, as well as any low-achieving stems. Before winter, you'll also want to cut back any long canes that could potentially break under heavy snow.

In addition to removing woody excess, in the first year you want to remove any blossoms. You won't harvest blueberries in this first year, and you may not even see any flowers. If you do see blossoms, however, it's important to take them off because doing so allows the canopy to develop. In later years this will be important when yield, and therefore weight, on the plant increases. You'll need a strong canopy for support.

Mulching Blueberries

Blueberries require about 1 inch of water a week, and they like moist soil. Mulching is an effective tool in helping the plants to retain water, as well as limiting weed growth and providing root protection. A light mulch of pine needles, chips, or bark works well and also helps to maintain the acidity of the soil.

Pest Control for Blueberries

Blueberries are rarely and only minimally affected by insect damage or disease. Animals are more likely to cause damage, but it is fairly easy to prevent crop loss or plant damage as long as you plan ahead. Able to destroy an entire crop quickly, birds are by far the most destructive enemy to a blueberry crop. Most blueberry plants will have ripe berries for about three weeks. During these weeks, you can cover your blueberry bushes with birdproof netting. Just draping the netting on individual bushes works only moderately well, as birds can still get to the berries by going underneath the net. If you have enough bushes that it seems worth your while, then you might want to consider building a frame around your blueberry bushes. During the harvest season, you can enclose the frame with the same birdproof netting. This will keep birds out as well as allow you inside for cultivation and harvesting.

In addition to birds, the young, tender branches of blueberry plants are a wintertime food source for small animals and rodents. Chicken fencing should suffice for protection, and if you decide to build a wooden frame for bird netting, chicken wire can easily be incorporated into this design to offer year-round protection. If you live in an area with heavy snowfall, build your fence high enough to account for the literal step up this snow will give small animals.

Bramble Fruits

Bramble fruits are the fruits produced on the thorny bramble plants that belong to the rose family. Raspberries and blackberries are the most popular bramble fruits for cultivation and consumption, and can continue producing for up to 20 years! Red raspberries are grown in every state except Hawaii and this plant's ability to grow in such a diverse array of climates is a testament to the many varieties available, as well as to the overall adaptability of this particular plant. Blackberries are more limited in their ability to grow in cold climates, but are still considered winter hardy to hardiness zone 6.

Bramble fruit plants are thorny bushes whose roots and crowns are perennial. The fruit-producing canes, however, operate on a biennial cycle, not producing fruit until their second year. Red raspberries are available in an everbearing variety that produces fruit twice on the same cane, first in the fall, then again the following summer. These varieties are also called *primocane fruiters* because of their ability to produce berries on the first-year cane.

Raspberries and blackberries can grow in a range of hardiness zones, and each variety is different. In the next section, the general adaptability and hardiness of different berry types is described, but it is important to note that each type contains varieties that vary greatly in hardiness.

Types of Bramble Fruit

Growing different types of bramble berries makes for a fun small-fruit garden that will offer a variety of taste to your year-round diet. Depending on your hardiness zone, you may be able to grow all different types of bramble berries or just one or two varieties. Understanding what types grow best in your particular climate will help you to have a vibrant and productive fruit garden.

Red Raspberry

Easily the most hardy, red raspberries are commonly grown throughout North America. Part of their adaptability comes from the availability of everbearing or primocane varieties. In zones with severe winters, the summer crop on primocane varieties is often sacrificed by cutting back the canes after a fall harvest in order to prevent cold damage during the winter. The plant won't produce the following summer, but the canes will grow back in time to produce a bountiful fall crop.

Black, Purple, and Yellow Raspberries

Black raspberries are not as adaptable or high-producing as red raspberries.

They tend not to be very winter hardy, although there are varieties available that are hardy in climates as cold as zone 3. Black raspberries are also more prone to disease than red raspberries. The flavor of these berries is recognizably different than red raspberry and typically less juicy.

Purple raspberries are next in line after red raspberries in winter hardiness. These berries are a hybrid of red and black raspberries. They are less susceptible to disease than black raspberries and can be almost as high-producing as red raspberries.

Yellow raspberries are less common than the darker berries. They tend to have a taste similar to the red raspberry but sweeter.

Blackberries

Blackberries differ from raspberries in taste and also because the fruits are not hollow like raspberries are after harvesting. This is because blackberries do not separate from the receptacle like raspberries do. Some blackberry plants grow similarly to raspberry plants as thorny, self-erect bushes. Other blackberry varieties grow in trailing, semi-erect, thorn-less bushes. These thornless varieties are popular for home gardening and small-scale berry production as the added work of regular trellising is often outweighed by the appeal of thorn-free harvesting.

Planting Bramble Berries

Bramble berries prefer a slightly acidic and nutrient-rich soil. A pH between 5.5

and 6.2 is best for these plants, and adding organic matter to the soil before planting is a must. The soil should be fertilized annually as well. These plants prefer full sun and a well-draining, sandy loam for soil.

Although considered to be self-erect (aside from the trailing blackberries), you will need to provide structural support for your raspberry and blackberry plants. Red raspberries do well when planted as a hedgerow because they fill out evenly as they grow and act as supports for one another as the hedge fills in. For this reason, red raspberries can be planted 2 feet apart. As they mature, you will want to maintain a base width of 12–18 inches per plant. The plants should be trellised; a standard *T* trellis works well. The crossbar on the *T* should be about 3½–4½ feet tall and 3½ feet wide. Wire is attached to each end of the crossbar and positioned so as to enclose the row of plants while connecting the *T*s at each end of the row.

T Trellis

Only red raspberries should be planted as a hedge, as other types of raspberries and blackberries do not fill out as well and should not be planted as close together.

Without the support of closely neighboring plants, these raspberries require a post to be positioned next to each plant. Plants and posts should be spaced at 4 feet, with wire connecting the posts at a height of 4½ feet. As the plants grow, you should assist them by placing fruiting canes on the connecting wire, and help to support canes by wiring them to the nearest post when necessary.

Disease and Pest Control

Raspberries and blackberries are more susceptible to disease than other berries. It is important to select varieties that are disease resistant and certified virus-free. Your local small-fruit nursery is a good resource for knowing which diseases to look for in your region, as well as which varieties of plants are best suited for this purpose. If you have wild raspberry or blackberry bushes growing in your area, these plants can carry disease to your bramble fruits. You should allow a distance of at least 600 feet between any wild plants and your domestic ones. It is better to plant your bramble berries a good distance away from the wild plants, rather than creating this distance by destroying the wild berries. Depending on your particular outdoor space, however, you may have to remove some wild plants.

Maintaining weed control will also help to keep pests and disease away from your plants. To stay on top of weed control, you can use mulch or even cover crops. Be sure to pay attention to how these additions affect the pH levels. Good airflow is also important for disease prevention. By practicing regular pruning and by following the plant-spacing guidelines outlined above, good airflow will be promoted.

Preserving Small Fruits

Berries are extremely perishable. After being picked, they will keep in your refrigerator for a week at most. Fortunately, they preserve well and you can enjoy your strawberries, blueberries, raspberries, and blackberries year-round by freezing, making preserves, and drying.

Freezing Berries

Freezing berries is the best way to keep small fruit if diversity of use is important to you. By freezing berries whole, in slices, or as freezer jam, you can use frozen berries in most of the same ways that you use fresh berries. There are a few different ways to freeze berries.

Tray-Freezing

The most effective and easy way to freeze whole or sliced berries is by tray-freezing. Simply wash the berries in cold water, drain well, and place them in one layer on a tray or cookie sheet covered in wax or freezer paper. Once they are completely frozen, you can pack them into freezer bags. You want these bags to be packed with the same amount of looseness that the frozen berries at the grocery store are packed with.

Freezing with Sugar

Frozen berries retain their texture when stored with sugar. This is also the best way to preserve berries for pies. After washing and draining your berries, coat them with sugar. Loosely pack the sweetened berries in freezer bags or other freezer-safe containers.

Freezer Jam

You can use your favorite cooked or uncooked jam recipe to make freezer jam. Simply store the jam in any freezer-safe container.

Drying

To dry berries you will need to use a dehydrator. Drying your berries is a good idea if you have limited freezer or pantry space. Berries can be dried whole and cooked with throughout the winter. You can also make fruit leather, which is a fun and healthy snack for kids and will last in the refrigerator for about 6 weeks.

Canning

Canned preserves are the classic way to store berries. Canned preserves store well, are delicious, and there are many recipes that use either a single type of berry or combinations of all the berries in your harvest. If you have a pantry or root cellar, making lots of preserves is a good idea, particularly if you don't want to take up your whole freezer with berries.

No matter how you preserve your berries, there are some steps that are always used. Following is a list of tips for preserving berries.

1. Harvest—Harvesting at the optimal time is particularly important for preserving food. It is always best to harvest berries in the morning.
2. Wash—You should make sure berries are clean before preserving them. The best way to do this is gently, by putting berries in a bowl of cold water, allowing any dirt or particles to separate from the fruit. Either gently strain or use a slotted spoon to remove the berries from the water.
3. Quality Check—Berries that are past their prime or slightly damaged should be separated from fresh berries in excellent condition. Use the less-than-perfect berries to make smoothies or other puréed forms. You can keep these berries whole as long as they are cleaned, or slice them up. Label the package accordingly.

Berries that are in excellent condition should be frozen whole and used in dishes where having firm berries is important, such as in pies. To keep strawberries from turning to mush, leave the hulls intact, only removing the green stem. High-quality berries should also be used when making preserves.

The following fruit-based recipes are delicious ways to enjoy your berries. Berries preserve well, and recipes using small fruit are also featured in Chapters 8 and 9.

Wild Strawberry Preserves

Makes 2½ pints

This classic recipe transports you from your kitchen to the countryside every time you open the lid.

> 4 cups ripe strawberries, mashed
> 4 cups sugar
> 1 tablespoon lemon juice (optional)

1. Mix sugar and berries in a bowl and let sit at room temperature for about 1 hour so they begin getting juicy.
2. Transfer to a pan. Add lemon juice and bring to a full rolling boil for 7 minutes, stirring constantly.
3. Pour into 8 pre-sterilized half-pint jars with ¼-inch headspace. Process in a boiling-water bath for 10 minutes. May be kept for one year in dark, cool area. May also be frozen.

Summer Strawberry Ice Cream

Makes 4 cups

Ice cream is a wonderful treat, especially during the warm months. If you want to personalize this recipe, try adding some flaked coconut to the egg yolk mixture or mixing strawberries and raspberries.

> 1¼ quarts fresh strawberries, hulled
> 1½ cups heavy cream, divided
> ¾ cup white sugar
> ½ teaspoon vanilla extract
> 3 egg yolks
> 3 tablespoons light corn syrup

1. Place the berries into a blender or food processor; purée until smooth.
2. Heat 1¼ cups cream in a saucepan over medium heat until it begins to bubble at the edge of the pan.
3. In a separate bowl, whisk together sugar, egg yolks, remaining ¼ cup cream, vanilla, and corn syrup.
4. Slowly pour the cream into the egg yolk mixture, whisking constantly.
5. Return the mixture to the saucepan. Simmer until mixture is thick enough to coat the back of a wooden spoon, about 5 minutes. Do not boil!
6. Mix berries and custard together; refrigerate until chilled.
7. Use an ice cream maker to get a really smooth dessert. If you don't have an ice cream maker, you can transfer the custard into a mixing bowl and put it in the freezer. After 30 minutes, beat thoroughly and return to freezer. Repeat until you achieve the desired texture.

Lavender Raspberry Jam

Makes 2 pints

This recipe makes use of both the lavender and raspberries that you've grown and is an adaptation of chef Linda Gilbert's Lavender Raspberry Jam recipe. Properly stored, it will keep for a month.

3 cups fresh or frozen, thawed raspberries
1 cup shredded, dried lavender
2½ cups fine sugar

1. Mix the raspberries and lavender leaves in a glass or stainless-steel bowl. Refrigerate overnight.
2. In the morning, heat the raspberry-lavender mixture over low heat. Once the raspberries begin releasing their juices, bring the mixture to a boil.
3. Add the sugar and stir until dissolved. Boil for another 5 minutes over low heat with constant stirring. Pour into jars.

Lavender Blueberry Jam

Makes 2 pints

Making use of both your blueberries and lavender, this recipe is an adaption of chef Linda Gilbert's Lavender Blueberry Jam recipe. Like the Lavender Raspberry Jam recipe, this jam will also store for a month.

2 tablespoons dried lavender flowers

11½-ounce can white grape juice concentrate

3 cups fresh blueberries

6-inch square of cheesecloth

10 inches of twine

1. Put the dried lavender flowers into the middle of the cheesecloth square and tie into a bundle with twine.
2. Put the can of white grape juice concentrate, blueberries, and the bundle of lavender blossoms into a heavy saucepan. Boil gently for about 20 minutes, stirring constantly to prevent sugar from sticking.
3. Remove the lavender bundle and cool. You can check if the jam is done by putting a little bit on your finger to see if it jells. If it's not done, you can continue cooking over low heat until it is ready.
4. Once the jam is done, pour into jars. This jam will keep in the refrigerator for up to a month.

Blackberry Preserves

Makes about 6 pints

This recipe is flexible; use raspberries or a blend of raspberries and blackberries if you prefer.

3 quarts blackberries
7½ cups granulated sugar
2 3-ounce pouches liquid pectin

1. Rinse fully ripe blackberries in cold water and drain.
2. Place blackberries into a stockpot.
3. Crush with a potato masher to extract juice. Stir in the sugar and mix well.
4. Bring to a full rolling boil over high heat, stirring constantly.
5. Add pectin and return to a full rolling boil. Boil hard for 1 minute.
6. Remove from heat.
7. Skim off foam. Ladle preserves into sterilized jars. Wipe rims. Cap and seal. Process in water-bath canner for 5 minutes.

Vegan Whole-Wheat Blueberry Muffins

Makes 1½ dozen muffins

These muffins are a healthier version of traditional blueberry muffins, and are more delicious when you incorporate your homegrown blueberries. Because these muffins have very little fat, they'll want to stick to the papers or the muffin tin. Letting them cool before removing them will help prevent this, and be sure to grease your muffin tin well.

2 cups whole-wheat flour

1 cup all-purpose flour

1¼ cups sugar

1 tablespoon baking powder

1 teaspoon salt

1½ cups soy milk

½ cup applesauce

½ teaspoon vanilla

2 cups blueberries

1. Preheat oven to 400°F.
2. In a large bowl, combine the flours, sugar, baking powder, and salt. Set aside.
3. In a separate small bowl, whisk together the soy milk, applesauce, and vanilla until well mixed.
4. Combine the wet ingredients with the dry ingredients, stirring just until mixed. Gently fold in half of the blueberries.
5. Spoon batter into lined or greased muffin tins, filling each about ⅔ full. Sprinkle remaining blueberries on top of muffins.
6. Bake for 20–25 minutes, or until lightly golden brown on top.

Raspberry Vinaigrette Dressing

Makes 1¼ cups dressing

Create a colorful and inviting salad with this purplish dressing. Dress up a plain fruit salad, or toss some cranberries, pine nuts, and baby spinach with this vinaigrette for a gourmet touch.

¼ cup balsamic or raspberry vinegar
2 tablespoons lime juice
¼ cup raspberry preserves
2 tablespoons Dijon mustard
½ teaspoon sugar
¾ cup olive oil
Salt and pepper to taste

1. Process together vinegar, lime juice, raspberry preserves, mustard, and sugar in a food processor or blender until smooth.
2. Slowly add olive oil, just a few drops at a time on high speed, to allow oil to emulsify.
3. Season generously with salt and pepper.

Raspberry Salsa

Makes 3 quarts

This fruity salsa works for snacking and as a topping for meat.

6 cups fresh raspberries

1¼ cups red onion, chopped

4 jalapeño peppers, seeded and finely chopped

1 large sweet red pepper, seeded and chopped

¾ cup cilantro, loosely packed and finely chopped

Juice and grated zest of 2 limes

½ cup white vinegar

4 tablespoons balsamic vinegar

3 tablespoons honey

3 cloves garlic, finely minced

1½ teaspoons ground cumin

½ teaspoon cayenne pepper

1 teaspoon ground coriander

½ teaspoon black pepper

1. Put half the raspberries in a large stockpot and mash lightly. Add the remaining raspberries and the remaining ingredients. Bring to a boil, stirring constantly to prevent scorching. Boil gently for 5 minutes.
2. Ladle into sterilized jars, leaving ¼-inch headspace. Wipe rims. Cap and seal. Process in water-bath canner for 15 minutes.

Strawberries and Beets Salad

Serves 4

Colorful and nutritious, this vibrant red salad can be made with roasted or canned beets, or even raw grated beets if you prefer.

3–4 small beets, chopped
Water for boiling
Spinach or other greens
1 cup sliced strawberries
½ cup chopped pecans
¼ cup olive oil
2 tablespoons red wine vinegar
2 tablespoons honey
2 tablespoons orange juice
Salt and pepper to taste

1. Boil beets in water until soft, about 20 minutes. Allow to cool completely.
2. In a large bowl, combine spinach, strawberries, pecans, and cooled beets.
3. In a separate small bowl, whisk together the olive oil, vinegar, and orange juice, and pour over salad, tossing well to coat.
4. Season generously with salt and pepper, to taste.

Blueberry Cobbler

Serves 8–10

A delicious and traditional way to use your blueberries year-round. This mouth-watering dish will have your kitchen smelling like summertime no matter what the season is.

6 cups fresh blueberries

⅓ cup light brown sugar

1 tablespoon molasses

¼ cup flour

Grated zest of 1 lemon

1 tablespoon fresh lemon juice

Cobbler Topping*

1 egg, beaten

1. Preheat the oven to 375°F and lightly butter a 8" × 10" baking dish.
2. Toss the berries with the flour, brown sugar, lemon zest, and lemon juice. Put the mixture in the baking dish and cover with the cobbler topping.*
3. Brush with the egg and sprinkle brown sugar on top. Bake for about 25 minutes, or until the fruit starts to bubble at the edges.
4. Serve warm with vanilla ice cream.

*Cobbler Topping

1½ cups flour (either all-purpose or whole-wheat pastry)

⅓ cup sugar

1 teaspoon baking powder

½ teaspoon baking soda

½ teaspoon salt

6 tablespoons butter

½ cup buttermilk

½ teaspoon vanilla

1. Combine flour, sugar, baking powder, baking soda, and salt.
2. Using a large fork or a pastry cutter, cut in 6 tablespoons butter.
3. Stir in ½ cup buttermilk and ½ teaspoon vanilla.

Berry Jam Bars

Makes approximately 20 bars

These bars are a favorite snack that can be packed for school lunches, hiking trips, or served as an after-dinner treat.

½ cup butter
½ cup powdered sugar
½ cup light brown sugar
1 teaspoon vanilla
1 egg
½ teaspoon baking powder
½ teaspoon ground cinnamon
1½ cups flour
¼ teaspoon salt
½–¾ cup raspberry preserves
¾ cup rolled oats

1. Preheat the oven to 350°F.
2. Cream butter with sugars until light and fluffy. Beat in the egg and vanilla, and mix until smooth.
3. Add the remaining ingredients except for the preserves and oats. Save ¾ of the dough and spread the rest into an 8" × 10" baking dish. Spread the preserves on top.
4. Mix the leftover dough with the oats and sprinkle on top. Bake about 40 minutes or until lightly browned.
5. Cool and cut into bars.

Blueberry Sauce

With a hint of lime and ginger, this sauce brings out the best in blueberries. Use on pancakes or ice cream, or in plain yogurt.

> 3 cups blueberries without stems
> 2 teaspoons molasses
> ⅓–½ cup sugar, to taste
> 1 teaspoon ground ginger
> Juice of 1 lime, to taste

1. Rinse the berries and immediately put into a saucepan while they are still wet. Add molasses, sugar, and ginger, and bring the mixture to a boil, stirring occasionally.
2. Once the berries fall apart, taste the sauce. Add the lime. Add more sugar if necessary.
3. Serve warm with chunks of fruit, or strain and serve chilled.

Blueberry Vinegar

Makes 2 quarts

This makes a unique and vibrant vinegar that has a sweet-sour quality.

> 3 cups fresh blueberries
> 3 cups rice vinegar
> 2 cinnamon sticks, about 2" each
> 4 whole allspice berries
> 2 tablespoons honey

1. In a stainless-steel or enamel saucepan, combine 1½ cups blueberries with rice vinegar, cinnamon sticks, and allspice berries. Bring to a boil; reduce heat.
2. Simmer uncovered for 3 minutes. Stir in honey. Remove from heat.
3. Pour mixture through a fine-mesh strainer and let it drain into a bowl. Discard blueberries.
4. Divide remaining 1½ cups blueberries evenly between two jars. Add 1 cinnamon stick and 2 whole allspice berries to each jar.
5. Ladle half of the vinegar into each jar. Remove air bubbles. Wipe rims.
6. Cap and seal in a hot-water bath for 10 minutes. Let sit in a cool place for 2–3 weeks before opening.
7. Strain through a colander lined with cheesecloth twice and discard berries and spices before using.

Raspberry Butter

Makes 1 cup

Fruit-infused butters are a special breakfast treat on toast, bagels, or muffins and are a fun way to show off your homegrown fruits to friends and family!

2 sticks butter
Handful of fresh or frozen raspberries
1 or 2 small glass containers

1. Cook raspberries in a saucepan over low heat. If fresh, add a little water to help release the juices. Cook until soft.
2. Gently mash the berries into their own liquid while they are still cooking. If you like the texture of the fruit chunks, leave as is. If you want a smooth butter, strain the liquid and discard the berries.
3. Add the butter sticks to the saucepan and continue to cook over low heat until butter is completely melted, stirring occasionally.
4. Once butter is melted and mixed well, pour the butter into glass containers. When serving, you can either serve the butter on a tray, gently using a hot knife to extract the butter from the glass container, or you can keep in the original container.
5. Store the butter in the refrigerator for up to 3 weeks.

Raspberry Sauce

Makes 2 cups sauce

A different flavor than the blueberry sauce, the raspberries add a sweet tartness that is perfect for topping sweet pastries or creamy desserts.

> 2 cups raspberries
> ¼–½ cup sugar, to taste
> 1 teaspoon kirsch (cherry brandy)
> ¼ cup water

1. Cook the berries, water, and sugar in a saucepan until the berries fall apart.
2. Crush the berries and strain if desired.
3. Add the kirsch and any extra sugar if needed. Serve warm.

PLANT TO PRESERVE— HERBS

Herbs are an essential element in any meal and any garden. In food, they add flavor and provide healthful properties, and the right combination can turn a simple dish into a culinary work of art. At the heart of sauces and marinades, or on their own as a gentle dusting or heavy rub, herbs bring out the flavor and texture of whatever they are paired with. Many herb combinations are famous as flavors in themselves, and even moreso than specific vegetables, herbs and the flavors that they produce are linked to the cultures, regions, and people who have historically grown and cooked with them. If you're serious about eating well with what you grow yourself, then growing and preserving your own herbs is a must.

Aside from their post-harvest use, herbs in the garden provide a balance of beauty and functionality. By adding to the diversity of what you grow, herbs add to the diversity and health of your soil, as well as attract other life to your garden. The birds and insects that are attracted to different varieties of herbs add to a healthy ecosystem, keeping one another in check. A garden that incorporates a variety of herbs looks more lush, diverse, textured, and colorful, and also smells wonderful. The aromatic and therapeutic qualities of herbs are reason enough to grow and preserve at least a few favorites. This chapter will guide you through the different uses of herbs, as well as the growing, preserving, and cooking of popular varieties.

Annual, Biennial, Perennial, and Evergreen Herbs

It's important to understand the growing period for the herbs that you will plant. Herbs, like all plants, fall into a few different categories of life cycles. Depending on whether or not an herb is an annual, biennial, perennial, or an evergreen plant, you can expect your plants to require different sorts of care, and to vary in whether they need to be replanted every year or if they will last longer than one season. Knowing how long certain plants will produce will help you plan your herb garden not only for your first season but also for seasons to come.

Annual

Annuals are plants that live for only one season—flowering, fruiting, and then dying at the end of this process. The length of this season depends on the specific plant. It is usually a good idea to stagger plantings of annual herbs that have a shorter season in order to produce a continuous supply for as long as possible. It is interesting to note that while some food plants are actually perennials or biennials, many are grown as annuals, either for convenience or because they won't survive the colder months. Carrots are actually biennials and tomatoes are true perennials, yet both are commonly grown as annuals.

Annual herbs must be preserved if you want to cook with them year-round, unless you plan to continue your supply through the winter by keeping some growing fresh indoors. Some common annual herbs are basil, chamomile, dill, garlic, and savory.

Biennial

Biennial plants are those that live for two seasons. These plants will not fruit until their second and final season. They often are planted as annuals because of the inconvenience that a biennial plant can pose to gardeners who cannot harvest the whole plant until after the seed has been dropped. Biennials are rare, and caraway, parsley, and evening primrose are a few of the most popular varieties.

Perennial

Easily the most cost-effective plants to grow and harvest, true perennials live indefinitely and return every spring. Some varieties of lesser strength, however, will eventually die off. The length of life in these plants can be affected by different factors of care and climate. Some perennials propagate via their underground roots or bulb systems. Some favorite perennial herbs (though not in all hardiness zones) are lavender, chives, lemongrass, lemon balm, mint, oregano, rosemary, sage, thyme, tarragon, and marjoram.

Evergreen

Evergreen herbs keep their leaves year-round. Depending on the specific plant and the growing zone you live in, this might mean that you can leave your evergreen herbs outdoors all winter. In some zones you will need to cover and protect your evergreen herbs, and in zones with the harshest winters, you will have to bring them inside during the colder months if you wish to maintain the same plant for the next season. Evergreen herbs do require pruning but if you are using them to cook with, then regular harvesting should take care of this. Some common evergreen herbs are rosemary, thyme, oregano, savory, and lavender.

Organizing Your Herbs According to Use

If herbs are already integral to your home, you may want to consider organizing your garden according to the different ways in which you use herbs. I divide my herbs into two main sections—a culinary garden and a tea garden. Within each section, I grow some herbs to be used fresh, some to preserve, and some I grow in larger quantities because they are staples in my home. Designing your garden and thinking about your herbs according to these guidelines is helpful in understanding the quantities of herbs that you want to produce, which herbs you will preserve and how, as well as any herbs you will only use fresh.

In Chapter 1, you began thinking about the herbs that are staples in your home—the ones you use regularly and consistently throughout the year. Using these herbs as a base to get started planning your herb garden is a good idea since they will take up the majority of your gardening space.

Culinary Herbs

Everyone's cooking style is different, and your culinary herb garden will be a reflection of your own unique cooking style. The following is a list of herbs that comprise a universally well-rounded and practical herb garden for culinary use. Adapt this list to meet your individual needs.

Basil

Common in many types of cuisine, basil is best eaten fresh; however, this herb is delicious enough in any form to be useful preserved as well. I preserve basil by making and freezing pesto, as well as by drying and then crushing the leaves. Basil is an annual plant and can be easily grown indoors in the colder months. Keeping a few pots of fresh basil in your kitchen, as well as freezing and drying some, should be enough to keep even the most devout basil worshipper satisfied throughout the year.

Chives

Chives offer the popular and flavorful taste signature of the allium (garlic and onion) family. With a milder taste than onions, green onions, or scallions, chives are a wonderful addition to salads, dips, or any food improved by a gentle onion flavor. Chives are a perennial plant, and you can count on them to add beauty and taste to your herb garden year after year. Their hollow, green stalks are ready in early spring and you can enjoy them in your meals well before most other alliums will be ready to harvest.

Cilantro and Coriander

Delicious in fresh salsas, marinades, soups, and anything else that you want to add a fragrant flavor to, cilantro is actually the leaves of the coriander plant. Coriander seed is produced and typically used as an ingredient in cakes, breads, and other sweet dishes, as well as having a reputation as a digestion aid. Cilantro is important to Asian, Latin, and Carribean cooking, and is best enjoyed fresh, although it can be dried or frozen in sauces and blended salsas.

Dill

Dill is an important herb to grow if you plan to incorporate pickling into your home food-preservation system. This herb grows easily, but does have a root system that likes to grow deeply, so planting in well-aerated soil is best. In warm climates, dill is a biennial herb, although it is typically grown as an annual. Dill does not live for very long, so reseeding every few weeks is a good idea if you want a constant supply of this herb.

In addition to its use in brines and pickling recipes, fresh dill leaves are wonderful when paired with fish; used in soups, egg, and veggie dishes; and in salads and sandwiches. Unfortunately, dill does not retain much flavor when dried. Freezing is the best way to preserve this herb, although it's best in its fresh form.

Garlic

Whereas most herbs are grown for their leaves or flowers, garlic is grown specifically for its flavorful bulb. One of the most powerful and recognizable flavors, garlic adds personality and pungency to any dish. Although it can be started from either seed or clove, garlic is more easily started from individual cloves. Garlic can be planted in either spring or late summer, but bulbs will grow larger and more successfully if planted a month or so before the first fall frost. This warmer period allows the roots to become established before the harshness of winter sets in. Garlic responds well to the cold, and bigger, more flavorful bulbs are produced when garlic grows over through the winter. Garlic does need to be mulched for protection from extreme cold. Depending on climate and soil variation, garlic can take 6 to 10 months to be ready to harvest, although the scapes can be harvested earlier (garlic scapes have a mild garlic flavor and are delicious to eat on their own, or when cooked with other foods). You'll know the whole garlic plant is ready to harvest when the leaves lowest on the stalk turn brown and dry out.

Garlic can be eaten fresh as soon as it is harvested, but is most commonly seen in its cured, dried form because it stores so well. To cure garlic, do not clean the plant after harvesting, and leave the bulb attached to the stalk. Lay the plants out on a screen or other area that will allow for even air circulation and will keep the plants off the ground. It's best to do this when you can expect dry weather. After the plants have been cured for several days to a week, you can braid the stalks of the plants together and hang them in your pantry or kitchen. When braiding, leaving enough room around each bulb to allow air circulation. You can simply cut a new bulb off this braid when you need more garlic.

Mint

There are many varieties of mint—all sharing the common traits of its signature fresh scent and a ferocious ability to quickly take over a garden! Spearmint is most commonly grown, although the type of mint you choose to grow depends on your personal taste. Mint is great in teas and fruit sauces and jellies, as well as for its pleasant scent. Take care to plant mint in containers, as it will quickly take over your garden or any space it is planted in. Mint is preserved best by drying.

Onion

Onion, like garlic, is an herb grown for its bulb. The strong flavor of these bulbs is necessary to many different dishes and types of cuisine. There are many types of onions, and varieties of red, yellow, and white are most common. Onions can be seeded indoors in the early spring and are one of the first transplants that can go into the ground. They can also be seeded directly or started from bulbs. Unlike garlic, which grows best planted in individual stalks, onions can be planted in small bunches of three plants. This allows enough room for each bulb to grow, and makes for easier cultivation and harvesting.

Onions have a long shelf life and preserve extremely well. They should be cured in the same way as garlic—remaining dirty after being harvested and allowed to dry thoroughly before storing. The stalks of onion plants are not strong enough to braid well, however, and once the plant is dry, the stalks can be snipped off.

Oregano

A Greek herb and a member of the mint family, oregano is often used in combination with basil and other herbs common in Mediterranean cuisines. Oregano is a perennial, evergreen herb, but is not hardy enough to survive the winters of colder zones. This herb does not do well in full sunlight, preferring partial shade, and is best suited for well-draining soil. This herb can also be kept growing indoors during the colder months. The flavor of oregano intensifies in its dried form.

Parsley

Often underestimated, parsley is so much more than a garnish! Packed with nutrients, this herb is rich in antioxidants and has a vibrant flavor. Parsley comes in flat-leaf and curly-leaf varieties. Flat-leaf parsley has a stronger flavor and holds up better than curly varieties for preserving. Parsley can be dried or frozen, although its flavor is best when fresh. A biennial herb, parsley is more practically grown as

an annual, since it becomes less desirable to cook with in its second year.

Rosemary

Rosemary is an evergreen herb, but it is not hardy enough in colder zones to survive an unprotected winter. Depending on your climate, you might need to cover your rosemary during the winter, bring it indoors, or simply uproot and dry the whole plant at the end of the season. Rosemary has a strong flavor and even if you use it regularly, a typical cook can get away with producing and using a moderate amount of rosemary, unlike herbs that tend to be used in larger quantities, such as basil or cilantro.

Savory

Savory is an annual herb of many uses. Flavorful with a peppery kick, this herb comes in a lighter summer variety as well as a more intense winter variety. Summer savory is tender and can be used fresh in salads, whereas the coarser winter savory is most commonly cooked, particularly with vegetables, beans, and lentils. Wonderful to add to soups and stews, you can easily dry savory and use it year-round. Savory is also easily grown indoors.

Thyme

Thyme is a perennial, a member of the mint family, and comes in many varieties, although English and French are the most common for culinary use. Thyme's flavor goes well with meat and egg dishes and is equally useful in both its dry and fresh forms. Preferring well-draining soil and full sun, thyme is easy to grow and is a useful plant outside of its kitchen use. Fragrant and healthful, thyme is rich in antioxidants, has anti-inflammatory properties, and improves skin condition along with many other health and medicinal properties.

Herbs for Tea

Herbs are multifaceted plants and in addition to adding delicious flavor and nutritional qualities to meals, herbs also provide medicinal and therapeutic qualities. Often processed for their essential oils and fragrance, the therapeutic qualities of different herbs can be absorbed in different ways. Whether applied directly to the skin as a poultice or balm; inhaled through the steam of fragrant oil; dried, crushed, and put into capsules; or consumed as a tea, herbs are truly diverse in the uses and benefits they provide.

In the spirit of consumption true to *The Year-Round Harvest*, the use of herbs as tea is described in this section. Many of the herbs described in the previous culinary section also have aromatic and therapeutic qualities and are enjoyable as teas. In particular, rosemary, thyme, and mint can be used in this capacity.

Catnip

Known for its popularity with cats, catnip is also useful to humans. Wonderful as a tea, catnip serves as both an antidepressant and as a sleep aid, as well as helping to fight off colds. This herb is a perennial and also a ferocious grower. Be sure to allow plenty of room for catnip to grow, otherwise it will overcrowd its neighboring plants. It's best to harvest the leaves of the plant just as the flowers begin to bloom. You can use the leaves fresh, dry, or frozen. With regular pruning, catnip plants will grow into full, bushy plants about 2 to 3 feet in size.

HERB HERITAGE

The growing and harvesting of herbs is as old as civilization. The earliest known writings of most cultures reference herbs used in preparing food, preserving food, scenting the body, and treating wounds and illnesses. Some of the herbs used 2,000 years ago are still used in drugs that modern doctors prescribe today.

Chamomile

One of the most popular tea herbs, chamomile plants are low and bushy, and both the flowers and leaves are harvested and used for tea. The fresh flowers can also be used as an edible and healthful garnish on salads and other fresh dishes. Commonly used for its anti-inflammatory properties, specifically for skin ailments, chamomile can be ground and applied as a poultice, or added to bath water to ease skin irritations. When used as a tea, chamomile is known for its relaxing effect on adults and also to ease teething and colic discomfort in babies.

Echinacea

Echinacea is famous for its ability to strengthen the immune system. It also grows a beautiful flower and is an attractive addition to any garden. Both the purple flower and the root of the plant can be used to make tea and balms. Echinacea plants like full and partial sun and well-drained soil. To use echinacea in teas and balms, both the root and flower can be used. They should be cut just as the first flowers are beginning to bloom. Take care if cutting the root—you only want to remove a small portion, leaving enough for the plant to continue growing. Both the root and the flower can be dried easily.

Evening Primrose

Evening primrose is well known for its ability to aid women with menstrual discomfort as well as for its usefulness in relieving common skin irritations like acne and eczema. The entire plant is edible, and you can harvest the seeds, leaves, flowers, and even the roots.

To make tea, use the leaves and flowers in dried form. You can boil the roots or cook them as you would any other root crop. Evening primrose is a biennial, and if you want to get the most out of your plant, you should wait to harvest the roots until after the seeds have been produced. The leaves and shoots and even the flowers of evening primrose can be eaten fresh in salads. This plant produces a beautiful yellow flower that will bloom at dusk, in the evening, and on cloudy days, adding some character to your garden.

Lavender

One of the most beloved fragrances, lavender is known for its ability to soothe, reduce stress and anxiety, and promote consistency in moods. Also recognized for its aid in treating headaches, lavender is most commonly used outside of the kitchen, although it does have some culinary use and is used well as an herbal tea. Lavender holds its fragrance extremely well in its dried form and should be harvested just as it begins to bloom in order to preserve the most fragrance. Lavender enjoys full sun and dry soil, although it is an adaptable plant and different varieties will take better to different climates. Lavender is a perennial, but you can only expect to get about 10 years out of a plant.

Lemon Balm

In warmer zones, lemon balm can be grown as a perennial if it is mulched. A member of the mint family, this herb is an aggressive grower, and like mint you might want to consider separating this plant from the rest of your garden. Lemon balm is traditionally used as a digestive aid and as a fever reducer. It is a favorite of bees and butterflies and its essential oils contain citronella, helping to keep away mosquitoes. Lemon balm should be harvested before it flowers, and the leaves can be chopped up fresh and are a great addition to fruit and vegetable salads. To make tea, you can dry the herbs, or use them fresh. Lemon balm preserves well through drying or freezing, although the flavor is much stronger in its fresh form.

Lemon Verbena

Lemon verbena is known primarily for its scent. It is a deciduous perennial, meaning that its leaves fall off before winter, when it lies dormant. Lemon verbena is not a hardy plant and only in the warmest zones can you expect it to winter over. It can be planted in containers and brought indoors in the winter; the bare, woody stalks will not be the most attractive window plants, but you'll be happy you saved this herb come spring. The leaves of lemon verbena are harvested and are delicious in teas, and also pair well with rosemary and mint. Lemon verbena tea tastes wonderful, and is also useful as an expectorant, a digestive aid, and a fever reducer. Lemon verbena can also be chopped up and added fresh to salads and salsas, or sprinkled on cooked dishes. Its fresh lemony taste goes well in baked goods, particularly in sweet quick breads.

Tea Basics

Making your own herbal teas is easy and extremely economical if drinking and serving tea is something you do often. Most teas can be made with fresh or dried herbs, and served either hot or cold. Herbs can be used in combinations or on their own for teas, depending on your personal taste. As one of the best ways to absorb the healthful properties of herbs, drinking tea is both good for you and delicious.

To brew tea with loose herb cuttings, you will need a mesh tea ball. These come in different sizes and it's a good idea to have a single-serving tea ball as well as one large enough to brew a pot of tea. Most herbs should be brewed in hot water (not quite boiling) for 3–5 minutes. To make a more powerful infusion, allow herbs to steep for as long as 20 minutes. Whenever drinking herbal teas or herbal infusions, be cautious of the effects of these herbs, as well as the interactions between herbs and any health conditions that you have.

Planting, Maintenance, and Harvest

All herbs are different, but they have many common needs. Most herbs will do well in soil lacking in fertility, as the lack of nutrients actually perpetuates the richness and depth of the essential oils in most herb plants. The root systems of many herbs can succumb to rot if planted in anything other than well-draining soil. Most herbs are best started indoors and raised to be transplanted directly into the garden, although you can successfully seed some herbs directly, depending on your climate.

Herbs, like any other plant, require consistent care in order to maintain control over weeds and pests. Additionally, herbs tend to require pruning, but since you will be harvesting regularly from your plants, most of the pruning needs will be taken care of if harvested appropriately. Prune and harvest evenly throughout the plant, allowing main branches to remain. Pinching off shoots and extra leaves will help the plant to become bushy and healthy, and reach its optimal mature size.

Most herbs are harvested for their leaves and as a general rule of thumb it is best to harvest just before, or just as, the first flowers begin to bloom. This is when the essential oils (where most of the nutritional and healthful properties are contained) are at their most potent and flavorful. Harvest in the morning, after the dew has dried on the leaves and before the heat of the day dries the plants. If harvesting to preserve, the same holds true and you will have the best results if you harvest at the peak of oil production: just as the first flowers are starting to bloom.

Preserving by Drying or Freezing

Aside from their inclusion in some canning and pickling recipes, herbs are typically preserved by either drying or freezing. Herbs that have stalks or sprigs long enough can be tied together in bunches and hung to dry. In some cases, such as preserving evergreen plants in zones where it's too harsh for them to survive outdoors in winter, the entire plant can be uprooted and hung to dry by its root stalk. Other herbs can be strung using a needle and string (smooth fishing line works well; it does not harm delicate plants). When piercing plants to string them, it's best to lead the needle through the main stalk of the plant, not the more tender leaf. This will help to keep the oils of the leaf intact, as well prevent any dampness or pathogens from entering the leaf. The stalk is also stronger to support the weight of the plant when it is hanging.

If you live in a humid or wet climate, you might consider using a dehydrator for more tender leaves, as they can succumb to mold or dampness more easily, although not as easily as most vegetable plants since herbs lack the juices and meat that veggies have. As a result, herbs tend to dry more successfully. After herbs are dried, they should be chopped and stored in an airtight container. Before chopping them, gently brush or wipe off any excess dirt, then chop and store.

Most herbs are better dried than frozen, although this depends on how you plan to use them. Herbs that you plan to use for tea are almost always better dried, whereas some culinary herbs function better in their frozen form. The two most common ways to freeze herbs are by cleaning and separating the leaves and placing them in one layer on a baking sheet. Place the sheet in the freezer until the leaves are consistently frozen, then store in a freezer-safe container or bag. The second method is to wash and then cut the herbs before placing them in water in ice cube trays. Freeze the cubes and then use them by dropping them directly into cooking soups, or quickly thawing before use.

The following recipes will help you get the most enjoyment out of your herb garden.

Lavender Jam

Makes 2 pints

This recipe is adapted from Linda Gilbert's Lavender Jam Recipe and is one of my favorite culinary ways to use lavender. Adaptations of this recipe that include fruit are featured in the small-fruit chapter in this book.

A handful of dried lavender blossoms
¼ cup sugar
⅔ cup port wine
⅓ cup crème de cassis
½ cup water

1. Mix together all ingredients and then bring to a slow, gentle boil in a saucepan until the liquid becomes syrupy, stirring occasionally to prevent sticking. This should take about 30 minutes.
2. Pour into a glass jar and refrigerate.

Garlic Bread Spread

Makes 5–6 pints

You can keep this spread on hand for fast and delicious garlic bread any time. A classic way to make use of your garlic. The refrigerated lifespan of this blend is 8 weeks. To use this spread, lightly butter a whole loaf of bread and then add this spread on top. Heat under the broiler until cheese melts, about 1 minute.

6 cups shredded mozzarella cheese at room temperature

1½ cups grated Parmesan cheese

1½ cups grated Romano cheese

1 tablespoon coarsely ground black pepper

1 cup minced garlic

1 cup extra-virgin olive oil

2 teaspoons freshly squeezed lemon juice

1. In a large mixing bowl, add 3 cups mozzarella cheese and half of each of the remaining ingredients. Using a large spatula, fold until blended.
2. Repeat with remaining ingredients.
3. Put into sterilized pint Mason jars. Put on sterilized lids and bands. Keep refrigerated.

Herb Garlic Blend

Makes 1 cup

Mix this with butter for garlic bread beyond compare.

4 tablespoons minced basil
4 tablespoons tarragon
4 tablespoons chervil
5 tablespoons minced thyme
1 teaspoon garlic powder

1. Put all ingredients into a blender or food processor; whirl until fine.
2. Store in a jar with an airtight cover.

Garlic Onion Pesto

Makes about 3 cups

This is the foundation for a great white pizza. Just brush it over the crust and add your favorite toppings.

2 cups fresh basil, packed
¼ cup pine nuts
¼ cup dried minced onion
⅛ cup minced garlic
¼ cup olive oil
1 tablespoon lemon juice

1. Place all ingredients into a nonreactive pan over a low flame; simmer 15 minutes.
2. Cool; transfer to ice cube trays. Freeze.
3. Pop out frozen pesto cubes and put in a food-storage bag in the freezer.

Garlic Stock

Makes 6 cups

Have fun experimenting with different types of garlic in this broth. For a milder but rich garlic taste, bake the garlic in olive oil before using it for the stock.

1½ tablespoons olive oil
½ head garlic, peeled and chopped
½ head elephant garlic, peeled and chopped
6 cups vegetable stock
1 bay leaf
¼ teaspoon dried thyme
1 pinch dried sage
Salt to taste
Pepper to taste

1. Warm the oil in a frying pan and very lightly sauté garlics.
2. Combine all ingredients; boil.
3. Reduce heat; simmer 30 minutes.
4. Strain; taste for saltiness.
5. Preserve as desired. If canning, use 10 pounds of pressure for 30 minutes for pints.

Garlic Quinoa

Serves 4

A simple way to spruce up plain quinoa when served as a side dish, or as a topping to cooked veggies.

2 tablespoons olive oil
1 yellow onion, diced
4 cloves garlic, minced
1½ cups quinoa
3 cups vegetable broth
½ teaspoon salt

1. In a large skillet, heat onion and garlic in oil or margarine for 3–4 minutes until onions are soft.
2. Add vegetable broth and quinoa, and bring to a simmer. Cook for 15 minutes until liquid is absorbed.
3. Fluff quinoa with a fork and stir in salt.

Quinoa and Fresh Herb Stuffing

Serves 6

Substitute dried herbs if you have to, but fresh is best in this untraditional stuffing recipe.

1 yellow onion, chopped
2 ribs celery, diced
¼ cup butter
1 teaspoon chopped fresh rosemary
2 teaspoons chopped fresh marjoram
1½ tablespoons chopped fresh thyme
1 tablespoon chopped fresh sage
6 slices dried bread, cubed
1¼ cups vegetable broth
2 cups cooked quinoa
¾ teaspoon salt
½ teaspoon pepper

1. Preheat oven to 400°F.
2. Heat onion and celery in butter and cook until soft, about 6–8 minutes. Add fresh herbs and heat for another minute, just until fragrant.
3. Remove from heat and add bread, combining well. Add vegetable broth to moisten bread; you may need a bit more or less than 1¼ cups.
4. Add cooked quinoa, salt, and pepper, and combine well.

Bulgur Wheat Tabbouleh Salad with Tomatoes

Serves 4

Though you'll need to adjust the cooking time, of course, you can try this tabbouleh (also called tabouli), recipe with just about any whole grain. Bulgur wheat is traditional, but quinoa, millet, or amaranth will also work.

1 cup bulgur wheat
1¼ cups boiling water or vegetable broth
3 tablespoons olive oil
¼ cup lemon juice
1 garlic clove, minced
½ teaspoon sea salt
½ teaspoon pepper
3 scallions, chopped
½ cup chopped fresh mint
½ cup chopped fresh parsley
3 large tomatoes, diced

1. Pour boiling water over bulgur wheat. Cover, and allow to sit for 30 minutes, or until bulgur wheat is soft.
2. Toss bulgur wheat with olive oil, lemon juice, garlic powder, and salt, stirring well to coat. Combine with remaining ingredients, adding in tomatoes last.
3. Allow to chill for at least 1 hour before serving.

Lemon Cilantro Couscous

Serves 4

This flavorful couscous is a light and easy side dish, or top it off with a vegetable stew or some stir-fried or roasted veggies.

2 cups vegetable broth
1 cup couscous
⅓ cup lemon juice
½ cup chopped fresh cilantro
¼ teaspoon sea salt, or to taste

1. Bring vegetable broth to a simmer and add couscous. Cover and let stand for 10 minutes, until soft, then fluff with a fork.
2. Stir in lemon juice and cilantro, and season generously with sea salt.

Fresh Basil Pomodoro

Pick out the finest fresh zucchinis and tomatoes for this one, as pomodoro is a simple pasta dish with little added flavor.

> 2 zucchinis, sliced
> 4 cloves garlic, minced
> 2 tablespoons olive oil
> 4 large tomatoes, diced
> ⅓ cup chopped fresh basil
> 2 cups prepared angel hair or spaghetti pasta
> Salt and pepper to taste
> Parmesan cheese

1. Heat zucchini and garlic in olive oil over low heat for just a minute or two until zucchini is just lightly softened. Add tomatoes and cook for another 4–5 minutes.
2. Toss zucchini and tomatoes with basil and pasta, and season with salt and pepper, to taste. Serve topped with a sprinkle of Parmesan cheese.

Savory Sage Pasta

Serves 6

The earthy rosemary and sage flavors would complement gnocchi well; otherwise, use a grooved pasta, such as corkscrews, to catch the sauce.

12 ounces pasta, cooked

½ cup fresh sage, chopped fine

½ cup sliced cooked bacon

2 tablespoons cream

1 tablespoon butter

½ teaspoon rosemary

Salt and pepper, to taste

Over low heat, combine the cooked pasta with the remaining ingredients, combining well and heating just until well mixed and heated through, about 3–4 minutes.

Lemon Thyme Orzo with Asparagus

Serves 4

If you have fresh thyme growing indoors when your asparagus is ready to harvest, this recipe is a perfect way to welcome this early spring veggie. The combination of lemon and thyme is understated and rustic, and will also work well with dried thyme. If you aren't growing asparagus, use this recipe later in the season with green peas or lightly steamed broccoli.

1½ cups orzo

2 tablespoons olive oil

1 bunch asparagus, chopped

Zest from 1 lemon

2 tablespoons lemon juice

½ teaspoon salt

¼ teaspoon pepper

2 teaspoons chopped fresh thyme

1. Cook orzo according to package instructions.
2. In a large skillet, heat asparagus in olive oil until just tender. Do not overcook.
3. Reduce heat to low and add in orzo and remaining ingredients, stirring to combine well. Cook for just a minute or two, until heated through, and adjust seasonings to taste.

Homemade Flavored Oil

A flavored oil will beautify your kitchen and add flavor to your food. Simply combine several of your favorite herbs, whole garlic cloves, peppercorns, dried lemon or orange zest, or dried chilies with a quality olive oil. Avoid fresh herbs and zests, and always use dried. Oils infused with dried herbs will keep for up to one year, while fresh herbs can cause spoilage after less than a week.

Lemon Verbena Sherbert

Makes 1 quart

A light and refreshing dessert, lemon verbena sherbert is the perfect end to any summer meal. The homemade version is a blast of rich flavor that you simply cannot buy in a store.

2 cups whole milk
2 cups lemon verbena
½ cup sugar, plus 2 tablespoons more
½ cup lemon juice
Pinch of salt
Extra lemon verbena leaves for garnish

1. In a saucepan, bring the lemon verbena leaves, milk, sugar, and salt to a slow boil.
2. Remove from heat and allow to stand for one hour. Stir occasionally.
3. After an hour, strain the liquid and add the lemon juice.
4. Freeze in an ice-cream maker and garnish with lemon verbena leaves.

Parsley Salad

Serves 2

Parsley is delicious and flavorful in this extremely simple dish.

2 cups fresh parsley, packed

2 tablespoons extra-virgin olive oil

1 teaspoon fresh-squeezed lemon juice (or more to taste)

Sea salt and pepper to taste

1. Toss parsley lightly with olive oil.
2. Season with lemon juice, salt, and pepper. Enjoy!

Freshly Herbed Beets

A delicious way to change any beet-haters' minds, this recipe can be served with strong-flavored cheese or dill cheese as a tasty complement.

1½ pounds cooked and peeled beets

2 tablespoons red onion, finely chopped

2 tablespoons chopped fresh parsley

2 tablespoons chopped fresh cilantro

1 tablespoon chopped fresh mint

Finely ground zest of 1 lemon, and 2 tablespoons juice

6 tablespoons extra-virgin olive oil

Salt and pepper

4 handfuls salad greens, like spinach, frisée, red leaf lettuce, or a combination

1. Quarter the beets.
2. Whisk together lemon zest and juice, onion, herbs, salt, pepper, and oil in a small bowl.
3. Taste the dressing on a beet and adjust to your preference. Toss the beets with just enough dressing to lightly coat them.
4. Use the remaining dressing to toss with salad greens.
5. To serve, arrange the salad on plates and add the beets.

Parsley and Mint Carrot Salad

A fast, easy, and delicious salad to use your fresh carrots and herbs in.

> 1 pound peeled and grated carrots
> 1 tablespoon fresh lemon juice or white wine vinegar
> 2 tablespoons olive oil
> Small handful of chopped, fresh parsley
> Couple pinches of finely chopped mint leaves
> Salt and pepper

Toss all ingredients in large bowl. Salt and pepper to taste.

Winter Herb Dressing

Makes approximately ¾ cup

A classic dried herb vinaigrette that can be used at any time of year but its conduciveness to dried herbs makes it ideal for wintertime, when fresh herbs are harder to come by.

1 clove garlic
¼ teaspoon peppercorn
¼ teaspoon fennel seeds
½ teaspoon dried tarragon
Pinch salt
1–2 tablespoons dried parsley
Zest of 1 lemon
¼ cup thinly sliced scallions
⅓ cup extra-virgin olive oil
2 tablespoons champagne vinegar
Salt to taste

1. Using a mortar and pestle, make a smooth paste with the garlic, peppercorn, fennel, tarragon, a pinch of salt, and half of the parsley.
2. Combine with all the other ingredients except vinegar.
3. Allow to sit for 30 minutes before adding the vinegar, and salt to taste.

Sweet and Spicy Sauce

Makes just under 1 pint

A favorite sauce of mine to liven up plain rice, or use as a dipping sauce or salad dressing.

Olive or canola oil
Rice vinegar
1 dried chili pepper, ground
1 tablespoon honey
1 garlic clove, pressed or minced
½ teaspoon freshly grated ginger root
Sea salt
Freshly ground black pepper

1. Using twice as much vinegar to oil, fill a pint jar halfway with the liquids. Depending on how spicy you want it, add as much of the ground chili pepper as you would like.
2. Add the other ingredients and with the lid securely fastened on the jar, shake the jar. Taste and adjust accordingly.
3. You can save this dressing for weeks in the refrigerator. It may solidify because of the oil, but will quickly turn back to liquid after it has been out of the fridge for a little while.

Fresh Mint Chutney

Makes 3 cups

You can serve this fresh chutney as a topping on a meat or fish dish, or as a salsa for crusty bread or crackers.

2 cups fresh mint leaves
1 onion, peeled and chopped coarsely
4 garlic cloves, peeled and chopped coarsely
4 jalapeño chilies, seeded and chopped
2 teaspoons cumin seeds, toasted in oven
⅔ cup almond slivers, chopped
Lemon juice to taste

Combine all ingredients in a food processor, pulse until just finely chopped, and serve!

Refresh Tea

You can use fresh or dried herbs for this tea. Just follow the ratios listed below and pack your tea-ball with dried herbs, or let fresh ones steep loosely. You can serve this tea hot or cold.

2 parts lemon balm

1 part lemon verbena

1 part spearmint

Hot Mediterranean Tea

You can use fresh or dried herbs for this tea. Just follow the ratios listed below and pack your tea ball with dried herbs, or let fresh ones steep loosely.

1 part summer savory

1 part marjoram

1 part rosemary

Lemon-Mint Sun Tea

This tea is great as a sun tea; just allow it to steep in the sun, covered, for a few hours. It is also good brewed as a traditional iced tea. To make a pitcher of sun tea,* take a handful of mint sprigs and quarter a whole lemon. Add both to a pitcher of clean water, and cover with a cheesecloth or other light fabric. Place in the sun for several hours and then pour over ice, allowing the mint and lemons to remain loose as a pretty garnish.

*Note that when making sun tea, it's best to use a glass or a ceramic pitcher. Some metals can react with the acidity in some herbs and fruit, affecting the flavor, and a plastic pitcher left in the sun tends to leach a bad taste into its contents.

Cucumber Basil Water

Makes 1 large pitcher

Not quite a traditional tea, this flavored water is a delicious accompaniment to any summertime meal, or on its own.

1 whole English cucumber or 2 pickling cucumbers
5–6 small sprigs of basil
2–3 lemon wedges (optional)

1. Wash and cut ends off cucumber(s). Leave the peel on, and slice into moderately thin slices (not so thin as to be totally translucent).
2. Gently wash the basil so as not to bruise the leaves.
3. Separate the leaves from the stems. Do not cut.
4. Add cucumber and basil to water, add ice, and chill in the refrigerator for at least an hour before serving.
5. You can keep a pitcher in the fridge, adding more water when necessary, for a few days or until the basil starts to lose its freshness. Mint is also a good substitute for the basil.

Herb Vinegars

Making herb-infused vinegars is easy and provides you with a useful diversity of herb flavors and vinegars for dressings, sauces, and cooking. Simply select any single herb or herb combination that you want to preserve. If maintaining color is important, then white wine vinegar is recommended. Red wine vinegar works well with strongly flavored herbs like garlic or basil. Whereas wine vinegars are gentle enough to allow the herb's flavor to come through, other vinegars (like cider or white vinegar) are too strong to do justice to your herbs.

You do need to sanitize your herbs, and *briefly* dipping them in a solution of 1 teaspoon of bleach—no more!—to 6 cups water will do the trick. Do not soak the herbs in the solution; just dip them briefly. Be sure to rinse the herbs well after sanitizing them and put them right away into a sterilized glass quart jar. Heat 3½ cups of vinegar to just below the boiling point, and pour over the herbs. Seal the jar and store in a cool, dark spot for 3–5 weeks. Your root cellar is an ideal place.

Every few days you'll want to give your jar a quick shake to help disperse the flavor. After a few weeks, taste the mixture. If it doesn't have the flavor you want, either add more vinegar or add fresh herbs. Once you get your mixture to the right flavor, strain out the liquid and remove the herbs. Continue straining the vinegar until any bits of herb residue have been removed. Pour the vinegar into dry, sterilized jars. Add some sprigs from fresh herbs and seal the jar. You don't need to can this vinegar, simply keep in your root cellar or similar environment, or even in the refrigerator.

Basic Balsamic Vinaigrette

Makes 1 cup

No need to purchase expensive and sugar-laden salad dressings at the grocery store! This simple vinaigrette will serve you well for a last-minute salad dressing.

- ¼ cup balsamic vinegar
- ¾ cup olive oil
- 1 tablespoon Dijon mustard
- ¼ teaspoon salt
- ⅛ teaspoon black pepper
- ½ teaspoon dried basil
- ½ teaspoon dried parsley

Whisk together all ingredients with a fork until well combined.

Vegan Pesto Vinaigrette

Makes 1¼ cups

Turn your herb pesto into a flavorful salad dressing. Perfect on a green salad with red onions, black olives, and diced avocado. You may need a little more or less liquid, depending on how thick your pesto is.

⅔ cup pesto such as Herb Pesto
¼ cup red wine vinegar
1 tablespoon lemon juice
⅓ cup olive oil
1 tablespoon Dijon mustard

Whisk together all ingredients until well combined.

Cabbage Salsa

Makes 6 cups

This recipe can be used as a salsa with chips, or as a taco topping. It also makes for a great side dish on its own.

5 cups shredded cabbage
1 cup firmly packed cilantro leaves, minced
¼ cup lime juice
1 tablespoon honey
Salt and pepper to taste

In a large nonmetal bowl, mix all the ingredients together.

Bob's Fabulous Yummy Marinade

Makes approximately ¾ cup

This recipe is adapted from Recipes from a Kitchen Garden *by Renee Shepherd and Fran Raboff and is a great marinade for tofu and meats, a pasta or rice sauce, and a salad dressing.*

5 tablespoons vegetable oil
⅓ cup packed fresh cilantro with stems
¼ cup fresh lime juice
¼ cup tamari soy sauce
1½-inch fresh ginger, cut into six ¼-inch slices
6 large cloves garlic
1½ tablespoons ground cumin
1 small jalapeño or other chili (optional)

Combine and blend all ingredients together in a food processor or blender until the chili, garlic, ginger, and cilantro are finely chopped.

Herb Pesto

Makes 1 cup

A variation of the classic, more simple pesto, this version will have your mouth watering and is a great way to use lots of fresh herbs.

½ cup packed fresh basil leaves
½ cup packed fresh parsley leaves
¼ cup packed fresh oregano leaves
3 garlic cloves
2 tablespoons grated Parmesan
2 tablespoons olive oil
2 teaspoons lemon juice
½ teaspoon salt
¼ teaspoon pepper
1 ounce walnuts (optional)

1. Combine all the ingredients except for the salt, pepper, oil, and lemon juice. Use a food processor or blender to mix until finely chopped.
2. Gradually mix in the lemon juice and oil, and stir in the salt and pepper last.

Red Chile Sauce

Makes 2–3 cups

This classic Southwestern sauce is perfect served over enchiladas or beans and is a great way to use your dried herbs, onion, and peppers in the wintertime.

> 2 tablespoons onion, chopped
> 2 tablespoons vegetable oil
> 1 large or 2 small garlic cloves, finely chopped
> 1 teaspoon dried oregano
> 2 tablespoons flour
> ½ teaspoon ground cumin
> ½ cup ground red chile
> Salt to taste

1. Heat the oil in a heavy saucepan and add the onion, garlic, and oregano in that order. Cook over medium heat for just over 5 minutes.
2. Add the flour and cumin and cook until the flour turns slightly brown, about 2 minutes, stirring constantly to make a roux.
3. Mix the chile with 2½ cups of water and whisk it into the roux. Continue cooking until the sauce thickens, about 15 minutes.
4. Add salt to taste.

Garden Herb Salad

Serves 2–3

This salad, adapted from Vegetarian Cooking for Everyone *by Deborah Madison, explodes with perfectly balanced gatherings from your garden. The perfect taste of summertime green, you'll find yourself dreaming of this salad year-round.*

2 cups lettuce leaves

2 cups spinach leaves

4 marjoram sprigs

2 tablespoons basil leaves

½ cup celery leaves

½ cup flat-leaf parsley leaves

Handful lemon verbena sprigs

1 cup purslane sprigs

Any available herb blossoms

Fresh lemon juice or apple cider vinegar

Extra-virgin olive oil

1. After washing, sorting, and drying all the lettuce and spinach leaves, tear or cut into bite-sized pieces.
2. Separate the marjoram leaves from stems, keeping leaves whole. Tear basil leaves into small pieces.
3. Keep the other herb leaves in their current condition.
4. Toss everything, with just a pinch of salt and a light application of oil.
5. Add lemon juice to taste and toss in the blossoms.

CHAPTER 7

STORING YOUR BOUNTY

Storing food for year-round use is one of the most enjoyable parts of creating your own food system. By creating a diverse storage system you can maximize your food supply, as well as store food in different levels of preparedness. In the following chapters you will learn about storing prepared foods by freezing, canning, pickling, and fermenting. In this chapter you will learn about the different types of spaces and structures for storing whole foods.

The Root Cellar

The purpose of a root cellar is to store your fresh fruits and veggies so you can eat them during the winter months. If you are just starting to think about building a root cellar, or if you already have one, this chapter will help you to learn how to get the most out of it. You will learn how to choose the best location and size, how to create the best conditions, and gain new knowledge about shelving and container options that will help you get the best possible results from your root cellar.

Size

The size of your root cellar will depend on how much food you want to store and what size root cellar you can build in a good location. A 10-foot by 12-foot root cellar will usually have plenty of space to store veggies, fruits, and both canned and dried goods for a family. Your requirements will vary, but if you are going to the expense of excavating or building a root cellar you need to make sure it is large enough that you are able to grow into it as you gain more experience storing your foods.

In addition to being a basic size, your root cellar should ideally have at least two rooms, one colder than the other. Having two rooms allows you to regulate the humidity, temperature, and air flow, giving you the best storage conditions for a variety of foods. You will learn more about the storage requirements of specific vegetables later in this chapter.

Location

Ideally you want your root cellar to be close to your garden so you will find it easy to put extra veggies directly into it when harvesting. You also want the root cellar to be easily accessible from your kitchen so you will be able to get to your stored foods without any difficulty, especially on those cold winter days. If you live on flat ground, without a hillside available for excavation, you will most likely need to build an above-ground cellar. Otherwise, it is best to build your root cellar below ground.

Below Ground

If you live on a site with a hillside or slope—one that can be easily excavated and faces away from prevailing winds—then you already have an ideal spot to build your root cellar. Using the earth as insulation is one of the best ways to protect your fruits and vegetables, and having three walls and the roof covered with soil is ideal. If at all possible, locating the entry door on the north side of the slope will help to insulate the structure and provide minimal exposure to direct sunlight. You will want to avoid building in a low-lying area and make sure your site has good drainage so that the cellar doesn't fill up with water.

Examine the soil content before you begin digging into your hillside; soil that is rocky or hardpan clay may not allow for easy hand digging, which means that renting or buying excavation equipment may be necessary. Sandy soil can also provide difficulties, such as walls collapsing as you dig. There can be a variety of different types of soil on any property, and it may be necessary to consider a few potential sites before you settle on the right one.

Another thing to look out for when choosing a site for your underground root cellar is large trees. Tree roots can reach amazing distances and may cause a lot of problems during the excavation of the site. They can also invade the walls of your root cellar later on. If at all possible, avoid areas with large trees and do not plant deep-rooted trees or shrubs nearby.

Walls, Doorways, and Insulation

A root cellar that has been dug into a hillside is an underground structure with one exposed wall and an access door. The wall can be made from a variety of materials such as wood, cement blocks, adobe, rammed earth, earth bags, and cob.

To create an access door for your underground cellar, first mark off a 32-inch space to serve as a rough opening for your doorway. Next, create the doorframe out of 2-foot by 8-foot lumber boards. An economical option is to install a previously used door, often found at salvage yards, Habitat for Humanity ReStores, and garage sales.

Depending on what material you choose to make your access wall and on the climate in your area, you may need to insulate your cellar. A wall made of wood will have to be insulated no matter what the climate, as wood alone will not keep the heat or cold from coming through. Two feet of insulation material, placed between the interior and exterior wall, is ideal for a wood-framed wall if using natural materials for insulation: A wall built with hollow cement blocks is easily insulated by filling in the hollow area between blocks with some common material such as sawdust, loose straw, or dry sand. Or, commercial insulation can be used. A wall made of adobe, rammed earth, or cob needs no additional insulation as it is thick enough and the material used functions as a natural insulator. Your access door will also need to be insulated. One way is to cover the inside of the door with standard home insulation. To do this, cut 2-foot by 4-foot boards long enough to make a frame around the inside of the door. Nail the wood to the door, then fill the two-inch recess with insulation. Nail a piece of plywood to this frame to hold the insulation in place. A much easier way to provide insulation is to tack a heavy blanket or cloth to the inside of the door, although this may not be effective if you live in a very cold climate.

If your underground root cellar has more than one room, you can help regulate temperature and humidity by having well-insulated walls and doorways. Hanging blankets on interior walls and over doorways is one way to regulate temperature throughout the cellar and provide an extra measure of insulation for your fruits and veggies.

Ventilation Below Ground

It may seem like common sense, but this bears repeating: Hot temperatures warm the earth while cold temperatures will freeze it. Both heat and cold affect the temperature inside your underground root cellar. All root cellars, whether they are built above or below the ground, require two air vents: one lower down on a wall to let in cool air and another higher up to allow the warm air to be released. Ventilation and good air circulation are required to keep the temperature regulated in any root cellar, and a ventilator may be necessary in certain root cellars.

Root Cellar

Above Ground

What if you want to store some of your own veggies for eating during the winter but do not have the type of property that will allow you to build an underground root cellar? An above-ground or partial above-ground structure is a viable option. You will have to build your structure above ground if you live on a flat property, which means making sure to provide proper insulation. Heat will penetrate the walls of your root cellar if the sun hits them, especially if they are made of concrete or wood, and this will warm the interior and cause the temperature to rise. Your stored fruits and veggies will dehydrate more quickly in those tepid conditions. The room may freeze without proper insulation in the winter when the temperature gets below freezing, causing the fruits and vegetables to rot more quickly. Wiring your root cellar with electricity is another way to solve this problem. Whichever method you choose, be sure to keep the temperature in your above-ground root cellar as consistent as possible.

DIY VENT

The most practical item to use as a vent is a 6-inch water or sewer pipe wrapped in duct insulation. Attaching an elbow at the end exposed to the outside will help keep the temperature consistent and prevent rain and water from getting inside. Do not glue this elbow; you want to make sure it is free to turn away from the prevailing wind.

A Partial Underground Structure

If your location is not ideal for excavating a root cellar, you can build a partial underground structure by digging just 4 feet or so into the ground. This type of structure is common in colder parts of the country, in areas where the ground is flat and rocky, or where the water table is high and there is very poor drainage. The walls of a partial underground root cellar are usually made of masonry blocks and banked with soil on three sides.

First you will need to decide on the size of your root cellar. For example, if you want a structure 12 feet by 8 feet that will stay solid for years, you will need to dig an area 16 feet by 12 feet that sits 4 feet deep, with an entrance ramp that is 4 feet wide and slopes 6 feet. You want the area to be larger than your structure so you have access to build your walls from all sides. You can fill in the extra space on the outside of the wall once it is built with the dirt from the excavation; this will provide even more insulation for your root cellar. The entrance ramp is 6 feet long and angled, giving you an area to make steps leading down to the main door of your cellar. Make sure you have the space to accommodate the size structure you want to build before you start digging.

This type of structure traditionally has a hatchway door with a stairway leading down to a second doorway. The "double entrance" offers great insulation from the outside temperatures because of the air space between the two doors. The roof is typically made of two-by-fours and then protected with roof sheathing and plastic film, with dirt piled on top of everything. Vents are installed for good air circulation, and a drainage system is used to eliminate water and reduce humidity.

Two big advantages to the partial underground structure are that it is affordable and easy to build. If you utilize common materials from your own property or a local building-supply store, you can build this structure in your spare time.

Completely underground root cellars usually stay at the ideal temperature for storing fruits and veggies due to the earth's natural insulation. However, you can still preserve successfully in an above-ground storage building so long as you build in the right location and provide insulation and proper drainage. Constructing a solid above-ground structure begins with choosing the right materials for its walls.

Brick, Concrete Blocks, or Stone Walls

Brick, concrete blocks, and stone are some of the most common materials used in building the walls of the traditional above-ground root cellar. Usually the cost and availability of these materials are the most important factors in determining which of these products you choose. As you probably know, bricks come in a wide variety of sizes. They are typically small and therefore easy to work with; but because they are small you will need more product and your structure will take longer to construct. Concrete blocks are a good choice for making heavy-duty walls. They are usually cheaper than brick and the construction will go much faster because of their larger size.

Above-Ground Root Cellar

Building with stone or large rocks is often the cheapest option since these materials can often be found on your own property. The construction can also be more challenging, however, since you'll need a good eye, a strong back, and lots of patience to build sturdy walls from rocks that are all different shapes and sizes. However, building with stone can also give you a huge sense of accomplishment; not only will your structure have been built from materials gathered from your own land, it will have a handcrafted look and quality.

If you are new to building with rock and are not yet familiar with cutting the material, you will want to start with the flattest-edged rocks you can find for your first layer. Choose rocks that are similar in height to start building up your wall, continuing along the full length of the wall. Fill in all the joints between the rocks with mortar. When the first course is complete, spread mortar across the top and continue building another layer. If you run out of similar-sized rocks, find two that can be stacked to match the others. Stand back and look at the wall to make sure the joints are all staggered; if not, your wall has more of a chance of breaking.

Walls from Wood

Cedar is your best option if you decide to build your root cellar out of wood because cedar offers greater resistance to rot and insects. Your first step when building walls with wood is to create an insulation pocket. To do this, build two walls 2 feet apart, and fill this cavity with either traditional insulation or somewhat unconventional options like straw, hay, or sawdust. It is important to cover the outside of your wood walls with a moisture-resistant material, especially if you are planning to pack soil against them.

Adobe Walls

Adobe is one of the first human-made building supplies, and was originally used where trees were scarce but there was an abundance of dirt and water. Making your own adobe takes a lot of time and work, but its considerable benefits make the investment worthwhile. Adobe provides natural insulation, consistent humidity, and fresh air exchange, all invaluable to your burgeoning root cellar.

You will need molds to make your own bricks, and these can be made by hand using pieces of wood two-by-fours that are cut and connected to the right size (to save time, build a mold that allows you to make multiple adobe bricks at once). The adobe mixture is made by combining soil, water, and cement. Begin by adding just enough water to the soil to make it slightly plastic, meaning you want the soil to be a muddy consistency but not watery and so it will hold its shape. Next add the cement, followed by enough water to bring the mix to a molding consistency. Use a blade-type mixer to ensure proper mixing, or mix well by hand with a hoe.

Adobe Wall

Building Walls with Rammed Earth

Rammed-earth walls are made from earth and water. The ideal soil to use for these structures is a blend of small gravel, coarse or fine sand, and clay. The best ratio for these materials is 70 percent sand

mixed with 30 percent clay. The soil in the area of your root cellar can be tested to see if it is suitable for this use; if not, you can have better soil brought in. Cement can also be added to the soil to increase its strength and to help keep moisture out of the walls. Steel reinforcing bars are often used in the foundation and walls for added structural support.

WITHSTANDING THE ELEMENTS

To test your soil to determine if it will work well for building a rammed-earth structure, construct a small sample block so it can be checked for strength and weather resistance. Spray the block with water from your garden hose at full force for an hour to see how it holds up. If necessary, modify your earth mix and make another test block.

The basic procedure for building a rammed-earth structure has not changed in the past two millennia. Suitable moist soil is compacted one layer at a time into a form that is constructed to where the wall is to be. The form can be made out of two pieces of plywood with wood connecting them. The form is constructed to the width and height of the wall you are building. Once the form is full and the last layer is compacted, the form is taken down and the process repeated for all remaining walls. The earth is compacted by hand or by machines.

The benefit to making rammed-earth walls is that earth is always readily available. In addition, it is unprocessed, low-cost, heat-storing, load-bearing, recyclable, and durable. A properly built rammed-earth root cellar gains free heat from the winter sun and stores that heat in its walls, preventing your food from freezing. During summer months, the walls absorb excess heat from the inside if the structure is properly shaded and ventilated, helping to keep the interior cool and allowing your food to stay fresh longer.

Rammed Wall

The Cob Structure

Cob is probably the oldest earth-building system and it also happens to be the simplest. A cob structure requires no framework, ramming, or additives, and is very easy to build. The word *cob* is an English term that means "mud building," so it's no surprise that a cob wall is made of a combination of sand, clay, straw, and water—all of which are readily available right on your own property!

The cob recipe:

* 50–85 percent sand
* 50–15 percent clay

* Straw (add as much as you can until each piece is surrounded by the sand/clay mixture—the more clay in the mix, the more straw can be added)
* Water (add enough so the earth mixture holds together)

After you thoroughly mix these four ingredients, the stiff mud is piled to make a wall and formed using your own hands.

A cob structure typically takes several weeks to build. First, a stone foundation is laid and stiff mud is shoveled onto it and tamped down. Next, about 18 inches of material, know as a "lift of cob," is piled on top of this foundation, then left for two weeks to dry before the next "lift" is added. The walls are trimmed back as they dry using a paring iron, leaving them straight and plumb (meaning the wall is exactly vertical) and between 20 and 36 inches thick. Openings for a door and windows are built in by framing in lintels of stone or wood at appropriate heights as the walls are constructed.

Cob structures need protection from prolonged soaking. Building a strong foundation and roof and adding the additional protection of a coating of exterior plaster will ensure that your structure withstands the elements.

The benefits of cob walls are the same as with rammed earth; whether your cellar is built underground or partially underground, these types of walls help keep the temperature consistent and therefore prevent your stored items from getting too warm or too cold. The dirt floor in these structures makes it easier to maintain the proper humidity as well. Additionally, you'll be buying a minimal amount of materials if you decide to build cob walls, making them an inexpensive option. Plus, they can be fun to construct, especially if you enlist the help of your family, friends, and neighbors!

Using Earthbags

Another cost-effective alternative for building the walls of your above-ground root cellar is to use soil-filled sacks, also known as earthbags. This more flexible version of rammed earth is preferred in areas where the soil has very low clay content, where wood is scarce, or where the site is prone to floods, hurricanes, or wildfires. When properly built, earthbag walls are very strong.

When choosing which bag to use, you'll want to seek out bag material that's strong. The most commonly used bags are made from either burlap (hessian) or polypropylene. Burlap is more durable than polypropylene, and burlap is biodegradable because it is made from plant fibers. Polypropylene bags are made of woven plastic and are photodegradable, meaning that they will deteriorate if exposed to ultraviolet rays from the sun. Recycled seed or feed sacks are good choices for either of these materials.

First, bags are filled with subsoil, removing any organic matter and topsoil. You can also fill the bags with gravel, which may be handy if you are using gravel for the foundation. Then all that's necessary is to stack the bags layer upon layer, in a staggered pattern to prevent rain from seeping into the wall.

The Roof

The roof will be made of soil in any underground root cellar. Interior framing may be supplied to support this dirt roof depending on the size of the cellar and the soil type, but that is all that is needed. A roof will need to be built in the case of an above-ground cellar because only the walls are supported with soil. Three of the most common roof types used in these cases are sloped roofs, gable roofs, and flat roofs.

The style of roof you choose will depend upon the overall appearance you want, the amount of money you want to spend, and the materials you have available. A flat or low-pitched roof is the most common style for a root cellar; however, a flat roof can be problematic if you live in a wet climate or where the snowfall is heavy. Whatever roofing style you choose, make sure it is properly built.

Unconventional Storage Spaces

Even if you live in a rental home, an apartment, or do not have any traditional space to build a root cellar, you can still find a place within your home to store preserves and fresh fruits and vegetables for winter eating.

Repurposing Areas in Your House

The average home usually has a few spots that would make great unconventional root cellars. When looking around your home, try to find areas that have good storage conditions—a cold, damp space for root vegetables like potatoes and carrots, a warm dry spot for storing squash, and a cool dry area for your garlic and onions.

An unheated room such as a spare bedroom, an unused bath, or a spare closet that doesn't see much use are all great candidates for your cold storage area. Close the door to the space, put in a thermometer, and record the temperature. If it is cool (32–40°F) and moist (80–90 percent relative humidity), you have found a great place to store your root veggies. If the area is cool (32–50°F) but dry (60–70 percent relative humidity), then it is the place to store your garlic and onions.

STORING ROOT VEGGIES

Before storing beets, carrots, rutabagas, and other root vegetables, make sure the leafy green tops are removed. Tops that are not removed will quickly deplete the nutrients found in the root vegetable. Leave an inch or so of stem so the peel of the vegetable is not broken. This practice will also help to keep your vegetables crisp longer.

An unheated attic is usually easily accessible and often has the ideal conditions for storing vegetables such as squash and green tomatoes. A warm attic is also a good spot for drying herbs, nuts, and beans. Make sure your vegetables, herbs, and nuts are in perfect condition before placing them in boxes or hanging them in your attic. Some vegetables, like tomatoes, will have to be checked regularly as they can ripen fairly quickly. Others, like good quality squash, can last up to 6 months when stored properly. Since most attics are unheated, you'll occasionally need to open the door to let in a little heat. Another option for storing your squash is under your bed—an area that is normally warm, dry, and unused.

Wall space along stairwells up to your attic or down to your basement can hold small containers or baskets of apples, onions, or garlic. On the floor under your kitchen table can even be a spot to store a few of those green tomatoes so they can easily be checked and pulled out to use when ripe.

Porches and Basements

Your living space may not be big enough or convenient if you have a large amount of food to store. In this case, an enclosed porch or basement may offer the perfect solution.

An enclosed porch is usually a dry, unheated room; in other words it is a great place for food storage. It would be a good spot to store potatoes for a short time while onions, garlic, nuts, canned goods, and dried goods could be stored there for a long time. Just make sure that they do not get direct sunlight and that the area does not freeze.

There are often crawlspaces under porches or patios that offer great storage conditions—dark, cold, and damp. One concern with a crawlspace is it is usually not insulated, meaning your food will need to be protected from freezing. If you live in an extremely cold climate, insulate with straw, sawdust, or leaves to help prevent severe fluctuations in temperature. A crawlspace can be difficult to get in and out of, so make sure you know exactly what you are putting into the area. A diagram that shows where items are placed can be helpful when you are searching for a particular vegetable in the middle of the winter.

Most basements have unused areas that are cool, dry, and easily accessible, making them another ideal area for use as an unconventional root cellar. You will want the basement to be well ventilated and to maintain a temperature between 50° and 60°F. This is a good area for ripening tomatoes as well as for storing squash, potatoes, carrots, and onions over a short period of time. If you can, build an insulated room away from your furnace since it will help these items to keep longer. Make sure any storage containers are set off the floor. The floor may also need to be dampened occasionally to keep the humidity high enough so the veggies do not shrivel. Damp sawdust scattered on the basement floor will also help.

Basement window wells can also be used for cold storage, and windows can be opened to provide extra cooling if needed. These areas are usually fairly small, but have the distinct advantage of being well off the floor. Place your veggies in a box or container in the window well, scattering some wood shavings around the outside of the container for extra insulation. It's important to make sure you are not storing food items near your furnace when using your basement, as this area is often too warm to successfully store any fruits or veggies. On the other hand, a furnace room with sturdy shelves offers a great place to store your jars of canning and preserves.

Outbuildings

If your home does not have a porch or basement, outbuildings such as a garage or gardening shed can be used to store your fruits and veggies. A garden shed can be used for hanging dried herbs, garlic, or onions, and the garage is great for storing root vegetables. Many garages are unheated, but most are insulated and therefore provide an ideal freeze-resistant spot to store a few boxes of potatoes, carrots, or beets.

The climate you live in will determine how long you can store items in an unheated garden shed. If you live in an area that gets long periods of below-freezing temperatures, your fruits and vegetables will probably freeze if stored there. A structure made of cement or rammed earth, as discussed in the previous section about above-ground root cellars, will be better able to support your food in these extreme conditions.

If the only space you have available is an unheated shed, you can pack your fruits and vegetables into containers with wood shavings, sawdust, straw, or peat moss between the layers to help insulate the food from extreme cold. Hanging blankets on the shed walls will add further insulation from the damaging cold. If your shed floor is made of dirt, digging a pit right under the shed will help to insulate your stored items even more. Your potatoes and carrots may not last all winter long in these conditions, but you will be able to enjoy them for a few months at least, so give it a try!

Pits and Trenches

If you have a lot of root vegetables such as potatoes, carrots, beets, and rutabagas to store and do not have a root cellar or other indoor space available, a pit or trench might be another option to utilize. A pit or trench can come close to creating the same conditions you would find in a root cellar—cool temperatures but not freezing, humid but not too damp, some type of ventilation, and protection from critters of all kinds.

A word of warning: A pit or trench is not a "for sure" thing. The spot you choose may look dry and suitable in September, but by January it may be a soggy mess, and mice and other creatures will have found their way into your food. Your climate is big a factor when using pits and trenches; if you live in an extremely cold climate the food will easily freeze no matter how much straw or leaves you use for insulation.

Pits should be small and it is best to store no more than a week's worth of food in each pit, so that it is emptied all at one time and its contents used (transferred inside to the refrigerator for the week's meals). A pit is great for storing potatoes, carrots, parsnips, Brussels sprouts, turnips, rutabaga, cabbages, and apples.

To create your pit, dig a hole 1 foot deep and 3 feet square in an area that you know has good drainage. Line the hole with 3 to 4 inches of straw, hay, or leaves. Gently place the vegetables into the pit in a pyramid shape—do not just throw the veggies in as they can be easily bruised or broken. Now cover them with a foot of straw or leaves, and then cover the straw with soil. If you think mice or other critters will be a problem, place hardware cloth or a screen over the vegetables before covering them with the straw and soil.

You now need to work on ventilating your pit. Loosely layered straw and hay might provide sufficient ventilation, or you can use a metal can or pipe that has both ends open. Place the can on top of the pile of vegetables, making sure the top of it is not covered with the straw or soil mulch. It is important to cover the top of the can with mesh to help prevent mice, birds, and other animals from using it as a doorway to their next meal.

Trenches are used to store leafy vegetables like cabbages, celery, Brussels sprouts, and Chinese cabbages. Again, like a pit, the trench will not keep your veggies from freezing if you live in a cold climate. To build your trench, dig a channel 1 foot deep (or more depending on what you are storing), 2 feet wide, and whatever length you may need. If the soil is loose, you may want to prop up the sides with boards.

Dig up the plants (including their roots), that you want to overwinter, then transplant them closely together in the trench. Make sure the roots are well covered with soil and that the top of the plant is not higher than the height of the trench. Once transplanted, water the plant roots, making sure the leaves do not get wet. Leave the plants for a few hours to settle and then place a board over the trench, covering the vegetables. Cover the board with a foot of straw, hay, or leaves and place a piece of plastic or a tarp over everything. To remove the plants, open one end of the trench, remove what you need, and then close it up again.

Burying a barrel is another way to store some veggies; a wooden barrel covered with straw would work well. You can use any type of barrel except plastic, and make sure there was nothing in the barrel previously that could poison your food. Stay completely away from anything that may have contained any pesticides or other toxic substances.

Dig a hole deep enough to contain the barrel. Make sure there is about 2 inches of the barrel left above ground, keeping in mind that you'll be placing a few inches of rocks or pea gravel in the bottom of the hole for the barrel to sit on. Cut a hole in the bottom of the barrel for drainage, making sure you cover it with mesh or screen to keep out any critters. Place your veggies into the barrel, layering with straw every foot or so. Cover the filled barrel with at least 3 to 4 inches of straw that extends several inches larger in diameter than the barrel. You may want to put in a ventilation pipe for better circulation; again, making sure you cover the top of the pipe with fine mesh screen.

Root-Cellar Conditions

Cool temperatures, high humidity, good air circulation, and proper ventilation are essential to having a well-functioning root cellar. If you lose more than 30 percent of your crop to spoilage each season, you will have to figure out which of these conditions are not being met.

Temperature

The optimum temperature for your root cellar is between 32° and 40°F. This fairly cool temperature helps to slow the release of ethylene gas from certain vegetables and will also slow the growth of microorganisms that cause foods to decompose. If the temperature gets too warm, the food will rot or get moldy; too cool a temperature and the food will freeze, causing it to become soft and mushy after it thaws again. Extreme temperatures will cause the food in your root cellar to deteriorate faster, so it is important to make sure you insulate well and regulate the temperature.

The temperature in a root cellar is never uniform, and knowing which areas are colder or warmer will enable you to store your produce in the proper areas. You will need at least two thermometers to regulate the temperature inside your root cellar. Place one in the coldest part of the cellar, and one on the outside of your structure, and closely monitor each area. Regulate the inside temperature by opening doors and windows, and by opening or closing ventilation pipes.

Humidity

The optimum relative humidity in a root cellar is between 85 and 95 percent, and every root cellar should have a hygrometer to properly regulate the humidity. Too much moisture and your food will rot and deteriorate more quickly; too little and your food will shrivel up, leaving nothing for you to eat.

A damp dirt floor will give you the best results for achieving the ideal humidity in your root cellar. A concrete floor will also work, but will tend to lower the humidity in the cellar and therefore it needs more regulating to get the best results.

Here are some easy ways to add moisture to your root cellar:

- Sprinkle the floor with water, especially a few days before you start bringing in the freshly harvested veggies.
- Leave large pans of water near the intake air vents.
- Cover the floors with wet materials such as damp straw or sawdust.

- Shovel some snow into the root cellar to cool and humidify the area.
- Pack vegetables in damp sawdust or peat moss.

Too much humidity can be just as damaging to the food stored in your root cellar as too little. Cold air does not hold as much moisture as warm air, so moisture will collect on the roof or shelves and cause condensation if the cellar has too high a humidity content. Keeping the humidity regulated so there is no condensation is your best practice for preserving your food. If condensation does appear, make sure no water is dripping directly onto your vegetables or fruits.

Ventilation and Air Circulation

You will want to make sure your root cellar is equipped with one vent allowing air to flow in and another vent allowing air to be released. Keep in mind that it is easiest to put these vents in when building your root cellar. Ideally you will want the intake vent to be low and the outflow vent to be placed higher up; cool air will be able to enter the cellar, and as warm air rises it will be released through the outlet vent. A mesh cover placed over each vent will prevent rodents from getting in.

As previously mentioned, the most practical item to use as a vent is a 6-inch water or sewer pipe wrapped in duct insulation. Attaching an elbow at the end exposed to the outside will help keep the temperature consistent. Do not glue this elbow; you want to make sure it is free to turn away from the prevailing wind.

The vents allow both the temperature to adjust and the air in the root cellar to circulate freely. In extremely cold or extremely warm climates, you have the option of blocking the intake vent to prevent intense temperatures from entering. Make sure you open it regularly to allow the air to circulate since this is a critical factor in minimizing any airborne mold. One way of maximizing airflow is to make sure your shelves sit a few inches away from the walls. Another is to store containers of food and jars of preserves with some space between each.

Shelving

In addition to keeping your cellar more organized, shelving helps keep your veggies fresher. Fruits and vegetables put directly onto the floor of a root cellar will rot and deteriorate more quickly because they will either become too moist or get too cold. Shelving allows the air to circulate freely around your stored foods. Some foods, such as cabbage, onions, and apples, give off ethylene gases, and so you'll want to make sure these foods are put in an out-of-the-way corner or on the topmost shelf to prevent them from affecting other produce.

There are many shelving options available for use in your root cellar. You can build sturdy wood shelves; use metal or plastic shelving; make use of recycled items such as old cabinetry or cement blocks with wood slats laid across them; or install any other item that will stack or can be easily hung on a wall. Make sure your shelves are the right height to allow your containers to get air circulation around the top as well as the sides. Your shelves should be sturdily built to hold heavy items. Shelves that use slats are one of the better options available since they will support those heavier items and allow for extra air circulation around your containers and jars. You will also want your shelves to be easily removed so they can be cleaned at least once a year.

Vegetable Storage

All vegetables have different storage characteristics. There are some that cannot be stored, while others will last for several months with only a little care or attention. Learning which vegetables will store best in your conditions is often based on trial and error. Every vegetable plant has different growing circumstances that will either let it store better or cause it to deteriorate more quickly, and the conditions in your root cellar or storage area may vary from year to year as well. This means you may have to deal with different successes or problems every season; but having fresh veggies to eat during the winter months is well worth the effort.

If you want to grow produce that will store for several weeks or months in your root cellar, choose vegetables such as onions, garlic, squash, root vegetables, and cabbage. These all require varying conditions in order for them to remain fresh and in good enough shape for you to eat them during the off-season.

The Best Storage Keepers for Your Root Cellar

Commodity	Temperature (°F)	Relative Humidity	Average Storage Life
Onions and Garlic	32°	65–70%	5–8 months
Winter Squash and Pumpkins	50–55°	70–75%	3–6 months
Root Crops	32°	90–95%	2–6 months
Cabbage	32°	90–95%	3–4 months

Root crops include beets, carrots, Jerusalem artichokes, parsnips, rutabagas, turnips, and potatoes.

CHAPTER 8

CANNING AND PRESERVING YOUR BOUNTY

Many climates are not conducive to growing a balanced diet of food year-round. For those of us who live in these seasonal regions, preserving food is a necessary part of an at-home food system. By allowing you to eat your own food year-round, food preservation is the final step and closing link in the home food system. The methods outlined in this chapter—freezing, drying, and canning—are also fun activities to do with family and friends. What better way to remember and appreciate the hard work and fun of summertime come winter than by sharing a meal of homegrown food with the loved ones who helped to produce it, preserve it, and perhaps cook it?

In addition to having a root cellar stocked with whole foods, adding canned, dried, and frozen foods to your supply will provide you and your family with a diversity of healthy food options throughout the year. Being able to experience the full system of growing, preserving, and eating your own food is a satisfying joy that you won't soon regret when your garden is dormant under snow or frost.

Determining the Best Method

When preserving food, it is important to know that there is usually a best way to preserve each food, and to also be aware that some foods can be preserved in multiple ways. With the basic objective of handling and keeping food so that it maintains quality flavors, textures, and colors while avoiding the spoilage and bacterial growth that cause illness, you want to choose the method of preservation that balances what is best for the food with what is conducive to your storage and preservation system. This chapter focuses on the methods of freezing, canning, drying, pickling, and fermenting, although there are even more ways to store food.

There are many vegetables that are best and easily frozen, but if you do not have access to freezer space, then you will have to consider other preservation methods. In some cases, employing a few different preservation techniques for the same vegetable is a good idea because it puts less strain on a single storage component (that is, less food in your freezer or less cans in your pantry) and foods preserved in different ways can be cooked differently, adding a fun variety to the meals that you prepare throughout the year.

Canning

Canning begins with good food and sterile jars. It's very important that the storage containers used in canning are properly cleaned to kill bacteria. Additionally, canning includes hot-water baths (for high-acid items) and pressure-cooking (for low-acid items) to create a vacuum and kill off any lingering, potentially harmful microbes, specifically botulism, which has no odor or taste and is potentially deadly.

Many people have rediscovered the art of canning because it offers flexibility and variety to an at-home food system. Canned food can last a long time, can be stored in lots of places, and won't take up room in a freezer. If you're nervous about canning food, the processes used today are very safe when you follow the directions carefully and understand what you're doing.

Hot-Water Bath or Pressure Cooker?

The most important piece of equipment is the canner itself, which is really nothing more than a pot large enough to fully submerge your biggest jars under water. To have as many options as possible when canning, having a pressure cooker of the same large size is also a good idea because some food must be canned under pressure, whereas some foods need only a hot-water bath in the canner. The simple rule of thumb is that all high-acid foods go into a hot-water bath canner and everything else must be processed in a pressure cooker. High-acid foods are all fruit products (jams, jellies, preserves, conserves, fruit butters, and marmalades) and anything pickled with vinegar such as pickles, relishes, and vinegar-based sauces. The hot-water bath increases the temperature in the canning jar enough to kill bacteria and it also pushes out air bubbles as the content expands. As the jars cool, the air pressure creates a seal that makes the lid pop.

Equipment

Hot-water bath canners are made of aluminum or porcelain-covered steel. They have removable perforated racks and fitted lids. The canner must be deep enough so that at least 1 inch of briskly boiling water covers the tops of jars during processing. Some boiling-water canners do not have flat bottoms, which are essential for use on an electric range. Either a flat or ridged bottom can be used on a gas burner. To ensure uniform processing of all jars with an electric range, the diameter of the canner should be no more than 4 inches wider than the element on which it is heated.

You need a hot-water canner that is deep enough to submerge the jars you're using. Look for one that has a rack for the jars so they don't clank together during boiling. Some home preservers use a large stockpot and homemade rack system, but it is also very easy to find affordable hot-water bath canning kits starting at around $30. The following is a list of basic canning equipment, some of which you probably already own.

Basic Canning Equipment

- One or more canning books with recipes (This book makes one!)
- Water-bath canner (You can use a large stockpot with a lid. Any pot used as a water-bath canner must have a rack to keep the jars off the bottom.)
- Pressure cooker if you intend to put up vegetables, meats, and nonacidic foods
- Canning jars—pints, quarts, and Mason jelly jars
- Lids and rings (also called screwbands)
- Canning funnel
- Colander and/or large strainer

- Squeezer or juicer
- Food mill, food processor, and/or blender
- Canning-jar lifter and lid wand
- Stirrer for getting air bubbles out of jars
- Kitchen timer
- Cheesecloth for making spice balls or large tea balls
- Pickling or canning salt, Fruit-Fresh, powdered and liquid pectin, and ClearJel A
- Disposable rubber gloves
- Long-handled jar scrubber
- Kitchen scale (optional)
- Jelly bags (optional)

Jars, Lids, and Rings (Screwbands)

Only Mason jars are safe for canning. Commercial jars such as mayonnaise and peanut butter jars are designed for one-time use only; they may crack or shatter in either a water-bath canner or a pressure cooker.

Use canning jars in sizes suitable for the product and your family's needs. Canning jars generally are sold in half-pint, pint, and quart sizes with wide and regular mouths. Wide-mouth jars are convenient for packing such foods as whole tomatoes and peach halves. Quart jars are convenient for vegetables and fruits if your family has four or more members.

Choosing Recipes for Canning

You cannot use just any recipe when canning food. Recipes specific to canning should be used, and only ones that have been tested to guarantee food safety. This is particularly true when canning foods that combine ingredients with different pH levels. Most recipes that you find that are specific to canning have been tested, but it is still a good idea to use only recipes from reputable sources. If you're sharing recipes with any friends, be sure to ask where they got the recipes from!

Preparation

Before you start canning, read your recipe at least twice and get your ingredients and supplies together. Prepare your workspace to allow for ample working room, and remember, canning projects require your uninterrupted attention from start to finish.

Determine how many jars your recipe calls for and examine these jars carefully, making certain there are no cracks or chips. You may put them through a sterilizing cycle in a dishwasher if you have one. Otherwise, use a bottle brush to scrub them inside and out, rinse them in hot water, and sterilize them in a stockpot or water-bath canner. Meanwhile, your lids should be placed in a bowl of hot water to soften the rubber sealing compound.

Processing

After following your recipe, fill your jars with the prepared food. Although the process is basically the same, the details will vary slightly depending on whether you are using a hot-water bath or a pressure cooker. If you are using the hot-water bath method, leave ¼ inch of headroom at the top of your jar. If you use a pressure cooker, leave 1 inch of headroom at the top.

For a hot-water bath, jars are placed on a rack and covered with 1–2 inches of boiling water. Put a lid on the bath and begin timing when water is boiling. Remove jars with a jar lifter and place them on a towel-covered counter to cool. Leave undisturbed for 12–24 hours. Check the seals and remove the screwbands.

When using a pressure cooker, jars are placed on a rack and boiling water is added according to the manufacturer's instructions, usually several inches. Lock the lid securely into place. Leave weight off the vent pipe or open the petcock (exhaust vent), and exhaust steam for 10 minutes. Place weight back onto vent pipe or close petcock. Canner should start to pressurize in 5–10 minutes. Once the canner has reached the required amount of pressure, start the cooking timer.

After cooking, allow the canner to come down to zero pounds on its own. Do not try to speed up this process by removing weight or opening the petcock, as it may cause jars to crack and/or lose liquid. Do not put the canner into cold water to hasten the process. Let jars sit in the canner for 5–10 minutes to allow them to cool down. Remove jars with a jar lifter and place them on a towel-covered counter to cool. Leave undisturbed for 12–24 hours. Check the seals and remove the screwbands (rings).

To check the seals on cooled jars, press your thumb in the middle of the lid. If the lid seems to give and come back up, the jar isn't sealed. If you're not sure, tap the lid with a knife in the same place. It should sound like a bell; a muffled sound means the jar isn't sealed right. Finally, there's the visual; the surface of the lid should be concave.

What happens if your jar doesn't seal properly? All is not lost! You can put the jar in the refrigerator and use it soon.

After Processing

Wash off all of your sealed jars, label them with the date of canning, and move them into a suitable storage place. To prevent spoiling, keep your jars away from places that are too hot or damp, and don't expose them to bright light. Use your canned goods within one year unless otherwise specified by the recipe. Either write expiration dates on your jars to remind you how long they will remain good, or write the canning date on the jar and figure the time accordingly.

When you use your canned goods, always check for signs of spoilage. The most obvious sign is the loss of a vacuum seal on the jar and mold growing inside. Other indicators include gas bubbles, odd coloring, and foul smells. When you open a can for use, you should hear the lid "pop" as the seal is broken. If there is no vacuum seal and the lid does not pop as the seal is broken, it means the lid did not seal properly. In that case, you must dispose of all food contents immediately. Never test suspect food—throw it out!

KEEPING TRACK OF CANNED GOODS

To make it easier to keep track of the cans you have in your pantry, post a piece of graph paper on the door or wall. Each time you place jars in the pantry, mark the appropriate number of squares next to it on the list—one square per jar. Each time you take a jar out, cross that square off with an X. This way you can easily tell how many jars of an item you have in stock.

Drying

Drying was one of the first preserving methods ever used, probably because of its simplicity. It's also a very effective way of preserving many foods because it decreases water, therefore thwarting or slowing any unhealthy organism's growth. Although you can get commercial equipment designed for drying, there are items already in your home that will fit the bill nicely. An additional advantage to drying is that food has a long shelf life when it's dried properly. Without water content, food packs neatly onto cupboard shelves or storage areas. Drying is best suited to meats, fruits, herbs, mushrooms, and grains.

DRIED FOOD REACHES COMMERCIAL POPULARITY

A large-scale food-drying effort occurred at the beginning of World War I when food was needed to feed the troops. The Great Depression in the 1930s led to more households using dry foods, as canning equipment was expensive and not readily available. During World War II, vegetable-dehydrating factories were opened all across the United States as dried food had the advantage of being lightweight, compact, easy to transport, and enjoyed a long shelf life.

Drying Methods

Temperature variations and humidity will both affect the drying process, specifically how long it will take. Pay attention to these things so that you can adjust your drying method accordingly. There are a variety of different ways to dry food.

Herbs and flowers are the most common air-dried foods. Remember to harvest in the morning and if you're hanging the plants, don't bundle too many together; about six stems to a bundle is good. Hang them upside down from a string in a dry, warm spot with a paper lunch bag draped loosely over the bundle to keep it free of dust and to protect against sunlight. Use a toothpick to make holes in the bag to allow air to circulate. The plant matter should be dry in 14 days.

Depending on what you're drying, another method of drying is to remove the flower petals or herb leaves from the stem and lay them on a screen. It's very important that the screening material be clean and that the plant pieces don't touch each other. Place a piece of cheesecloth (or a large paper bag with pinholes in it) over the top of the screens. Again, this protects the flowers and herbs from airborne dust and dirt. Keep the trays out of the sunlight and in a cool, dry area. As with hanging, it takes about 2 weeks to dry the plant matter.

Oven Drying

Oven drying can be costly because your oven is not designed to maintain a low heat efficiently. Using your oven to dry food is only recommended if you won't be drying enough food to warrant buying a dehydrator. Because you're leaving food on low heat for many hours, if you regularly use your oven to dry food, the resulting energy costs will end up being more than the cost of a new dehydrator.

On the other hand, oven drying is very simple. Simply preheat your oven to 140°F, and pre-prepare your food according to instructions. Most oven trays hold up to 2 pounds of food. Unless you have a very large oven, it's suggested that you dry no more than three trays at a time, shifting their position and turning the food every 30 minutes for best results. Finally, try to keep the door of the oven open about 2 inches throughout this time. This improves air circulation and decreases the amount of heat you lose when you circulate the drying items.

Food Dehydrator

Using a commercial electric dehydrator takes half the time as drying in an oven, making it perfect for the energy-conscious consumer. These devices are created specifically to maintain air circulation, sustain even heating, and safeguard nutritional value. Fruits, herbs, and meats are good candidates for the dehydrator.

The market for dehydrators has grown, which means you can find some great optional features. You can pay more than $300 for a stainless-steel dehumidifier with 16 cubic square feet of interior space, but most home preservers don't need anything quite so elaborate. If you plan to spend between $60 and $75, you can easily find a good quality machine.

When you look to purchase a dehydrator, it's best to buy the type that heats and fans from the sides, as opposed to the bottom. Drying from the sides produces better results when you want to preserve a variety of items at one time because it doesn't allow the flavors to mix.

For Drying Success: Freshness, Attentiveness, and Airflow

In drying, "fresh is best" is your mantra. The sooner you begin drying items after they've been harvested, the happier you'll be with the results. This is also one of the few times in cooking when you'll hear "faster is better." When you carefully and quickly dry food once it is harvested, it helps create a continuity of texture and ensures that the center of the item doesn't retain moisture. Nonetheless, most drying techniques do take a little while, so allow for the time in your schedule. If you have to stop in the middle of drying something, you're opening the door for microbial growth.

Freezing

Freezing and refrigeration are the most common types of home food preservation. Where refrigeration slows bacterial action, freezing comes close to totally stopping microbes' development. This happens because the water in frozen food turns to ice, in which bacteria cannot continue to grow. Enzyme activity, on the other hand, isn't completely deterred by freezing, which is why many vegetables are blanched before being packaged. Except for eggs in the shell, nearly all raw foods can be frozen, or frozen after blanching or cooking.

If you're ever in doubt about how to best prepare an item for freezing, the National Center for Home Food Preservation (*www.uga.edu/nchfp*) is a great online resource. It offers tips on how to freeze various items ranging from pie and prepared food to oysters and artichokes.

Equipment

Once you're ready to begin freezing food, assemble all the items you need. For example, if you're freezing fruit, you'll want a clean cutting board, a sharp knife, and your choice of storage containers. If you're doing any preparation of the fruit before freezing it, you'll also need cooking pans. Stainless steel is highly recommended; galvanized pans may give off zinc when fruit is left in them because of the fruit's acid content.

If it's in your budget, a vacuum sealer is another great piece of equipment. Vacuum sealers come in a variety of sizes with a similar variety of bags that are perfect for people who like freezing and drying methods. They're fairly cost-effective when compared to freezer bags or plastic containers, and they eliminate the excess air that contributes to ice crystals. Keeping air and ice crystals out of your frozen food packages will greatly enhance your food quality for longer periods of time, helping to prevent freezer burn. A third item that you shouldn't be without is a freezer-proof label system that includes the packaging date as well as the name of the item.

Location and Space

Consider your space constraints. Where are you going to put the freezer? Does that space have a suitable electrical outlet? Many new appliances require a 220-volt electrical line for them to run effectively. Placing the freezer in a cooler area of your home will help keep the cost of operating your freezer down. Once you've found a spot, measure it. That measurement will tell you pretty quickly if you can get an upright or chest freezer.

Upright or Chest Freezer

An upright is very easy to access, especially if someone in your family has back problems. When you open the door, a fast visual survey will tell you what's inside. Uprights also typically offer conveniences like auto defrost and ice makers. Chest freezers, by comparison, hold more food. They allow you to store oddly shaped items inside, and the internal temperature varies less than in an upright. On the down side, you may forget what's in the bottom, and you'll have to manually defrost these foods. However, foods will last longer in a chest freezer that requires manual defrosting—auto defrost features suck the humidity out of frozen foods and thus tend to promote freezer burn. While you're looking at features, see if there's a defrosting hose.

Help and Hints

The first step in freezing is keeping those items cold until you're ready to prepare them. This is very important with meat, but it also makes a difference in how fruits and vegetables come out of the freezer.

Blanching has several benefits. It stops enzyme action that decreases vegetables' textural quality, flavor, and color, and it cleans off any lingering dirt. To blanch vegetables, fill a pan with water and bring it to a rolling boil. Add the vegetables and make sure they're immersed. Follow the blanching time recommended in the recipe and then turn the vegetables into a bowl of ice. The ice retains the vegetables' vitamins and firmness.

If there's no specific blanching time provided in your preserving recipe,

here's a brief overview to get you started. Remember to move your vegetables into an ice bath immediately after blanching until they're totally cooled.

Timing and Techniques for Blanching Vegetables

- **Asparagus:** Remove the tough ends from the asparagus. Depending on the storage container, you may need to cut the stems in half. If your stalks are thin, they'll only need 2 minutes of blanching; thick stalks require twice as much.
- **Beans (green or wax):** Remove any tips. Leave the beans whole and blanch them for 3 minutes.
- **Brussels sprouts:** Clean off outer leaves, then soak the sprouts in cold salt water for 30 minutes. Drain and blanch for 4 minutes.
- **Cabbage:** Remove the outer leaves. Shred the cabbage and blanch for just over 1 minute and leave in the water for another 30 seconds before icing.
- **Carrots:** Clean the skins, then slice into ¼-inch pieces. Blanch for 3 minutes. Whole baby carrots need 5 minutes of blanching.
- **Cauliflower and broccoli:** Break off the pieces from the central core and clean well (a spray nozzle at the sink works very well). Soak in a gallon of salt water (3–4 teaspoons salt) for 30 minutes. Pour off the salt water. Rinse and blanch for 3 minutes.
- **Corn:** Rinse, remove from the cob, and blanch for 5 minutes.

- **Greens (including spinach):** Rinse. Remove any leaves that have spots or other damage. Blanch for 3 minutes.
- **Mushrooms (small):** These can be frozen whole. (They can also be dried.) Toss with a little fresh lemon juice and blanch for 4 minutes.
- **Peas:** Blanch out of the husk for 90 seconds.
- **Peas in the pod:** Trim the ends and remove strings. Blanch for 1–2 minutes, depending on the size of the pod.
- **Peppers:** Slice open and remove the seeds. Cut into desired size and blanch for 2 minutes.
- **Potatoes:** Wash and scrub thoroughly. Remove the peel and blanch for 4 minutes.
- **Tomatoes:** To easily peel the skins, use a straining spoon and dip the tomatoes in boiling water for 30 seconds. Peel and remove the core. These can be stored whole or diced to desired size.
- **Zucchini and squash:** Peel. Cut into ½-inch slices and blanch for 3 minutes.

Packing Frozen Foods

It's always a good idea to use bags and containers that are rated for freezing, and to provide an extra layer of protection with aluminum foil or freezer wrap, particularly on meats. It's especially important to keep as much air out of the containers as possible, thus the benefit of using a vacuum sealer. Avoid using waxed cartons; they don't retain the food's quality very well and defrosted food often becomes limp and unstable for handling. Your packaging materials should also be leak-proof and oil-resistant, and all packing materials should be able to withstand freezing.

Another consideration with your containers is size. Think about how many people you plan to serve and choose freezing containers accordingly. If you're going to put several servings in one large container, separate them with a piece of aluminum foil or plastic wrap so you can take out one at a time fairly easily.

Most important, remember to label and date everything. This will help you gauge what should be eaten first so it retains the greatest quality.

Safe Storage Times and Defrosting

Frozen food can be kept nearly indefinitely at 0°F or colder. Nonetheless, the longer the food stays frozen, the more nutrients you lose and the greater the likelihood that ice crystals or freezer burn will form and decrease the overall color, taste, or textural quality of the product. One great way to deter this is by rotating foods so that the most recent entry to the freezer goes to the back.

USING GLASS IN THE FREEZER

Glass containers can be used in the freezer, but you need to be very careful if you choose to do this! Test your containers first by putting a jar into a plastic bag and placing it in the freezer overnight. This way the pieces will be contained in the bag if it shatters. Even after testing, it is advisable to freeze glass jars in plastic bags, as accidents may happen.

After all the hard work that went into raising and storing your food, you'll want to defrost the food properly. The first rule of defrosting is that you don't leave anything at room temperature for hours at a time. Instead, there are three tried-and-true ways to safely defrost your food.

1. Leave the food in your refrigerator to defrost. This takes a while, and it's wise to put some paper towels down or a platter underneath the item to catch any water or juices that run out during defrosting.
2. Put the food in a cold-water bath; do not use warm or hot water. Keep the item in the wrapper or container, and if need be put it in an additional resealable bag for protection. It's recommended that you refresh the water every 30 minutes until the item is defrosted.
3. Use the defrost setting on your microwave. Microwave powers vary greatly from machine to machine, so watch carefully to make sure your food isn't being partially cooked because that can give your food a rubbery texture.

The following recipes can be easily frozen and reheated to serve throughout the year.

Blueberry Chutney

A fun way to use your blueberries in unexpected ways. Top savory and sweet dishes with this delicious chutney. Try this sweet chutney on goose, turkey, chicken, hen, and other fowl.

8 cups fresh blueberries, rinsed and stemmed

2 medium onions, finely chopped

3 cups red wine vinegar

1 cup golden yellow raisins

1 cup dark brown sugar, firmly packed

1 tablespoon yellow mustard seeds

2 tablespoons freshly grated gingerroot

1 teaspoon ground cinnamon

1 pinch salt

¼ teaspoon ground nutmeg

½ teaspoon dried red pepper flakes

1. Rinse and stem blueberries.
2. Place all ingredients in a large stockpot. Bring mixture to a boil.
3. Lower heat; simmer, stirring occasionally, about 45 minutes, or until chutney is thick.
4. Ladle hot chutney into sterilized jars, leaving ½-inch headspace. Wipe rims; cap and seal.
5. Process in water-bath canner for 15 minutes. Cool.
6. Put in a cool, dark place; leave 6–8 weeks before using.

Green Tomato Piccalilli

Makes 6–8 pints

A delicious relish that you can serve year-round as a side dish or as a brightly colored condiment, especially for hamburgers and hot dogs.

16 cups green tomatoes, finely chopped
½ head green cabbage, finely chopped
½ cup pickling salt
Water to cover vegetables
4 cups cider vinegar
1½ cups dark brown sugar
½ tablespoon yellow mustard seed
½ tablespoon ground cinnamon
1 tablespoon black pepper
⅛ teaspoon crushed red pepper flakes
½ tablespoon ground allspice
1 tablespoon ground ginger
1 tablespoon dill seed

1. Combine vegetables and salt; cover with water and soak overnight. Drain and rinse vegetables.
2. In a large pot, combine remaining ingredients; bring to a boil. Add drained vegetables; return mixture to a boil. Reduce heat; simmer until vegetables are tender, about 30 minutes.
3. Pack hot mixture into sterilized pint jars. Cover; process in boiling bath for 15 minutes.

Green Tomato Medley

Makes 10 pints

While this is not a traditional pickling recipe, it does use pickling salt and vinegar as preservatives.

2 tablespoons pickling salt
2 quarts green tomatoes, cored and chopped
Water to cover
4 tablespoons dried orange peel
⅔ cup peeled, seeded, and chopped orange
2½ quarts peeled, cored, and chopped apples
1 pound golden yellow raisins
3½ cups packed dark brown
Sugar
½ cup cider vinegar
Juice of 1 lemon
2 teaspoons cinnamon
1 teaspoon pure vanilla extract
1 teaspoon nutmeg
1 teaspoon ginger
1 teaspoon cloves

1. Sprinkle salt over green tomatoes and let sit for 1 hour.
2. Rinse well in cold water and drain. Cover tomatoes with boiling water and let sit for 5 minutes. Drain.
3. Combine tomatoes and remaining ingredients in a large stockpot. Bring to a boil. Ladle into sterilized jars, leaving 1-inch headspace. Wipe rims. Cap and seal. Process in a pressure canner at 10 pounds pressure for 25 minutes.

Fruit or Vegetable?

Have you ever wondered why the tomato is classified as a fruit? When we cook, we generally use fruits when we want a sweet dish. But tomatoes are more savory and are often used with vegetables. Technically, tomatoes are in the fruit family because they contain the seeds of the plants; vegetables do not.

Spiced Tomato Paste

Makes 12 paste roll-ups

This recipe uses a dehydrator to make tomato paste roll-ups that are best either kept in a dark airtight container or well wrapped in the freezer. Rehydrate the paste as needed.

2 quarts ripe Roma tomatoes
1 teaspoon oregano
½ cup finely diced onion
¼ teaspoon garlic powder
1 teaspoon garlic purée
1 teaspoon fresh basil leaves
⅓ cup dry white wine

1. Dice the tomatoes and put them through a food processor, then use a sieve to remove the seeds.
2. Add tomatoes and remaining ingredients to a pan; simmer over low heat until mix thickens.
3. Keep stirring for another 30 minutes or until the consistency thickens and becomes paste-like.
4. Spread the paste on a lightly oiled fruit roll-up sheet for the dehydrator. Paste should be no more than ¼-inch thick.
5. Dry at about 115–120°F for 12 hours or until the paste is not sticky. Store as desired.

Garlic Jelly

This different kind of jelly can be used as a condiment. It's wonderful added to a marinade or brushed directly on meat while cooking.

¼ pound peeled garlic cloves
2 cups white vinegar
5 cups granulated sugar
1 3-ounce pouch liquid pectin

1. Blend garlic and ½ cup vinegar in a food processor or blender until smooth.
2. Combine garlic mixture, remaining vinegar, and sugar in a stockpot. Bring mixture to a boil over high heat, stirring constantly.
3. Quickly stir in pectin; return to a boil and boil hard 1 minute, stirring constantly.
4. Remove from heat; ladle into sterilized jars, leaving ¼-inch headspace. Wipe jar rims; cap and seal.
5. Process in a water-bath canner for 10 minutes.

Green Tomato Raspberry Jam

Makes 8–9 pints

You can use whatever type gelatin you like in this. No one will ever know there are tomatoes in it!

> 8 cups shredded green tomatoes
> ½ cup lemon juice
> 2 teaspoons orange extract
> 3 tablespoons dried, home-grated orange peel
> 8 cups white sugar
> 2 6-ounce packages raspberry-flavored gelatin mix

1. Combine tomatoes, lemon juice, orange extract, dried orange peel, and sugar in a large saucepan; bring to a boil over medium heat. Stir and cook about 10 minutes.
2. Add gelatin; reduce heat to low and simmer 20 minutes. Spoon into hot, sterilized jars. Cap and seal.
3. Process in water-bath canner for 10 minutes or pour into freezer containers and freeze.

Garlic Dill Pickles

Makes 8 quarts

Dill and garlic form a classic combo in these crunchy, tart pickles—they're a perennial favorite!

8 pounds pickling cucumbers
4 cups white vinegar
12 cups water
⅔ cup pickling salt
16 whole cloves garlic
4 teaspoons minced garlic
16 sprigs fresh dill weed
4 teaspoons dry dill weed

1. Wash cucumbers and soak in ice water for 2 hours. If you're planning to slice these, wait until just before canning.
2. Bring the vinegar, water, and salt to a boil.
3. Place 2 cloves of garlic, 2 sprigs of dill, ¼ teaspoon minced garlic, and ¼ teaspoon dry dill into each of the 8-quart jars. Pack each jar with about 1 pound of cucumbers.
4. Fill jars with brine, leaving 1" headspace and making sure the cucumbers are fully covered.
5. Cap and process jars for 15 minutes in a hot-water bath. Age for 2 months before eating.

Pickled Walnuts

Makes 5 pounds

Pickled walnuts make a unique addition to barbecued meats, especially venison and other game animals. You can also mix them with cheese or toss them into Thai and Indian recipes.

5 pounds fresh black walnuts
Water to cover
2 cups pickling salt
1 quart malt vinegar
1 pound brown sugar
1 teaspoon allspice
1 teaspoon cloves
1 teaspoon cinnamon
1 teaspoon ginger

1. Pierce each nut with a fork in several places. Place walnuts in a bowl, covering with water and salt. Place a weight on top so the nuts stay below the brine. Let set 7 days.
2. Drain and make a fresh brine. Let stand another 7 days.
3. Dry the walnuts on a tray using a light cloth over the top to keep dust and dirt out. When the nuts turn black, they're ready for the pickle solution.
4. Combine vinegar, sugar, and spices and bring to a boil.
5. Add nuts, reduce heat, and simmer for 15 minutes.
6. Pack into canning jars, covered with syrup, leaving ½-inch headspace.
7. Process in a hot-water bath 10 minutes for pints, 15 minutes for quarts.

Heirloom Mustard Pickles

Makes 4 quarts

These are the kinds of pickles often seen on our grandparents' tables. While the spices may change a little, the passion that these pickles inspire remains consistent.

4 cups onions
4 cups cucumbers
4 cups small green tomatoes
1 medium cauliflower
2 sweet peppers
2 cups salt
1 gallon water
Pinch of alum (optional)
4 cups sugar
3 tablespoons celery seed
⅔ cup mustard
4¼ cups vinegar

1. Cut vegetables into 1-inch pieces. Put in a large bowl; cover with water, salt, and alum.
2. Put a plate over top of vegetables so they stay below brine; leave at room temperature for 24 hours.
3. The next day, warm entire mixture to scalding; remove from heat and drain vegetables. Immediately put into sterilized jars (if canning) or freezer-safe containers (if freezing).
4. Put remaining ingredients in a large pot; simmer until thickened.
5. Pour sauce evenly over pickles. Make sure to get all the air bubbles out if canning. Leave ¼-inch headspace in the jars; process 10 minutes in a hot-water bath. If freezing, remember to leave extra space for freezer expansion.
6. Canned pickles have a shelf life of 1 year. Frozen pickles last 6–8 months.

Caramelized Red Onion Relish

Makes 6 pints

This relish will quickly be a staple condiment in your home. Tangy and sweet, add to any sandwich or use as a spread for bread or crackers.

6 large red onions, peeled and sliced very thinly
¾ cup brown sugar, firmly packed
1 tablespoon extra-virgin olive oil
3 cups dry red wine
½ cup aged balsamic vinegar
½ teaspoon fine sea salt
½ teaspoon freshly ground black pepper

1. In a heavy nonstick skillet, combine onions and sugar with olive oil; heat over medium-high heat.
2. Cook uncovered for 25 minutes, or until onions turn golden and start to caramelize, stirring frequently.
3. Stir in wine, vinegar, salt, and pepper; bring to a boil over high heat. Reduce heat to low; cook 15 minutes, or until most of the liquid has evaporated, stirring frequently.
4. Ladle into sterilized jars, leaving ½-inch headspace. Remove air bubbles.
5. Wipe rims. Cap and seal. Process in a water-bath canner for 10 minutes.

Pickled Ginger Sauce

This is a wonderful Asian-styled dipping sauce that can be canned or frozen. If you cannot find enough pickled ginger juice, many stores carry regular ginger juice.

½ cup rice wine vinegar
¼ cup fresh lime juice
1 tablespoon dried onion flakes
½ tablespoon chives
1 teaspoon freshly ground pepper
1½ teaspoons pickled ginger, minced, plus 1 cup juice
1 teaspoon dark soy sauce
Green onion, chopped (optional garnish)

1. Mix all the ingredients together in a nonaluminum pan over medium heat.
2. Let the sauce come to a low rolling boil; reduce by about ½ cup.
3. Cool and preserve. Add fresh chopped green onion when serving.

Burnt Onion Concentrate

Makes 8 pints

This recipe was adapted from a Victorian-era blend that can act as either a sauce or a marinade. It's also great for flavoring gravies, soups, and stews.

> 3 pounds onions, peeled and coarsely chopped
> 7½ cups cold water
> 3 cups brown sugar
> 7½ cups cider vinegar
> 3 tablespoons dried French tarragon
> 1 teaspoon salt
> 1 teaspoon coarsely ground black pepper

1. In a large stockpot, combine onions and water. Cover; bring to a boil. Reduce heat; simmer until onion is soft. Add sugar; stir well.
2. Continue to simmer until mixture has turned a very dark brown and has reduced by about half. This will take at least 1 hour. Stir occasionally to prevent sticking.
3. In a separate pan, bring vinegar, French tarragon, salt, and pepper to a boil. Reduce heat; simmer 10 minutes.
4. Slowly pour vinegar mixture into onion mixture; stir well. Bring to a boil; reduce heat, and simmer 10 minutes.
5. Ladle into sterilized pint jars, leaving 1-inch headspace. Wipe rims. Cap and seal. Process in a water-bath canner for 10 minutes.

Ukrainian Cabbage Soup

Makes 7–8 quarts

You can thicken the soup before freezing or after defrosting by making a butter-flour roux consisting of 4 tablespoons butter or margarine and 4 tablespoons all-purpose flour.

5–6 pounds pork neck bones
2 whole bay leaves
2 teaspoons ground black pepper
Water to cover neck bones
1 large head cabbage, cored and shredded
2 28-ounce cans sauerkraut
2 large onions, finely chopped
4 tablespoons whole caraway seeds

1. Put neck bones in a large stockpot.
2. Add bay leaves and pepper; cover with water. Start on high heat to boil; reduce heat and cook 1 hour.
3. Add shredded cabbage, sauerkraut (including juice), and chopped onions. Continue to cook about 45 minutes; meat will start falling off bones.
4. Add caraway seeds. Remove and discard bay leaves. Remove bones with slotted spoon.
5. After cooling bones, remove meat and discard bones. Add meat back to soup.
6. Freeze. Or, if canning, ladle soup into sterilized wide-mouth quart jars, leaving 1-inch headspace. Wipe rims. Cap and seal.
7. Process in a pressure cooker at 10 pounds pressure for 1 hour and 5 minutes.

Vegetable Juice

Makes about 6 quarts

This is a healthy beverage that can be canned and drunk just like you would commercial vegetable drinks. It can also be frozen.

15 pounds fresh, ripe tomatoes, cut up

1 small yellow, orange, or red pepper, chopped

1 small green pepper, chopped

1 cup diced celery

2 diced carrots

2 bay leaves

2 teaspoons dried basil

1 tablespoon salt

1 tablespoon freshly grated horseradish root

½ teaspoon pepper

1 teaspoon sugar

2 teaspoons Worcestershire sauce

1. Put all ingredients in a nonreactive pot (either stainless steel or nonstick); simmer 45 minutes. Stir periodically.
2. Put entire blend through a sieve or juicer to remove any fibers, skins, and seeds. Repeat to get a fine consistency.
3. Return to pan; boil. Pour liquid into hot quart jars, leaving ½-inch headspace.
4. Process in hot-water canner for 30 minutes. Let cool; then test lids.

Fruit Leather

This is a great way to use up berries that are in less-than-perfect condition. You can use combinations of different fruits or even vegetables.

1. Simply make a purée of fruit and sweetener (sugar or honey work well, and you can use as much or as little as you like) that is thin enough to pour (add water or juice if necessary).
2. Place parchment paper on your dehydrator sheets and pour the purée out, spreading it across the tray. You will want to make the edges twice as thick as the center since the edges will dry out first.
3. Turn your dehydrator to a low heat, about 135°F, depending on the specific berry or fruit combination, and let it run until you can easily remove the fruit from the paper in one piece and it is not sticky to the touch (usually 4–6 hours).
4. When rolled and wrapped up in plastic wrap or wax paper, your fruit leather can last for 6–8 weeks in the refrigerator.

Squash Chips

A great alternative to greasy, store-bought chips, squash chips are a healthier choice that your kids will love.

1. Wash and cut a summer squash into ½-inch slices. Do not peel.
2. Place the slices in the dehydrator at 120°F for 6–8 hours, turning once.
3. Cool and store in airtight containers.

Vegetable Leather

You can use any veggies that you like to make vegetable leather. This is a particularly good way to store soup bases. A tomato purée mixed with oregano and basil to be rehydrated later for use as tomato sauce is handy to have on hand, and leathers take up minimal space.

1. Simply steam your veggies until tender.
2. Purée and mix with herbs and spices.
3. Spread the purée on parchment paper or dehydrator sheet, making the edges twice as thick as the center since the edges will dry out first, and dry at 125°F until done.

Candied Strawberries

Makes ½ cup

You can use any berries you like for this recipe, but if making a combination, be sure to separate the berries inside the dehydrator in case one type is ready first.

1 pint fresh strawberries
¼ pound sugar

1. Slice the strawberries and dip each berry into the sugar.
2. Dry according to your dehydrator instructions, usually around 130°F for at least 6 hours.

Tomato Basil Flax Crackers

Serves 8 when served as a snack

These crackers are great to serve with cheese or spreads as an appetizer or as a nutrient-rich snack on a camping or hiking trip.

1 cup golden flaxseed, soaked for at least 2 hours

8 dried tomatoes, cut into pieces and soaked for 30 minutes

⅓ red bell pepper

1 tablespoon olive oil

1 teaspoon sea salt

2 fresh tomatoes, chopped

1 red onion, chopped

1 garlic clove, pressed

¼ cup basil

Salt and pepper to taste

Cayenne to taste

1. Using a food processor, mix all ingredients except for the flaxseed.
2. Once everything is well mixed, add the seed by hand. Spread the mixture onto your dehydrator sheets, evenly but not too thinly.
3. Dry at 110°F for 8–12 hours.
4. Turn over and continue drying for another 8 hours.

Sweet Potato Bark

Makes ¾ cup

A great recipe for a snack, to add to a meal, or to take on a backpacking trip.

> 1 large sweet potato, peeled and cut into chunks
> ½ cup apple juice
> 3 tablespoons maple syrup
> ½ teaspoon cinnamon
> ½ teaspoon nutmeg

1. Boil the sweet potato chunks until soft enough to mash.
2. Stir in the other ingredients and use either a mixer or blender to mix until completely smooth.
3. Spread the purée to ⅛-inch thickness on dehydrator sheets and dry at 135°F for at least 8 hours.
4. Turn over halfway through, at about 5 hours.

Dried Tomatoes and Herb Quiche

Serves 6–8

Use your own dried tomatoes and herbs in this delicious recipe.

1 unbaked pastry shell
¾ cup dried tomatoes (home-dried, not in oil)
Boiling water
1 tablespoon olive oil
½ cup finely chopped onion
1½ cups chopped spinach
1 garlic clove, minced
1 teaspoon dried basil
½ teaspoon dried thyme
1½ cups grated Gruyère cheese
5 large eggs, at room temperature
1½ cups light cream
½ teaspoon salt
¼ teaspoon pepper

1. Preheat oven to 425°F.
2. Put pastry shell into a 9-inch pie pan. Bake for 10 minutes. Once you take the crust out of the oven, lower the heat to 325°F.
3. While the oven cools, cut dried tomatoes into small pieces using scissors.
4. To rehydrate, pour boiling water over the tomatoes, cover, and let sit for 10 minutes before draining the water.
5. Heat olive oil over medium heat in a skillet.
6. Add the onion and cook for 3 minutes, then add the tomatoes, spinach, garlic, basil, and thyme. Cook just until the spinach wilts.
7. Fill the pastry shell with this mixture and cover with cheese. In a large bowl, whisk the eggs, cream, salt, and pepper. Pour over the cheese. Bake for 40 minutes until golden brown.

Greek Rub

This dry rub is great for grilling meats or vegetables.

¼ cup dried garlic cloves
½ tablespoon dried lemon peel
¼ cup kosher salt
2 tablespoons dried oregano
1 tablespoon dried thyme
1 tablespoon fresh-ground black pepper

1. Using a spice grinder or coffee grinder (make sure it's clean!), grind the garlic and lemon peel.
2. Combine with the other ingredients and store in an airtight container.

Cream of Cauliflower Soup

Serves 8–10

If keeping lots of dried vegetables on hand is a favorite way to store food, then this soup recipe is perfect for you.

4½ cups water
1 cup dry milk
1½ cups dehydrated cauliflower
1 tablespoon dehydrated onions
⅛ cup dehydrated carrots

Simply combine all ingredients in a large pot over low heat. You can add light cream or milk once all the food is rehydrated, as well as any seasoning to taste.

Cheesy Dried Potato Chips

Makes approximately 2 cups

Cheesy and filling, these chips are so delicious you won't be able to stop snacking on them!

> 3 cups potatoes, peeled, boiled, and mashed
> 1½ cups sharp Cheddar cheese, grated
> ½ cup Parmesan cheese, grated
> ½ teaspoon salt

1. Combine all ingredients in a food processor and mix until smooth.
2. Spread onto dehydrator sheets and dry at 145°F for at least 5 hours.
3. Turn sheet over in the fourth hour, or when one side is dry.

Dried Sour Cream and Onion Chips

Makes 2–3 cups

Slightly chewier than traditional sour cream and onion chips, these chips are a zesty, tangy, and satisfying snack. They also pack well and are great to bring on trips.

4 cups potatoes, peeled, boiled, and mashed
1 cup plain yogurt
¼ cup onion, chopped
½ teaspoon salt

1. Combine all ingredients in a food processor and mix until smooth.
2. Spread onto dehydrator sheets and dry at 145°F for at least 5 hours.
3. Turn sheet over in the fourth hour, or when one side is dry.

Homemade Garlic and Herb Gnocchi

Serves 4

Use your own dried herbs to make this a truly homegrown and homemade dish.

2 large potatoes
1 garlic clove, minced
½ teaspoon dried basil
½ teaspoon dried parsley
¾ teaspoon salt
1½ cups all-purpose flour
Water for boiling

1. Bake potatoes until done, about 50 minutes at 400°F. Allow to cool, then peel skins.
2. Using a fork, mash potatoes with garlic powder, basil, parsley, and salt until potatoes are completely smooth, with no lumps.
3. On a floured work surface, place half of the flour, and the potatoes on top. Use your hands to work the flour into the potatoes to form a dough. Continue to add only as much flour as is needed to form a dough. Knead smooth.
4. Working in batches, roll out a rope of dough about 1-inch thick. Slice into 1-inch-long pieces, and gently roll against a fork to make grooves in the dough. This helps the sauce stick to the dough.
5. Cook gnocchi in boiling water for 2–3 minutes until they rise to the surface. Serve immediately.

Salad Topping

Makes about 4 cups

You do not have to be exactly precise with this recipe. Just use up your vegetable ends and pieces and toss them with a little seasoning.

1½ cups sweet peppers, diced
1 cup green onions, diced
1 cup red onions, diced
1 cup celery, chopped
1 cup carrots, chopped
1 cup cherry tomatoes, quartered
1 cup cabbage, diced
½ cup banana pepper, diced (optional)
1 teaspoon Worcestershire sauce
1 teaspoon garlic powder (optional)
1 teaspoon salt
1 teaspoon ground pepper
2 tablespoons sesame seeds
2 tablespoons sunflower seeds
½ cup chow mein noodles

1. Preheat oven to 150°F. If you are using a dehydrator, follow the manufacturer's suggested setting for vegetables.
2. In a bowl, mix all ingredients except the sesame seeds, sunflower seeds, and noodles; toss vegetables to evenly coat in the spices.
3. Spread mixture evenly onto nonstick cooking trays. Dry in the oven; stir periodically to make sure nothing sticks or burns.
4. When the mixture is crunchy (about 3–4 hours), cool and mix with sesame seeds, sunflower seeds, and noodles.
5. Store in an airtight container with the rest of your spices. The topping has a shelf life of 6 months.

Brown Sauce Sheets

Makes 5 cups

These roll-up style sauce sheets can be sliced and placed over meat while it's cooking or used a little at a time in soups and stews for additional flavor.

1 tablespoon olive oil
2 large sweet onions, roughly chopped
½ cup tamarind paste
2 tablespoons garlic, minced
2 tablespoons ginger, minced
¼ cup tomato paste
2 tablespoons freshly cracked black pepper
½ cup dark corn syrup
1 cup black strap molasses
2 cups white vinegar
1 cup balsamic vinegar
1 cup dark beer
½ cup orange juice
¼ cup soy sauce
2 tablespoons coarsely ground mustard
2 tablespoons liquid smoke
2 cups low-fat beef stock

1. Heat olive oil in a frying pan. Add onions; sauté until soft. If you like a sweeter sauce, sprinkle a few pinches of sugar on them as they sauté.
2. Put onions and all remaining ingredients in a large saucepan; bring to a boil. Stir regularly.
3. Reduce to a simmer. Continue to stir regularly over the next 2–3 hours until it reduces by about 1 cup. Increase simmering time for a thicker sauce with more concentrated flavors.
4. Place an even coating of the sauce on waxed paper or the fruit roll-up sheets of your dehydrator. For the latter, follow the manufacturer's recommended temperature. If drying in the oven, set the temperature for 150°F; cook until no longer sticky. This can take up to 12 hours depending on the environment.
5. Slice to preferred sizes. Wrap in waxed paper; store in a jar or food storage bag for future use.

All-Purpose Dry Marinade

Makes 1½ cups

To use the dry marinade, simply sprinkle 1–2 teaspoons on each side of your meat, poultry, fish, or vegetables, and let sit. Meat and poultry improves from a full day in the refrigerator with the dry marinade rubbed in. Fish and vegetables can go on the stove or grill almost immediately.

Fresh Ingredients for Drying

1 medium onion, diced

5 cloves garlic, diced

¼ cup fresh oregano, diced

¼ cup chives, chopped

1 orange

1 lemon

1–2 chili peppers

Remaining Base Ingredients

⅓ cup brown sugar

⅓ cup paprika

⅓ cup kosher salt

⅓ cup coarse pepper corns

2 tablespoons dry mustard

2 tablespoons dry Worcestershire sauce powder

1. Dice the onion, garlic, oregano, and chives.
2. Place the herbs, evenly spaced, in the dehydrator or on a lightly oiled baking sheet.
3. Zest the orange and lemon peels; put them on a second layer or sheet.
4. Finely dice the orange and lemon; place on a third layer or sheet.
5. Carefully seed the hot pepper(s); dice. Place on a fourth layer or sheet.
6. Dry the herbs, fruit, and pepper in the oven at 150°F until crunchy. The mixture will dry in about 2 hours but make sure that everything is crunchy (not rubbery). Any rubbery items should remain in the heat until fully dried. If using a dehydrator, follow the manufacturer's recommended time and temperature guidelines, leaving longer if the items aren't fully crunchy.
7. Place all the freshly dried goods in a spice grinder and grind for consistency.
8. Add spices to the remaining base ingredients; mix well. Store in an airtight container located in a cool, dark area. Dry marinade is good for approximately 1 year.

Dried Vegetable Soup Mix

Makes 4 cups

This recipe can be made in bulk and put into food storage bags with instructions for gift giving. While it takes time to dry the vegetables, the resulting product saves a lot of shelf space and can be used just like instant soup mixes.

2 stalks celery, chopped
2 carrots, chopped
1 cup diced broccoli
1 cup diced cauliflower
1 cup diced cabbage
1 cup thinly sliced potatoes
1 cup diced onion
1 cup diced mixed sweet peppers
1 cup cherry tomatoes, quartered
½ cup diced leeks
1 cup fresh peas
1 cup powdered vegetable soup stock

1. Place each vegetable on a separate layer of your dehydrator. Set dehydrator to appropriate temperature as specified by the manufacturer (otherwise use your lowest oven setting). If you are drying vegetables in the oven, dry each type of vegetable separately because some will dry faster than others. Bake at 150°F. On average, vegetables take 6–12 hours to dry completely to a crunchy texture. Beets, carrots, and onions take 3–6 hours; corn and garlic 6–8 hours; and potatoes, mushrooms, and peas 8–11 hours.
2. Mix all vegetables together with soup stock. Store in a cool, dry area for use in flavoring soup or stews or as instant soup mix.

Dried Hot Pepper Flakes

Makes 1 cup

This is a good way to use up those leftovers from the garden, or a good reason for a trip to the farmers' market. It doesn't matter how many varieties you mix together.

| 5 cups fresh hot peppers, any variety

1. Rinse any lingering dirt off peppers.
2. Remove pepper stems and ends; clean off seeds.
3. Chop peppers no more than ¼-inch thick.
4. Line a cookie sheet with heavy-duty aluminum foil; lightly spray with cooking spray. Evenly spread chopped peppers onto cookie sheet.
5. Place in 200°F oven. Leave oven door slightly ajar. Bake 3–4 hours, turning with a long-handled spatula every 30 minutes. Peppers should be bone dry.
6. Leave on kitchen counter for a few days to make sure flakes crumble when picked up. Store in a Mason jar with a tight-fitting cover. Label clearly.

Herbed Rice Mix

Makes 10 cups

This is a nice recipe for using up some of the herbs and spices you've already dried. You can also add small dehydrated vegetables to this for a unique touch.

Rice Blend
3 pounds long-grain or brown rice

2 cups previously preserved celery flakes

⅔ cup preserved minced onion

½ cup preserved parsley flakes

2 tablespoons preserved chives

1 tablespoon dried tarragon

1 tablespoon garlic powder

½ tablespoon Italian seasonings (optional)

3–4 teaspoons salt

2 teaspoons pepper

Ready to Eat
2 teaspoons butter

1 cup rice blend

2 cups water

1. Mix Rice Blend ingredients together. Divide into bags, 2 cups of mix per bag.
2. To prepare rice, melt butter in a saucepan. Add rice mix; let it brown gently. Add water; bring to a full boil.
3. Reduce heat; simmer 20 minutes, covered. Let stand 5 minutes, then serve.

Herb Paste

Basil is one of the most common herb pastes, often used to make pesto, but you can blend any herbs you want with oil in order to make a paste that can be frozen. You can also keep herb pastes in the refrigerator, although they will only last for about a month.

1. To make an herb paste, simply chop up about 2 cups of the herbs that you want to use and put them in a blender or food processor.
2. Add ⅓ cup of a high-quality olive oil by gently drizzling the oil over the herbs. Blend until you achieve a smooth paste.
3. Freeze paste for individual use by dropping tablespoons of paste onto a baking sheet lined with wax paper. Put the sheet in the freezer. Once the paste mounds are frozen solid, you can transfer them to a freezer container or plastic freezer bag and put them back in the freezer. Or,
4. For quantities greater than for individual use, add portions of paste to vacuum-sealer freezer bags, adding a layer of oil to top of paste before vacuum-sealing. Place sealed bags in freezer.

Freezer Coleslaw

Makes 4 pints

If you love coleslaw then keeping a batch from this recipe on hand is an easy way to enjoy this tasty side dish year-round.

| 1 cabbage
| 1 carrot
| 1 green pepper
| 2 tablespoons pickling salt
| 1 cup cider vinegar
| 1¼ cups sugar
| ¼ cup water
| 1 teaspoon celery seed

1. Shred the vegetables, sprinkle with salt, and mix well.
2. Cover and let stand for one hour. Before the hour is up, mix the vinegar, water, sugar, and celery seed in a saucepan and boil for 1 minute.
3. At the end of the hour, rinse the vegetables with cold water and drain. Squeeze out as much water as you can.
4. In a bowl, pour the brine over the veggie mixture, stir well, and cool.
5. Pack the mixture into containers, leaving 1 inch of headspace, and freeze.

Frozen Strained Tomato Purée

This is the best way to store tomatoes in the freezer, as whole tomatoes will turn to mush after defrosting.

1. Wash, core, and quarter your tomatoes.
2. Purée them through a hand-cranked strainer, run them through a food mill, or use a blender, then push them through a sieve to remove seeds and skin.
3. You want a smooth liquid, free of skin and seeds. Pack the liquid into fairly rigid, freezer-safe containers, allowing for 1 inch of headspace. Freeze.

Frozen Stir-Fry Greens

Keeping cooked, frozen greens in the freezer will come in handy when fresh greens aren't available.

1. Simply wash, sort, and drain any greens that you want to cook (collards and spinach work well).
2. Cut the greens into strips, removing any thick stems.
3. Stir-fry for 2–3 minutes, just until the greens are wilted.
4. Pack into boilable bags and let them cool. Dry the bags off before putting them in the freezer.

Beet Burgers

Makes 24 patties

This is one of my all-time favorite freezer recipes. These burgers are delicious fresh, but if you're going to make enough for one meal, you might as well stock your freezer. Much more nutritious than any processed veggie burger you can buy at the store, these real vegetable burgers will satisfy even the most devout meat-eater. They are great to have on hand for last-minute meals year-round.

1 cup sesame seeds
2 cups sunflower seeds
4 cups peeled, grated beets
4 cups grated carrots
1 cup minced onion
4 eggs, lightly beaten
2 cups cooked brown rice
2 cups grated Cheddar cheese
1 cup vegetable oil
1 cup fresh parsley, chopped finely
6 tablespoons flour
4 tablespoons tamari
2 garlic cloves
½ teaspoon cayenne pepper
Butter to grease baking sheet

1. Preheat oven to 350°F and lightly grease a baking sheet with butter.
2. Lightly fry the sesame seeds in an ungreased skillet over medium heat—just long enough to release fragrance.
3. Start by mixing the beets, carrots, and onions with your hands in a large bowl. Next, add all the remaining ingredients and continue to mix thoroughly with your hands.
4. Add the cayenne pepper last.
5. Shape your beet mixture into 24 patties and place them on the baking sheet (or as many patties as you can easily fit on the sheet).
6. Bake for about 20 minutes, or until the edges brown. You should not have to turn them unless they are very thick.
7. You can eat some right away, but after cooling, wrap the individual patties in plastic wrap or aluminum foil before putting into a freezer bag or container. Label and put in the freezer.

Frozen Fruit Cups

Serves 20–30

These are healthy summer treats that can also be helpful for little ones with wintertime sore throats.

> 1 watermelon, cut into bite-sized pieces, seeds removed
> 2 cantaloupes, cut into bite-sized pieces
> 2 cups berries, washed
> ½ cup mint leaves, chopped coarsely
> 4 cups sugar
> 1 can lemonade concentrate
> 1 can orange juice concentrate

1. Mix together watermelon, cantaloupe, berries, and mint leaves.
2. Fill individual containers with fruit mixture.
3. Bring water and sugar to a boil, and stir in lemonade and orange concentrates. Pour hot into fruit cups. Cool, seal, and freeze.

Nana's Tomato Sauce

Makes 2 quarts

This is my great-grandmother's tomato sauce recipe, and a wonderful one to have on hand in your freezer. It's a simple, smooth sauce and freezes well. To defrost, simply add the frozen block to a saucepan and heat on low until thoroughly thawed. This sauce is perfect to cook meatballs in. Just add baked or pan-fried meatballs to the defrosted sauce and cook on a low heat for 1–2 hours. Keep an eye on the pot to make sure the meatballs don't fall apart.

1 yellow onion, chopped finely
3–4 garlic cloves, chopped finely
1 cup tomato purée
1½ cups stewed tomatoes
½ cup tomato paste
Pinch of dried oregano
Pinch of dried basil
1 tablespoon olive oil

1. In a saucepan, sauté the onion and garlic in olive oil until browned.
2. Add the other ingredients and cook on low heat for 20 minutes.
3. Remove from heat and pour into a freezer container. Freeze.

Salsa Verde

Makes 1 pint

More than just a salsa to serve with chips, salsa verde is delicious as a chutney or to add flavor and thickness to soups. It also freezes extremely well and is a wonderfully fresh taste to pull from the freezer in wintertime. This boil-only recipe is easily adapted to different batch sizes.

1 pound tomatillos, husked
½ cup finely chopped onion
1 garlic clove, minced
1 serrano chili pepper, minced
2 tablespoons chopped cilantro
1 tablespoon chopped fresh oregano
½ teaspoon ground cumin
1½ teaspoons salt, or to taste
2 cups water

1. Combine all the ingredients and bring to a boil.
2. Reduce heat and simmer for 10–15 minutes.
3. Pour into a blender or food processor and mix until smooth.
4. Pour into freezer containers and transfer to the freezer. To defrost, place in the refrigerator until soft enough to use.

Gazpacho

Serves 6–8

A classic summer meal, this gazpacho recipe is rich enough in flavor to serve as a main course, but light and refreshing enough to serve with just about any other dish.

4 medium tomatoes, peeled

2 cucumbers, peeled and sliced

½ green bell pepper, seeded and sliced

1 garlic clove, minced

2 tablespoons olive oil

3 tablespoons white wine vinegar

6 slices bread, cubed (whatever bread you prefer)

3½ cups water

4 ice cubes

1½ teaspoons pepper

1. Mix all ingredients in a blender or food processor until smooth. Don't worry if it is a little too thick, you can add water when you defrost it.
2. Pour into freezer-safe containers and store. To defrost, put in the refrigerator and serve chilled.

Eggplant Casserole

Serves 10–12

The ultimate comfort food on a cold winter day is a warm, filling casserole. One that only needs to be moved from the freezer to the oven is even better.

1 large eggplant

3 eggs, beaten

1 cup dry bread crumbs

Olive oil

¾ cup Parmesan cheese

2 teaspoons dried oregano, or 1 tablespoon fresh

½ pound mozzarella cheese, sliced

3 cups tomato sauce

1. Preheat the oven to 350°F.
2. Peel the eggplant and slice into ¼-inch slices, and place in a bowl.
3. Pour the beaten eggs over the eggplant pieces, making sure to coat evenly.
4. Coat the eggplant in bread crumbs. Heat the oil in a skillet until hot. Pan-fry the eggplant until golden brown. Remove from heat.
5. Layer the eggplant in a casserole dish with the Parmesan, mozzarella, and oregano.
6. Cover with tomato sauce. Bake for 20 minutes. Let cool to room temperature. Wrap the casserole dish in aluminum foil, followed by layers of plastic wrap. Label and freeze. To reheat, bake at 350°F until hot all the way through.

Tomato Corn Casserole

Serves 8

This recipe is easy to make when there is excess harvest during the summer.

2½ cups tomatoes, peeled
2½ cups loose corn kernels, cooked
1 green bell pepper, chopped
½ cup dry bread crumbs
2 tablespoons melted butter
1 teaspoon onion salt
Pinch of pepper
½ cup Cheddar cheese, grated
Butter

1. Combine the tomatoes, corn, pepper, bread crumbs, and melted butter.
2. Stir in onion salt and pepper.
3. Add to a greased casserole dish and top with cheese. Wrap and freeze. To bake, place frozen casserole in the oven and bake at 350°F until browned and heated all the way through.

Frozen Pickles

Makes 2 quarts

For pickle fans, keeping these in your freezer is one of the best ways to stock up on homemade pickles. These sweet and spicy pickles thaw quickly and stay crisp when defrosted.

2 quarts cucumbers, sliced
2 tablespoons sea salt
3 onions, thinly sliced
1½ cups vinegar
3 cups sugar
¼ teaspoon celery seed

1. Sprinkle salt over cucumber slices.
2. Heat sugar and vinegar until sugar is dissolved. Gently press cucumber slices to remove water, being careful not to remove salt.
3. Pour syrup over the cucumbers, coating them.
4. Place cucumbers in freezer containers and sprinkle the celery seed on cucumbers. Seal the containers. Freeze.

Vegetable Marinara

Serves 4

Use this sauce on pasta, with rice and grain dishes, with meatballs, or as a soup base. It's a great way to use your canned tomatoes and dried herbs when made to serve in the wintertime, or use fresh ingredients during summer. Either way, this recipe freezes well.

4 cloves garlic, minced
1 carrot, sliced thin
2 ribs celery, chopped
2 tablespoons olive oil
1 28-ounce can diced or stewed tomatoes
1 6-ounce tomato paste
1 teaspoon oregano
1 teaspoon parsley
2 tablespoons chopped fresh basil
2 bay leaves
½ cup corn (optional)
½ cup sliced black olives
1 tablespoon balsamic vinegar
½ teaspoon crushed red pepper flakes
½ teaspoon salt

1. Heat garlic, carrot, and celery in olive oil over medium heat, stirring frequently, for 4–5 minutes.
2. Reduce heat to medium low, then add diced tomatoes, tomato paste, oregano, parsley, basil, and bay leaves, stirring well to combine.
3. Cover and heat for at least 30 minutes, stirring frequently.
4. Add corn, olives, balsamic vinegar, red pepper, and salt, and simmer for another 5 minutes uncovered.
5. Remove bay leaves before serving, and adjust seasonings to taste.
6. Allow to cool to room temperature, then store in freezer container, label, and freeze.

Millet and Butternut Squash Casserole

Serves 4

Slightly sweet, slightly savory, this casserole is great to pull out of the freezer.

1 cup millet
2 cups vegetable broth
1 small butternut squash, peeled, seeded, and chopped
½ cup water
1 teaspoon curry powder
½ cup orange juice
½ teaspoon sea salt

1. In a small pot, cook millet in vegetable broth until done, about 20–30 minutes.
2. In a separate pan, heat butternut squash in water. Cover and cook for 10–15 minutes until squash is almost soft. Remove lid and drain extra water.
3. Combine millet with squash over low heat and add curry and orange juice, stirring to combine well. Heat for 3–4 more minutes and season with sea salt.
4. Allow to cool to room temperature, and pour into a freezer-safe baking dish. Wrap well, label, and freeze. To defrost, unwrap the dish, leaving aluminum foil in place, and bake at 350°F for 45 minutes or until done.

Bell Peppers Stuffed with Couscous

Serves 4

Baked stuffed peppers are delicious and filling, and make for a great individually packaged frozen meal.

4 cups water or vegetable broth
3 cups couscous
2 tablespoons olive oil
2 tablespoons lemon or lime juice
1 cup frozen peas or corn, thawed
2 green onions, sliced
½ teaspoon cumin
½ teaspoon chili powder
4 green bell peppers

1. Bring water or vegetable broth to a boil and add couscous. Cover, turn off heat, and let sit for 10–15 minutes until couscous is cooked. Fluff with a fork.
2. Combine couscous with olive oil, lemon or lime juice, peas or corn, green onions, cumin, and chili powder.
3. Cut tops off bell peppers and remove seeds.
4. Stuff couscous into bell peppers and place the tops back on, using a toothpick to secure if needed.
5. Freezer-wrap each pepper in a layer of foil, followed by plastic wrap. Store in freezer bags and put in the freezer.
6. To defrost; preheat oven to 350°F and transfer pepper(s) to a baking dish, leaving one layer of aluminum foil on. Bake for 15 minutes, remove foil, and continue baking until brown.

Italian Veggie and Pasta Casserole

Serves 6

Veggies and pasta are baked into an Italian-spiced casserole with a crumbly topping. Add in a handful of TVP (textured vegetable protein) crumbles or some kidney beans if you want a protein boost.

> 1 16-ounce package pasta (use a medium pasta such as bowties, corkscrews, or small shells)
> 1 onion, chopped
> 3 zucchinis, sliced
> 1 red bell pepper, chopped
> 4 cloves garlic, minced
> 2 tablespoons olive oil
> 1 28-ounce can diced tomatoes
> ¾ cup corn kernels
> 1 teaspoon parsley
> 1 teaspoon basil
> ½ teaspoon oregano
> ½ teaspoon crushed red pepper flakes
> ¼ teaspoon pepper
> 1 cup bread crumbs
> ½ cup grated cheese

1. Cook pasta according to package instructions, drain well, and layer in a baking dish.
2. Sauté onion, zucchini, bell pepper, and garlic in olive oil just until soft, about 3–4 minutes. Add tomatoes, corn, parsley, basil, oregano, and crushed red pepper. Simmer for 8–10 minutes and season with black pepper.
3. Cover pasta with zucchini and tomato mixture. Sprinkle with bread crumbs and cheese.
4. Wrap in aluminum foil, followed by plastic wrap. Freeze.
5. To bake, preheat the oven to 425°F. Remove plastic wrap and transfer frozen casserole to oven, covered in aluminum foil. Bake for 10–12 minutes, then remove the foil and bake until browned and heated through.

Raspberry Reduction Marinade

Makes 5 cups

Fruited meats were very popular on the finest tables during the Middle Ages and Renaissance.

1 red onion, minced
1 teaspoon olive oil
2 cups juiced raspberries
2 cups dry red wine
½ cup beef broth
½ cup golden raisins
½ cup raspberry vinegar
2 tablespoons fresh ginger, minced
¼ cup sugar
1 tablespoon Dijon mustard

1. Gently sauté the minced onions in oil until golden brown.
2. Add the remaining ingredients to the onions; simmer.
3. Let the liquid reduce by about 1 cup; cool.
4. Move to freezer containers or pour over the desired meat and freeze everything together. Use within 8 months.

Pickled Onion Sauce

Makes 3 cups

This is an intense onion sauce that marries nicely with bratwurst, garlic sausage, and kielbasa. Other herbs worth trying in this blend include cumin, ginger, and allspice.

1 large red onion, thinly sliced
2 chili peppers, seeded and diced
10 cloves fresh garlic
1½ cups white vinegar
½ cup sugar
1 tablespoon mustard seed
1 tablespoon celery seed
½ cup dark beer
¼ cup dark honey
1 teaspoon salt

1. Blanch the onions and peppers 2 minutes.
2. Place onions, peppers, and remaining ingredients in a sauce pan; bring to a boil.
3. Reduce heat; simmer until sauce reduces by ¼ cup.
4. Cool; run through a blender or food processor for consistent texture.
5. Store in freezer containers, leaving space for expansion. Use within 8 months.

CHAPTER 9

PICKLING AND FERMENTING YOUR BOUNTY

Fermentation is one of the oldest ways to preserve food. The unique flavors and qualities of fermented food makes fermentation as popular for taste reasons, as for preservation reasons. Pickling, while more modern than fermentation, creates similar flavors in food and is also a form of preservation. Both fermentation and pickling add distinct flavors to food, with undertones of sweet, spice, and tartness, with the largest difference between the two methods being the inclusion or exclusion of vinegar. Pickling uses vinegar and fermentation does not. In this chapter you will learn how to ferment different foods, as well as how to pickle food.

Pickling 101

There are four basic types of pickles. The first is fresh pack, which is blissfully simple to prepare. Second are fruit pickles that are prepared with a sugar-vinegar syrup. Third is chutney and relish, and finally, the most popular is salt-cured or brined pickles. No matter what type of pickle you intend to preserve, always start with firm fruits or vegetables, fresh spices, and clean water. If you're harvesting your own fruits and vegetables, do so early in the morning and refrigerate them immediately before preparing all your pickling equipment. This is also true of store-bought items. Heat makes pickled items softer.

Basic Equipment

One of the great beauties of pickling is that it doesn't require a lot of fancy equipment. Stainless steel and glass are ideal for pickling projects. Aluminum, enamel, and iron pots or tools aren't recommended because of brine's natural acidity; when the acid reacts with those bases it changes the flavor of the resulting food items. The following list includes some of the items you'll want for pickling:

- Paring knife
- Vegetable peeler
- Stone jar or crockery for fermenting (Note: You will need a plate or other cover that fits inside your fermenting jar. This holds the pickles beneath the brine. Kitchen plates work well.)
- Large bowl, plastic Ziploc bag, or plastic food container (These may substitute for the stone jar or crockery as a fermenting vessel.)
- Pots large enough for simmering the brine and spices
- Ladle
- Funnel
- Measuring tools
- Storage jars or containers
- Hot-water canner (if you're planning to put up the pickles)

Embracing Brine

Brining has become a very popular method in cooking, not just for pickling but also for marinade. For example, some people who love deep-fried turkey swear by herb-laced brine as one method for making a truly flavorful bird. The longer an item remains in brine, the more it changes the taste and texture of the food.

Brining is very easy and very popular for meat because the salt helps keep it moist during the cooking process. To the foundation of salt and water, many cooks now add other flavorings to transport taste to every part of the meat (rather than just the exterior, as sometimes happens with a marinade). Meats that benefit from brining include lean poultry, pork, and seafood.

The same concept holds true for vegetables, fruits, and flowers. Whatever spices you add to fermenting or pickling brine are transported with the salt into the vegetable. This typically results in a unique texture that not everyone likes, so start your brining efforts small until you find a process that's pleasing.

Salt

Table salt and sea salt are most commonly used in brining, and some folks like a gourmet touch like Fleur de Sel and Hawaiian salt—but these get costly. Recipes will usually specify which salt they recommend. If you're going to substitute, 1 cup of table salt becomes 1½ cups of kosher salt.

Brine Containers

Food storage containers, large cooking bowls, and stainless-steel stockpots all work very well as brine receptacles. Alternatively, if you're doing a large amount of brining, try a clean cooler (this needs to be sterilized). Remember that you'll need enough brine to completely cover the food. If you can't guess, put the food in the container and cover it with plain water. Measure that water and add your salt accordingly. Note that no matter how much you might like a blend, you should never reuse brine.

Temperature

Some cooks adjust their meat brine according to the temperature at which they plan to cook it. Slow- and low-cooked meat receives more sugar and salt compared to high-heat (grilling or broiling) meat. Generally, the brine for slow-cooked meats takes ¼ cup of kosher salt and sugar to 1 pint of water. For items that will require high-heat cooking, use 1 quart water, 1 tablespoon sugar, and ⅛ cup of kosher salt. In terms of brining time, about 1 hour per pound is a good measure.

Pickle Brining

Pickle brine includes vinegar for curing along with the traditional salt and/or sugar. Cucumbers are far and away the most popular vegetable for pickling. They are best purchased or harvested unwaxed, when they're small and very firm. Brining waxed cucumbers won't work because the salt cannot penetrate the skin. The basic brine for pickling is 1 quart water to ½ cup salt. It's important that the vegetables remain under the brine throughout the fermenting period. It takes about a month for a whole pickle to be completely fermented. The best test is to cut one open and look for uniform color.

Fermentation

Fermentation, or lacto-fermentation, is possibly the most simple, safe, and healthy way to preserve food. It's also one of the oldest methods of food preservation, and almost every culture has a fermented dish in its food repertoire. Kimchi and sauerkraut are probably the two most famous lacto-fermented dishes, and you can ferment any other vegetables, as well as fruit, fish, dairy, and grains. Lacto-fermentation differs from other food preservation techniques for two main reasons: the unique taste and the added nutritional benefit that the process creates. Whereas other preservation methods can negatively affect the nutritional value of food, lacto-fermentation results in a finished food product that is packed with essential nutrients, boosts your immune system, and aids digestion by putting healthy bacteria into your body. In some vegetables, such as cabbage, lacto-fermentation actually increases significantly the vitamin C levels in the food.

What Makes Fermentation Safe and How Does It Work?

Dr. Fred Breidt, microbiologist for the USDA Agricultural Research Service, says that lacto-fermented vegetables are actually safer than raw vegetables, which can be exposed to pathogens such as *E. coli*. Breidt's concern about *E. coli* applies much less to your backyard veggies than it does to commercial farms, but the point about the safety of lacto-fermentation holds true.

There are essentially three stages to the food lacto-fermentation process. In the first stage, oxygen is removed by anaerobic bacteria (the good bacteria), creating an environment where good bacteria can flourish and bad bacteria cannot survive. In the second stage, lactic acid is produced, effectively killing off any aerobic bacteria (the bad bacteria that will make you sick), as well as creating an environment that allows vitamin C to stabilize. In the third stage, lactic acid increases, the overall pH level decreases further, vitamin C levels increase, and flavor begins to develop, resulting in a mild sauerkraut flavor. To get to this stage takes about a week or less, and at this point the fermented food is ready to eat. If allowed to continue fermenting, and to reach the fourth stage, the pH level will decrease further, and flavor will develop into a bolder taste. It is completely up to you and your taste when you decide to eat your fermented food, but it will be safe and ready to go after just a few days to a week, depending on temperature.

What You Will Need

All you need to start lacto-fermenting food is a cutting board, chopping knife, grater, bowl, noniodized salt, clean water, and either a clean glass jar or ceramic vessel.

How to Lacto-Ferment Foods

Although you can lacto-ferment many different foods, the following description is specific to vegetables. The same process and steps can be applied to other food groups, although you'll want to do a little research to learn any tricks or recommendations. The book *Wild Fermentation: The Flavor, Nutrition, and Craft of Live-Culture Foods*, by Sandor Ellix Katz, is a great resource to learn the ins and outs of lacto-fermentation.

Step One: Create Surface Area

Create surface area by chopping, grating, or slicing your veggies, and then place them in any bowl. Sauerkraut is typically grated cabbage, carrots, and chopped garlic, but whether you chop, grate, or slice makes no difference and is entirely up to you.

Step Two: Break Down Cells

The objective here is to help break down cells in the food in order to make it easier for it to be thoroughly penetrated. Depending on what food you are fermenting, you either want to mash it or rub it until it becomes wet. In the case of grated foods, you can mash it between your hands. With some other foods, like greens, rubbing it in your hands might be more effective. As long as liquid is produced from the food, cells are breaking down and the process is working.

Step Three: Add Salt and Pack It

With your food in the bowl, sprinkle salt on it. It is important that this salt is not iodized, so any sea salt will work. The amount of salt you use depends on your taste, but more salt will slow the fermentation process, and less will speed it up.

It will also affect the taste of your food. A good ratio is 1 teaspoon salt per pound of cut vegetables. In most cases, a filled pint jar will equal a pound. If you decide to use whole vegetables, you will want to increase the salt levels, and 1 tablespoon of salt per quart is generally a good ratio.

If you're using cut vegetables, add the salt as you pack it into your glass jar or other vessel. It is very important that you really mash and punch the cut veggies into the vessel so that all air pockets will be removed. After you've filled the container, pour clean water over the food, making sure that all the vegetables are completely covered. With whole vegetables, simply place them into the vessel and pour the saltwater brine over them, making sure to fully submerge the food in liquid. Cover your vessel. If you're using a jar, screw the lid on but be sure to unscrew the top regularly to release the pressure that will build up. This is important! If you're using a ceramic vessel, cover it with a plate but weigh this plate down with something heavy. Otherwise, the pressure will end up moving the plate.

Step Four: Wait

Place your fermentation vessel somewhere where the temperature is between 65°F and 80°F. Most likely this is room temperature, but depending on the season and how warm you keep your house, it can vary. Most likely you will want to wait at least a week before eating your lacto-fermented food, but you can start taste-testing it after day three in order to get a feel for the way the flavor develops. You will also need to check on the food regularly before eating it to remove any mold, to possibly add water, and to release any pressure. If any surface mold develops, simply scrape it off. The food underneath is still totally safe. Add more water if necessary to make sure that your veggies stay submerged, and be sure to release pressure by opening any lids.

Step Five: Eat!

Once your lacto-fermented food reaches the flavor that you like, you can eat it or refrigerate it. Refrigeration will halt the process of fermentation and therefore flavor development. Lacto-fermented foods can also be stored in your root cellar, and so long as temperatures don't go above 50°F, it should keep for a very long time wherever you store it.

Lacto-fermentation is an acquired taste for some, and if you don't already love the flavor of sauerkraut, you might want to ease yourself into this preservation technique by allowing foods to ferment for a limited time, so that the flavor is mild, as well as by trying lots of different recipes. You may find that while you dislike traditional cabbage sauerkraut, you love fermented eggplant or green beans. You might not want all of your preserved food to have the signature lacto-fermented taste, so using this method as one component of your food preservation system works well.

Lacto-Fermentation Recipes

Here are some recipes that highlight this method of fermentation.

Pickled Beets

Makes 8 quarts

Pickled beets are intense in flavor and in texture. The perfect blend of softness and firmness, pick-led beets are a great addition to sandwiches, as well as being a delicious side for meat dishes.

6–10 medium size beets or enough to fill 8 quart-sized jars

4 cups beet juice (can be diluted with water if necessary)

2 cups vinegar

4 cups sugar

1 teaspoon salt

1. Boil the beets until you can easily insert a fork into them; about 20 minutes.
2. Mix the beet juice, vinegar, and sugar and boil this liquid mixture.
3. Add the beets to the liquid and continue cooking until beets are soft enough to eat, about 10 minutes.
4. Pack the beets into the jars and cover with beet juice mixture, being sure to leave ½-inch to 1-inch headspace.
5. Submerge the jars long enough to seal the lids.

Pickled Garlic

Makes approximately 4 cups

For garlic lovers, this recipe is a must. The end result is a mild garlic flavor, well infused by the accompanying herbs.

1 cup dry white wine
1 cup white wine vinegar
2 dried hot peppers
2 rosemary sprigs
2 thyme sprigs
2 bay leaves
20 black peppercorns, whole
4 teaspoons sugar
1 teaspoon sea salt
2 cup garlic cloves, peeled

1. In a saucepan, combine all ingredients except the garlic.
2. Bring to a boil and add garlic. Return to a boil and continue boiling for 5 minutes. Cover and allow to stand at room temperature for 24 hours.
3. The next day, bring to a boil once again and pour immediately into a pint jar. Allow to cool. If desired, you can seal in the contents with a layer of olive oil (makes for a nice appetizer).
4. Cap the jar, leaving 1 inch of headroom. Store in the root cellar or similar environment for 5 days before eating and/or transferring to the refrigerator. This garlic will keep for a year in the fridge.

Fermented Mint Chutney

Makes 3 cups

This chutney recipe is adapted from Sally Fallon's book, Nourishing Traditions, *and is wonderful as a topping to any meat dish.*

2 cups fresh mint leaves

1 onion, coarsely chopped

4 garlic cloves, coarsely chopped

4 jalapeño chilis, seeded and chopped

⅔ cup almonds, finely chopped

1 tablespoon sea salt

1 cup water

1. Use a food processor to mix all the ingredients except salt and water.
2. Place in a glass quart jar and press down lightly to remove any air bubbles.
3. Mix salt water and pour into the jar, covering the chutney. Allow 1 inch of headspace and cover tightly. To allow flavor to develop, wait at least 2 days before putting in the refrigerator.

Pickled Garlic Scapes

Makes 1 quart

Use only the most tender scapes to enjoy in this simply delicious recipe.

About 1½ teaspoons unrefined sea salt
Enough tender garlic scapes, trimmed with hard stems removed, to fit in a 1-quart jar

1. Stir sea salt together with one quart fresh water until the salt is dissolved.
2. Pack a glass quart jar with the garlic scapes.
3. Pour the salt water over the scapes, completely covering them. Ferment for a minimum of a week, and up to four weeks, to achieve the flavor you like.

Fiery Fermented Jalapeños

Makes 1 quart

These are hot!

> 1 quart fresh jalapeño jeppers
> ½ onion, sliced
> 3–4 cloves garlic
> 3 tablespoons sea salt
> 1 quart water

1. Gently wash and clean the jalapeños, sorting out any bruised or damaged peppers.
2. Pack the peppers, garlic, and onion into quart jar or ceramic crock.
3. Combine the salt and water until the salt is dissolved. Pour this brine over the vegetables, making sure they are fully submerged.
4. Cover your container and store at room temperature. Wait for the peppers to turn an olive green, in about 5–7 days, before tasting.

Fermented Salsa

Makes 1 quart

The tangier, fermented version of classic, fresh salsa.

4 large tomatoes, peeled, seeded and diced
2 onions, finely chopped
¾ cup chili pepper, chopped
8 garlic cloves, finely chopped
1 bunch cilantro, chopped
Juice of 2 lemons
2 tablespoons sea salt
¼ cup water

1. Pack all ingredients except water and salt into quart-sized jar. Pack well, and if necessary, use a meat hammer to ensure that all air bubbles are out.
2. Mix salt and water and pour over the vegetables, making sure to fully submerge. Allow 1 inch of space between the veggies and the top of the jar. Cover and check the taste after the second day.

Kimchi (Korean Sauerkraut)

Makes 2 quarts

Kimchi is an important Korean dish, served at every meal. The thin-leafed Napa cabbage is the traditional cabbage used in kimchi, and it can easily be grown in many North American climates.

1 head Napa cabbage, cored and shredded
1 bunch green onions, chopped
1 cup carrots, grated
1 tablespoon freshly grated ginger
3 garlic cloves, minced
½ teaspoon dried chili flakes
2 tablespoons sea salt

1. Combine everything except the whey in a large bowl.
2. Using your hands or a meat hammer, pound the mixture to release juices. Continue pounding until the juices are just below the top of the mixture.
3. Pack into quart-sized jars and pour water over, fully submerging the vegetable mixture. Allow 1 inch of headspace before covering. Keep at room temperature for at least 3 days before refrigerating.

Sauerkraut

Makes 1 quart

Here's a traditional sauerkraut recipe that pairs perfectly with sausages and hot dogs or works as a hearty side dish to any meal.

> 1 medium cabbage, cored and shredded
> 1 tablespoon caraway seeds
> 2 garlic cloves
> 2 tablespoons sea salt

1. Mix all the ingredients in a bowl using your hands and a meat pounder. Pound and squeeze the mixture until the juices begin to fill the bowl.
2. Pack tightly into your quart jar and pour water in until the mixture is submerged. Allow 1-inch space between the top of the cabbage mixture and the top of the jar. Ferment for at least 3 days before refrigerating.

Pickled Ginger

Makes 1 quart

Not only to be eaten with sushi, you can enjoy pickled ginger on its own, or with meat and fish dishes at home.

> 3 pounds fresh gingerroots
> 2 tablespoons sea salt
> 1 quart water

1. Using a vegetable peeler, peel the ginger and slice it very thinly.
2. Place the slices in a bowl and using a meat pounder, pound the ginger to release juices.
3. Pack into the quart jar, pressing down as you pack.
4. Mix the salt with the water and pour over the ginger. Allow 1 inch of room at the top of the jar and cover. Wait at least 3 days before refrigerating.

Sour Berry Syrup

Makes 1 quart

This fermented version of classic berry syrup has a tangy sweet and sour taste that is delicious on ice cream, pastries, or pancakes.

4 cups fresh berries (anything other than strawberries, which are too acidic)
3 teaspoons sea salt
¼ cup sugar
2 teaspoons pectin

1. Wash berries and place in a bowl with the other ingredients.
2. Mash until well crushed.
3. Pour the mixture into the quart jar and push down lightly. Pour in enough water to just reach the same level as the berries. Make sure the tops of the berries are 1 inch from the top of the jar, and cover. After 2 days at room temperature, taste and transfer to the refrigerator.

Corn Relish

Makes 1 quart

Including sweet corn in a zesty relish is a genius way to add color and summer flavor to meals year-round. Serve as a dip for tortilla chips, as a side dish, or spread on a wrap or sandwich.

3 cups fresh corn kernels

1 tomato, peeled, seeded, and diced

½ red pepper, seeded and diced

2 tablespoons fresh cilantro, chopped

½ teaspoon red pepper flakes

2 tablespoons sea salt

1. In a large bowl, mix all the ingredients. Pound with a meat pounder to release juices.
2. Pack and pound the mixture into a quart-sized jar until the juices are covering the relish. You should not have to add any additional water. Allow 1 inch of space between the top of the relish and the top of the jar. Cover and keep at room temperature for 3 days before refrigerating.

Snap Beans

Makes 1 quart

Use this recipe only with fresh, tender green beans. The ones you grow yourself will work best!

Enough green beans to fill a quart jar, trimmed
2 small dried hot peppers
2 garlic cloves, chopped
4 whole black peppercorns, crushed
2 dill heads
2 tablespoons sea salt

1. Pack all the ingredients into the quart jar, including the salt.
2. Cover with water, making sure to submerge all the vegetables. Allow 1 inch of room between the tops of the beans and the top of the jar. Cover and keep at room temperature for at least 3 days before tasting.

Sour Mustard Greens

Makes 2 quarts

This Vietnamese dish is mild, with a lighter fermented taste than most lacto-fermented foods.

> 1½ pounds mustard greens, cut into small pieces
> 6 scallions, cut into small pieces
> 1 tablespoon sea salt
> 1½ teaspoons sugar
> 1 quart water

1. Wilt the greens and scallions slowly at a low heat in the oven, or if it's a warm day you can put them outside in the sun.
2. Mix the water and salt until the salt is dissolved. Once the greens are wilted, pack in quart jars, layering the greens with the brine.
3. Make sure the greens are completely submerged and allow 1 inch of space at the top. Cover the jar and store at room temperature for 3–4 days or until the greens are sour enough. Refrigerate.

Pickled Cherry Tomatoes

Makes 2 quarts

This Russian tomato recipe is adapted from Linda Ziedrich's book, The Joy of Pickling, *and works best with tomatoes that are not yet fully ripe.*

1¾ pounds cherry tomatoes
5–6 dill heads
¼ cup horseradish, coarsely grated
5 garlic cloves, halved
3 sprigs parsley
3 sprigs tarragon
½ fresh hot pepper, seeded
Several dill sprigs
2 tablespoons sea salt
1 quart water

1. Pack all the ingredients into quart jars, except for the salt and water.
2. Mix the salt in the water until dissolved, then pour over the tomato mixture. Use just enough brine to fully cover the tomatoes.
3. Allow at least 1 inch of space between the top of the tomatoes and the top of the jar. Let the jars sit at room temperature for at least a week before tasting. Refrigerate.

CONCLUSION

This book was written during the late spring in New England when the gardens are beginning to bloom with life and activity. Writing the methods, recipes, and ideas found here allowed me to put the excitement that I feel at this time of year into words. Each plant description, recipe, and bit of advice is tied to a person, a place, an experience, or a memory. Food, and the art of growing and caring for it, connects me to the people I love to feed, and the land that grows everything I need. I hope that you enjoyed this book and that it serves as a tool to connect what you eat to the people and places you love.

Eat well.

RESOURCES

The Berry Grower's Companion by Barbara L. Bowling. A helpful book to teach you everything you need to know about growing small fruit.

Feed the Soil by Edwin McLeod is a wonderful book to teach you exactly what different plants need from the soil.

Fresh Food from Small Spaces by R. J. Ruppenthal is an extremely useful tool for anyone with small gardening or food-storage space, or anyone who simply wants to make the most of the space they do have.

In the Green Kitchen by Alice Waters is a helpful book to have on hand if you're new to stocking a pantry and cooking from whole foods.

The Johnny's Selected Seeds Catalog. In print and online at *www.johnnyseeds.com*, this catalog is more than just a source to order seeds from, it also provides a wealth of information and a necessary resource to any farmer or gardener.

The Joy of Pickling by Linda Ziedrich contains 250 recipes. If you love lacto-fermentation and pickling, this is the book for you.

Mother Earth News, online at *www.motherearthnews.com*, is a great resource to find helpful gardening articles and advice for the organic gardener.

Mother Nature's Herbal by Judith Griffin, PhD, is a fun and useful guide for the blossoming herbalist interested in learning more about herbs than just how they taste.

The New Organic Grower: A Master's Manual of Tools and Techniques for the Home and Market Gardener, by Eliot Coleman, is a seriously useful book for anyone wanting to grow food efficiently and organically.

Nourishing Traditions: The Cookbook That Challenges Politically Correct Nutrition and the Diet Dictocrats, by Sally Fallon, includes many lacto-fermentation recipes and information, as well as traditional approaches to cooking.

Seed Savers Exchange, a nonprofit heirloom seed company that offers lots of choices and helpful information: *www.seedsavers.org*

Vegetarian Cooking for Everyone by Deborah Madison is stocked with 1,400 recipes to help you use everything you grow.

Wild Fermentation by Sandor Ellix Katz is a great introduction and in-depth summary of the art of lacto-fermentation.

Worms Eat My Garbage by Mary Appelhof is a comprehensive guide to at-home vermiculture.

INDEX

Green manures, 32
Greens. *See also* Collards;
  Spinach
    about: blanching, 206;
      choosing right varieties, 13
    Frozen Stir-Fry Greens, *243*
    Sour Mustard Greens, 277
Green tomatoes. *See* Tomatoes

Hand watering, 6–7
Hardening off, 47
Hardiness plant zones, 2–3
Health of plants. *See* Plant
  health
Heirloom Mustard Pickles, *216*
Heirlooms, 15–16
Herbs
    about. *See also specific herbs*:
      annual, 140–41; benefits
      of, 14; biennial, 141; for
      culinary use, 142–45;
      deciding to plant, 14;
      drying, 148; evergreen, 141;
      freezing, 148; historical
      perspective, 145; organizing
      according to use, 141;
      perennial, 141; planting/
      maintaining/harvesting,
      147–48; preserving, 148;
      salads with. *See* Salads; for
      tea, 145–47; tea basics, 147;
      understanding growing
      period, 140
    Dried Tomatoes and Herb
      Quiche, *228*
    Freshly Herbed Beets, 164
    Herbed Rice Mix, *239*
    Herb Garlic Blend, 151
    Herb Paste, *240*
    Herb Pesto, 178
    Herb Vinegars, 173
    Homemade Flavored Oil, 161
    Winter Herb Dressing, 166
  Homemade Flavored Oil, 161
  Homemade Garlic and Herb
    Gnocchi, *233*
  Hoop houses, 41, 42–44
  Hybrid houses, 43–44

Insects. *See* Pests and diseases
Italian Veggie and Pasta
  Casserole, *255*

Jams and preserves
    Berry Jam Bars, 134
    Green Tomato Raspberry
      Jam, *213*
    Lavender Blueberry Jam, 127
    Lavender Jam, 149
    Lavender Raspberry Jam,
      126
    Raspberry Butter, 137
    Wild Strawberry Preserves,
      124

Kale, 43, 62–63
Kimchi (Korean Sauerkraut),
  271

Lacto-fermentation, 262–64.
  See also Pickled and fermented
  food recipes
Latin Rice with Corn and
  Peppers, 101
Lavender
    about: growing, 146; uses
      and characteristics, 146
    Lavender Blueberry Jam, 127
    Lavender Jam, 149
    Lavender Raspberry Jam,
      126
Leeks
    about: growing, 56–57;
      harvesting, 57
    Potato and Leek Soup, 84
    Vegetable Stock, 65
Lemon. *See* Citrus
Lemon balm
    about: growing, 146; making
      tea with, 146; uses and
      characteristics, 146
    Refresh Tea, 169
Lemon verbena
    about: uses and
      characteristics, 147

Lemon Verbena Sherbert,
  162
Refresh Tea, 169
Low tunnels, 41–42

Maintenance and upkeep. *See*
  Pests and diseases; Water;
  Weeds
Maple-Glazed Roasted Veggies,
  97
Marinades. *See* Sauces, dips, and
  relishes
Mediterranean Potato Salad,
  109
Melon, in Frozen Fruit Cups,
  245
Millet and Butternut Squash
  Casserole, *253*
Mint
    about: preserving, 143; uses
      and characteristics, 143;
      varieties, 143
    Fermented Mint Chutney,
      267
    Fresh Mint Chutney, 168
    Lemon-Mint Sun Tea, 171
    Parsley and Mint Carrot
      Salad, 165
Mulch
    for blueberries, 119
    disadvantages of, 29
    leaves, biodegradables for,
      40–41, 47
    moisture control with, 32
    overwintering with, 47
    plastic, 40
    as season extender, 40–41
    weed control with, 29
Mushrooms
    about: blanching, 206
    Mushroom and Rosemary
      Wild Rice, 102
    Sesame Soy Asparagus and
      Mushrooms, 89
    Tomato, Mushroom, and
      Barley Soup, 66

ABOUT THE AUTHORS

Catherine Abbott grew up on a farm in Northern Alberta. She grew vegetables in her suburban backyard until 2000, when she decided to make a lifestyle change and started a small-scale vegetable farm. She now grows fabulous vegetables that she sells in her local community. She also teaches gardening classes and has developed a popular website called *www.your-vegetable-gardening-helper.com*. She lives in British Columbia, Canada.

Alison Woitunski works at The Food Project, a leading agricultural and gardening organization, where she writes and teaches curriculum about backyard gardening, agriculture, food preservation, and food culture. Along with a personal love for at-home growing, seed sprouting, cooking, and food preservation, Alison is passionate about sharing her food knowledge with others. She lives in the Boston area.